Joel and Dana's journey into preserving began with an innocent lesson in making jam. Almost a decade later, WellPreserved.ca is an extraordinary resource for both beginners and experts alike. Their much-anticipated first cookbook showcases seven different preserving techniques—waterbath canning, pressure canning, dehydrating, fermenting, cellaring, salting & smoking, and infusing—and takes readers on a trip to the market in twenty-five ingredients. Within each ingredient chapter, you'll find multiple preserving recipes using the different methods. From apples, pears, peaches and rhubarb, to asparagus, peppers, mushrooms, and tomatoes, and covering a variety of meat and fish, *Batch* teaches you everything you need to know to get the most out of your kitchen.

With their signature approachable and fun style, Joel and Dana showcase techniques for a variety of skill levels, explain how to batch your recipes to make two preserves at once, give you multiple options for preserving in ten minutes or less, and serve up mouthwatering center-of-the-plate meals that take your preserves from the pantry to the table. With personal anecdotes, creative and incredible recipes, and beautiful photography and illustrations, *Batch* will show you how to incorporate preserving into your life and your community.

Batch

Batch

OVER 200 RECIPES, TIPS & TECHNIQUES
FOR A WELL PRESERVED KITCHEN

JOEL MacCHARLES & DANA HARRISON

PHOTOGRAPHS BY REENA NEWMAN & MARGARET MULLIGAN

appetite
by RANDOM HOUSE

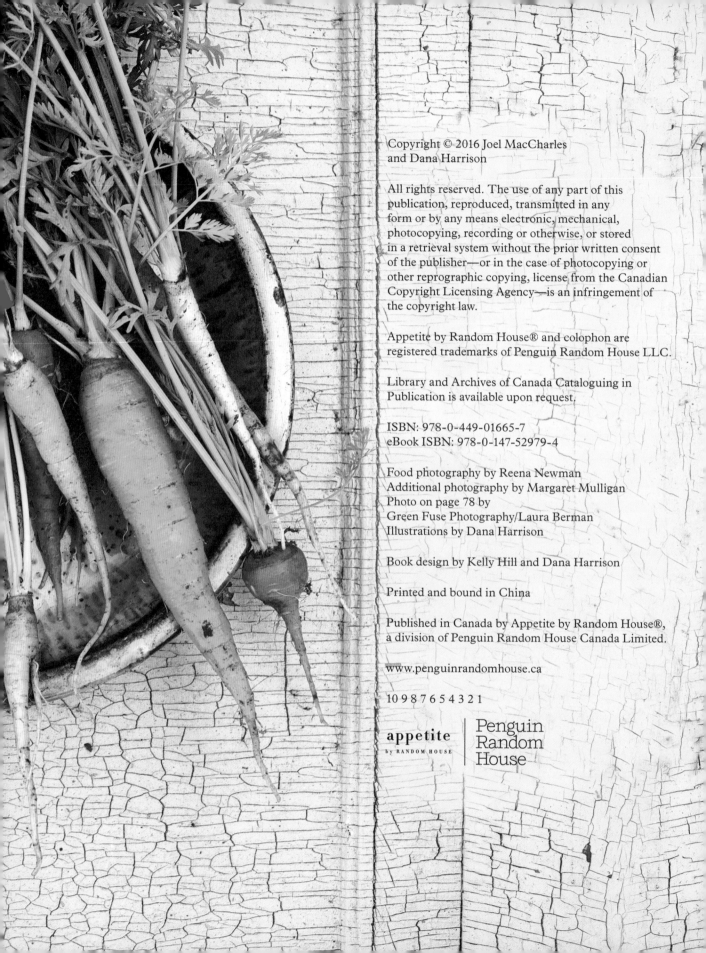

Appetite by Random House® and colophon are
registered trademarks of Penguin Random House LLC.

Library and Archives of Canada Cataloguing in
Publication is available upon request.

ISBN: 978-0-449-01665-7
eBook ISBN: 978-0-147-52979-4

Food photography by Reena Newman
Additional photography by Margaret Mulligan
Photo on page 78 by
Green Fuse Photography/Laura Berman
Illustrations by Dana Harrison

Book design by Kelly Hill and Dana Harrison

Printed and bound in China

Published in Canada by Appetite by Random House®,
a division of Penguin Random House Canada Limited.

www.penguinrandomhouse.ca

10 9 8 7 6 5 4 3 2 1

appetite
by RANDOM HOUSE

Penguin
Random
House

To our family and friends who pulled up a chair to this crazy table and dug in: thank you. We couldn't have done this without your support and love.

Contents

---

7 Methods for Preserving

A Trip to the Market in 25 Ingredients

Introduction

Why We Wrote *Batch*

"I wish I could preserve. I can't because . . ."

I've often heard those words. In fact, I said them for more than fifteen years.

People give many reasons for why they don't preserve food. Time, money, skill, and safety are the most common. Those were my reasons for not preserving food—I didn't know where to start.

Yet I grew up in a house where we preserved food all the time. My parents made strawberry jam, mustard pickles, pickled beets, wine (albeit from a home-brew store), tomato sauce, and more. They had a system for freezing food in a chest freezer, and routinely kept onions and carrots fresh by storing them in our garage, which was naturally cool.

After years of good intentions, I finally asked my parents to teach me how to make jam. My partner, Dana, and I made our first jam with them and were shocked to see how quick and easy it was to preserve. Within six months we preserved more than 300 jars of food and were excited to learn more.

When people think of preserving, they often remember the stories of past generations who spent long days in the heat of the kitchen, working to near exhaustion. The work is hard to justify when the imagined results are limited to condiments such as jam, jelly, or pickles. By limiting our understanding of preserving to canning—the way most of these preserves are made—we limit ourselves to a tiny portion of the nearly endless possibilities, many of which can be done in minutes.

As we began this process, we discovered at least seven different ways to preserve food. Each has its own set of advantages and weaknesses. Preserving can be easy, fast, and cheap. It doesn't necessarily require a lot of equipment and it can be done by people of all cooking abilities. The results range from staple ingredients that help you cook a meal in minutes to fully prepared meals.

And that is why we bring you *Batch: Over 200 Recipes, Tips & Techniques for a Well Preserved Kitchen*. We want to show you how easy it can be to transform fresh ingredients into preserves, and then to use those preserves to whip up tasty meals.

What Is "Batch" Preserving?

The name of this book is inspired by the way we preserve. Instead of making a single preserve at a time, we often make several recipes at once. For example, if I'm making a batch of raspberry jam, I might also cover a few berries in vinegar or vodka to make an infusion. This extra step takes seconds and means that I make two preserves in the time it would otherwise take to make one.

Creating batches isn't only about saving time; it's also about making the most of the ingredients we work with. Inspired by Fergus Henderson and the world of Nose to Tail cuisine, Dana and I look at the different parts of an ingredient to see how we can preserve each part in a way that makes the most of it. For example, we preserve strawberries in three different ways: we dehydrate the tips after thinly slicing them, use the top of the berry to make jam, and dry the hulls for tea or smoking fish.

Who We Are

On the morning of December 28, 2008, Dana changed our lives by accident when she spontaneously created a food blog called "WellPreserved.ca." We started by posting recipes and food-related articles. I quickly became obsessed and published a daily article for the next 1,500 consecutive days. The blog contains more than 700 recipes and is still updated often.

"WellPreserved" became the home of many creative projects beyond the blog. Almost fifty pop-up events, a full food festival, posters, articles, a graphic design company, and other collaborations have all been created under its moniker.

Moving from a blog to a cookbook was a completely new project for us. Dana art-directed and illustrated all of the images in *Batch*. She provided the book's visual expression. I created the recipes and wrote the text.

From the overall concept to the recipe testing and tasting, this book has been the center of our lives for a good long time now. Unlike the blog, where recipes are developed one at a time, this project has felt like creating a box set of concept albums. A change to one recipe affected another, and that changed yet another. It forced us to look at preserving in a way that we've never done.

You'll find recipes that are adaptations of family classics, as well as those inspired by our friends and the many cultures that mingle in the amazing city of Toronto. We have tried to respect the traditions of many of the preserving techniques of the world, while also infusing the tastes and practicality of modern city living into them as well.

How the Book Is Organized

The first half of the book introduces you to the fundamentals of the seven styles of preserving and walks you through the basics. If you're new to preserving, you'll find the building blocks to get you started; if you're experienced, you can treat these chapters as a refresher course. If you're guided more by your stomach than logic, as I am, you can skip these chapters and come back to them after choosing the recipes you'd like to try.

The second half of the book is organized by ingredient. This will be handy if you come home from the market with a flat of peaches or berries, or if you're at the end of the gardening season and want to preserve your bounty of hot peppers, for example.

Each ingredient chapter has six different preserving recipes and uses at least three techniques. Some preserves can be done in a few minutes and are easy to combine with others, while others will make a fun afternoon project when you have the time. We also share "Batch-It" recipes, which show you how simple it is to make two different preserves at once.

When we were learning to preserve, we found the biggest challenge wasn't making the products but finding ways to use them. We've given you some ideas for how to use the preserves in many of the recipes, and at the end of each chapter, you'll find delicious recipes for bringing the preserves you've just made into the center of the plate, as a feature ingredient in a meal.

Say Hello

hello@wellpreserved.ca
or on Twitter and
Instagram:
@WellPreserved
#BatchCookBook

Onward and Upward

We hope that some of these recipes find their way into your kitchen, pantries and to your friends and family. Get your hands dirty. Turn the fruits of your labor into something beautiful, memorable, and delicious. And don't be intimidated!

Joel

Dana

How to Use This Book

Here are a few tips and tricks for my perspective on cooking. Use this as your cheat sheet to help understand the approaches I take:

- Water. There are two types of water referred to in the book. Tap water is the default, but all ferments will call for filtered water (check the fermenting section to learn what that is and why we use it).
- When you encounter the term "cover loosely with a towel," use whatever you have. A loose lid, piece of cheesecloth, or a dishcloth. Anything that will keep the flies away and let air escape if pressure builds in the jar.
- My default salt is always non-iodized coarse salt. I avoid iodized salt because it can inhibit fermentation.
- Salt is generally measured in volume and should be adjusted to taste. There are rare times I insist on weighing salt (and other ingredients) when it is a critical component for the success or safety of a recipe (curing bacon is one such example).
- "Sterilization" is a term you'll run into during waterbath or pressure canning. See the note in the waterbath chapter (page 17) to learn more about it. Other preserving techniques don't call for it, as they don't rely on a sterile environment for preserving. However, some styles of ferments demand "sanitizing," which is explained on page 48.
- Reducing liquids. When I reduce a liquid to intensify its flavor, I do so on a large burner in a pan with a wide surface area. This allows for evaporation to happen faster than in a small pan on a small burner. Times will vary drastically depending on the size of your pot and your simmer temperature.
- Yield. All preserving recipes estimate yield in a way to guide you with their storage. Waterbath and pressure canning are the only two preserving techniques that demand jars, so the sizes of those jars are specified in the yield. Other recipes give you an approximate volume so that you can choose an appropriate container to store them. While we often use Mason jars for this purpose, knowing the volume should help you choose any other vessel. Freezer bags, storage containers, and yogurt tubs all have volumes listed on them.
- Although I prefer organic when possible, I specify organic when eating the skins of an ingredient (e.g., the rind of a lemon).
- I simmer a lot. Simmering, to me, is barely a boil unless otherwise specified (i.e., called a vigorous boil or strong simmer).

Conversions & Jar Sizes

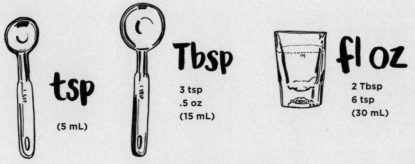

3 TSP ....1 TBSP	2 TBSP ....1 FL. OZ	8 FL. OZ...................1 CUP
2 CUPS ....1 PINT	2 PINTS ....1 QUART	4 QUARTS..............1 GALLON

tsp

(5 mL)

Tbsp

3 tsp
.5 oz
(15 mL)

fl oz

2 Tbsp
6 tsp
(30 mL)

Half Cup

4 oz
8 Tbsp
(125 mL)

Half Pint

1 cup
8 oz
16 Tbsp
(250 mL)

Pint

2 cups
16 oz
32 Tbsp
(500 mL)

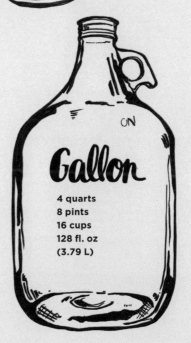

Quart

2 pints
4 cups
(1 L)

Half Gallon

2 quarts
4 pints
8 cups
(1.9 L)

Gallon

4 quarts
8 pints
16 cups
128 fl. oz
(3.79 L)

Based on American volume measurements. For those of you who use the metric system (we use both), note that most measuring cups describe 1 cup as 250 mL, and 1 quart as being equal to a liter when they are not exact equivalents.

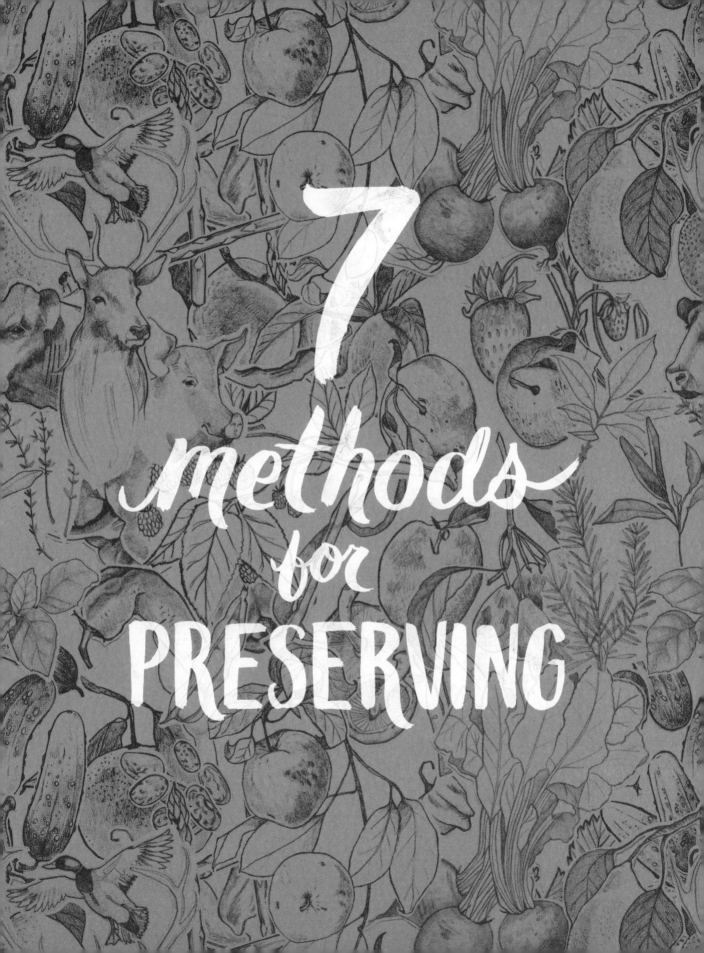

7 methods for PRESERVING

Waterbath Canning

How We Got Hooked

The Evergreen Brick Works Farmers' Market is one of the jewels in the farmers' market crown in Toronto. It's a massive market with humble beginnings: there were twenty-five vendors when it began in 2007. Back then, markets were seen as curiosities, destinations for a family outing (but not regular shopping), and were sometimes criticized, along with the local food scene, as elite or naïve. But I loved them from the first time I went, due to a fortuitous run-in with a cowboy.

As I walked through the market that first time, I saw local food champion and chef Jamie Kennedy walk toward me with an entire flat of strawberries. I swear he was walking in slow motion with the sun cutting a perfect silhouette around him like he was a sheriff in a Western movie.

And as superficial as it seems, I wanted to be like that.

The next weekend, I went back to the market with Dana, bought a half-flat of strawberries, and headed to my parents to learn how to make jam. We were shocked by how easy it was, and I was instantly hooked. I canned more than 250 jars of preserves that summer, and we launched our blog a few months later.

What I learned that summer, and what fueled my whole preserving journey, was this: If you can boil water, you can waterbath! Once you've got that basic step nailed, you'll be ready for just about anything.

What Is Waterbath Canning?

The term "waterbath canning" describes the technique of submerging jars under boiling water for a specific time. It's used for high-acid foods, such as fruit or pickles made with vinegar and is the most common type of home preserving in North America.

Fruit is sometimes cooked with sugar—for example, jam or jelly—or preserved in simple syrup made of sugar and water. Vegetables are covered in a vinegar-based brine after a brief cooking, though they're also sometimes raw-packed.

If you can boil water, you can waterbath

The Basic Process for Mason Jars with Two-Piece Lids:

1 **PREP THE CANNER AND JARS:**

Place a rack or towel on the bottom of your canner. Place your jars (without lids) inside. Cover the jars in water and boil for at least 10 minutes in order to sterilize them. Leave the jars in the water until step 4.

2 **PREP YOUR PRESERVE:**

Follow the prepping instructions in the recipe you're using. Some recipes involve cooking the vegetables (called "hot packing"); others involve only cooking the liquid and then packing raw vegetables into the jars with the liquid (called "cold packing").

3 **PREP THE LIDS:**

Place the lids in a clean bowl and cover with very hot or boiling water 5–10 minutes before canning.

4 **FILL THE JARS AND PLACE THEIR LIDS ON TOP:**

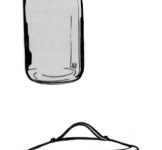
Headspace

Using special tongs, remove the jars from the canner and drain them well. You can place them on a rack on a clean countertop now, but be careful not to touch the rims. Turn the heat to high to boil the water again. Fill the jars with your preserve ingredients. Use a spoon to press between the food and the wall of the jar to remove any air bubbles. Take care to wipe the rims clean. The recipe should specify how much headspace (air) to leave. Screw the jar ring in place, finger-tight only.

5 **PROCESS IN THE WATERBATH:**

Immediately place the jars in the waterbath, ensuring they are covered by at least 1 inch of boiling water. The recipe will specify the processing time, which is the time they must stay submerged. If the water stops boiling when you add your jars, you must wait until it's boiling again before you start timing.

6 **REMOVE THE JARS FROM CANNER:**

Use tongs to remove the jars. I leave them on a cutting board overnight to cool.

7 **CHECK THE SEALS:**

Remove the rings (use them for other preserves), and check for any unsealed jars. Those should be stored in the fridge or reprocessed. Wipe clean, label, and store on a shelf for one or more years.

 **Batch-It** It is possible to do small batches of waterbath preserves. I will often cook a small batch of jam or pickles while preparing dinner. Learning to ferment, infuse, cure, properly freeze, and dehydrate will help you make other products using these methods while you are waterbathing, increasing your productivity significantly. If you're making strawberry jam, for example, set aside a few berries and infuse some vinegar or vodka!

Common Equipment and Costs

MY MUST-HAVES

PRESERVING JARS, SEALS, AND RINGS. Your basic essentials.

A BIG POT ($0–100). You may already have one and it doesn't have to be fancy. Ideally the pot will fit 4–6 large Mason jars and be tall enough to cover them with 2 inches of water (20–25 quarts of water in total). I use the pot from my pressure canner, which saves cost and storage space.

SMALL RACK ($0–$10). You need a small rack that will fit in the waterbath pot. See the Tip on page 84 to learn how to make one for free.

CANNING FUNNEL ($5–$15). These aren't vital, but they save a lot of cleanup. I prefer the stainless steel funnels over the plastic versions, although the metal ones can be harder to find and more expensive.

MAGNETIC WAND ($5). These are truly magic. They allow you to pick up jar lids without touching them.

JAR TONGS ($10–$15). I preserved for a long time without a pair of tongs. It wasn't worth it. A good set of jar tongs will make preserving safer and avoid breakage.

MANDOLIN WITH CRINKLE CUTTER ($15–$200). A crinkle cutter makes the wavy cuts common in many pickles. These cuts have a purpose: the increased surface area allows for greater and more intense exposure to flavors.

A PERMANENT MARKER ($3–$5). I use the marker to describe the contents of a jar on its lid. I'll often write the description before putting the jar in the waterbath and as long as the ink is dry, the label will survive the waterbath.

NON-REACTIVE BOWLS ($5+). Bowls made from stainless steel, ceramic, glass, and metal are all non-reactive (aluminum, copper, and cast iron are not). Reactive cookware can transfer metallic flavors to acidic foods (such as jams and jellies).

MY NICE-TO-HAVES

CANDY THERMOMETER ($15–$45). Some use it to tell when jam is set, though it's not essential.

SLOTTED SPOON OR SKIMMER ($5–$15). Very useful when skimming foam off boiling jam or jelly during cooking.

STRAINERS ($10–$20 EACH). Often used for making jelly and removing seeds from boiled fruit. I like to use multiple strainers, starting with larger holes before getting progressively smaller.

CHEESECLOTH OR MUSLIN ($5). These can be used in place of strainers or placed inside a colander. They're also used to make a "jelly sack," which holds spices without letting them become a part of the finished product (much the same as a tea bag).

STRONG BREAD RACK ($10). I like to rest my jars on a bread rack once they come out of the boiling water. This helps them to cool faster.

A GOOD RASP AND/OR PEELER ($10–$15). I use a bow-shaped peeler and have two rasps with different shaped teeth. They are vital for making apple sauce, zesting a lemon, or peeling veggies for pickles.

HIGH-SPEED BLENDER OR FOOD PROCESSOR ($100–$800). These are extremely handy for making relish or chutneys. We bought our first high-speed blender seven years after we started preserving, and it really sped up the process of making certain recipes.

JUICER/STEAM JUICER ($100–$400). This is a luxury for waterbathing, though it's become a fairly common tool for preserving juice or jelly in our house. See the notes in the fermenting section (page 42).

FOOD MILL OR TOMATO SQUEEZER ($30–$1,000). These devices separate the juice from the seeds and skin of tomatoes and berries, and are often used in making jelly or sauce.

Filling Your Pantry

You can probably think of a vast number of preserves made by waterbath canning—jam, jelly, marmalade, fruit butters, sauces, pickles, salsa . . . the list goes on—but here are a few of the less common options:

CHUTNEY

Traditional in India (though it's been adopted all over the planet), this is a chunky spread often characterized by its use of vegetables and spices.

CONSERVES

Similar to chutney, though often made with dried fruits, nuts, vinegar, and sugar.

CORDIAL

A concentrated fruit juice often added to water, alcohol, or other beverages, or used as a cooking ingredient. Cordial can also refer to a boozy preserve associated with fermenting fruit.

Setting Jam and Jelly

The best tip for making jam consistent comes from our friend Marisa McClellan of the blog Food in Jars. She insists that jam be made in a wide skillet with sloped sides. Her logic? "The wide base gives the fruit a lot of surface area on which to cook and the sloped sides encourage evaporation."

Jam is made thick by boiling the fruit with sugar and natural or added pectin. As the water is removed, the pectin breaks down, becomes water-soluble, and binds with the sugars and acids in the food to make the jelly texture. A thick jam is said to have set.

Testing the set of a jam can be done in multiple ways. From easiest to hardest (in my mind):

TEMPERATURE TEST. Most jams set at 220°F. Use a candy thermometer to check, and you'll know when it's done. This is a great way to learn—and you'll likely regift the thermometer before long.

PLATE TEST. Place a small plate in the freezer when you start making jam or jelly. When you think it's ready to test, place a small spoonful of the jam or jelly on the plate and place it in the freezer for 2 minutes. Run your finger through the jam; if it stays separated, it's ready to go!

SPOON/DRIP TEST. Dip a spoon in the jam or jelly and lift it over the surface of your jam. When it comes off in clumps (as opposed to drips), you're done!

SIGHT AND SOUND. Experience will teach you all you need to know. I can generally tell that a jam or jelly is set by the sound it makes as it simmers; a quick look at it is all I need to confirm that it's good to go!

Occasionally, jam and jelly will continue to thicken for one to two weeks after processing.

ALTERNATIVES TO COMMERCIAL PECTIN

I am not firmly (pun intended) against pectin; most jellies require it (see, for example, the Lemon-Mint Fridge Jelly recipe on page 226). Before using it, though, I highly recommend tasting it. Most pectin is extremely bitter and requires an inordinate amount of sugar to offset the taste. Your jam becomes less healthy and tastes less like its ingredients.

You can make your own pectin (see page 84 in the Apples chapter) and help achieve set by adding it a few tablespoons at a time to jam or jelly that's too thin. In most cases, I simply use and create recipes that don't require added pectin.

ALTERNATIVES TO WHITE SUGAR

Brown sugar, maple sugar, and cane sugar can all replace white sugar (and vice versa). However, if you're using pectin, for best results do not substitute sugar for other sweeteners (you'll notice that in many recipes I suggest honey instead of sugar—my standard ratio is to replace sugar with half its volume of honey). If you want to minimize the added sweeteners, choose recipes developed with low (or no) sugar, preserve whole fruit in light syrup, and avoid recipes with added pectin (its bitterness means extra sweeteners are required). If you're using a recipe that doesn't call for pectin, you can generally replace the sugar with half to one-third of its volume of honey or maple syrup.

JELLY SACKS

Solid ingredients (often spices such as cloves or peppercorns) are tied in a jelly sack to form a teabag-like flavor enhancer. You can buy jelly sacks or make your own with cheesecloth.

Advantages and Disadvantages

ADVANTAGES

- Minimal special equipment required.
- Reusable equipment.
- Long shelf life.
- Easy storage. They can be stored on a shelf, though you should avoid direct sunlight.
- Larger batches can be made at any one time.

DISADVANTAGES

- Changes taste and texture of original product—of course, this isn't always a bad thing.
- Often uses large amounts of sugar or vinegar, which could decrease the health benefits of some produce.
- Can take more time than other techniques.
- Can add a lot of heat to your kitchen and can be energy-intensive.
- Limited room for creativity because of the reliance on high-acidity ingredients.

Fundamentals of Waterbath Canning

SAFETY

People will joke that they want to learn to preserve but "don't want to kill" their family or friends. These worries stem from a combination of legitimate concerns and simple fear of the unknown. It is possible through improper canning to create an environment that will produce the botulinum toxin. Botulism is the worst possible type of food poisoning. It can cause irreversible damage and, in the worst cases, death.

Although botulism is a very real concern, it is important to stress that it is also both avoidable and rare. According to the US Centers for Disease Control and Prevention, there were eighteen reported cases of botulism directly related to home-canning vegetables between 1996 and 2008 (see www.cdc.gov/nczved/divisions/dfbmd/diseases/botulism/consumers.html). The rarity is magnified when you consider the same resource estimates that 20% of American households can their own food, with 13% of the population canning low-acid foods!

Why did the eighteen people eating home-preserved food get botulism? Were they unlucky? According to the CDC, "These outbreaks often occur because home canners did not follow canning instructions, did not use pressure cookers, ignored signs of food spoilage, and were unaware of the risk of botulism from improperly preserving vegetables."

I make every conscious effort to follow the standards set forth in the *USDA Complete Guide to Home Canning*, which can be found and downloaded online. It is a relatively brief guide, and I highly recommend referring to it or the online resource The National Center for Home Food Preservation (http://nchfp.uga.edu) to further your knowledge about and comfort with canning.

Most spoilage is recognizable. Mold appears on the surface, or a lid becomes unsealed as gases in a jar expand. The most common signs that a jar may be contaminated (in general, not just for botulism) include:

- Leaking containers; loose or bulging seals.
- Cracked or damaged jars.
- The jar "explodes" liquid when opened.
- Food is discolored or moldy, or smells bad.

Despite the relatively low risk of severe illness, the absolute best advice to follow is:

When in doubt toss it out

There are specific procedures to follow should you suspect a jar is spoiled or contaminated. Because it's incredibly rare (I've lost two jars in the thousands we've preserved), I recommend checking the website of the Centers for Disease Control and Prevention (see above for the URL) for the most current advice on how to dispose of it.

V IS FOR VINEGAR

All vinegar should have its percentage of acidity clearly marked on the label: 5% is standard for most white vinegar and is the default percentage most recipes use unless otherwise specified. Pickling vinegar (usually 7% or higher) is far more acidic and shouldn't be used unless specified. Lower percentage vinegar should be avoided unless a recipe calls for it, in which case it is likely being used for its flavor and not its acidity.

Storing

Waterbath preserves should be stored with the rings removed, out of direct sunlight. Avoid extreme temperatures. If you want to stack them in layers, separate the jars with a piece of cardboard. Once opened, these preserves should be stored in the fridge where they will last for a long time.

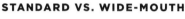

Weck   **Mason**

Standard

Wide-mouth

Types of Jars

Other than safety concerns, the biggest consideration when waterbath canning comes down to jar selection.

Avoid swing-top bottles (the type you find on some beer, maple syrup, or olive oil bottles) and use jars made specifically for preserving. The most common types are those with two-piece lids (a seal, the flat cover, plus a band to hold it in place), typically called Mason jars, and others with glass lids, a gasket, and clamps, popularized by a company called Weck.

Both jar types are reusable. Mason jars require you to purchase new seals (the flat part that sits directly on the glass) though you can reuse the bands. The other jars are completely reusable, and come in many different and pretty styles, but they are usually more expensive than Mason jars.

STANDARD VS. WIDE-MOUTH

Regardless of style, most jars are available in standard or wide-mouth. I'm picky about the style of jar I use for each preserve.

I use standard jars for pickles and preserves that have large pieces of food that I want to stop from floating (see Seatbelting on page 18).

Jam, jellies, marmalade, and other single-consistency preserves can be poured into either a wide-mouth or a standard jar.

SIZE OF JAR

A good preserving recipe should specify the quantity of jars and their size, as it affects processing time. Make sure to follow the directions, otherwise the results could be unpredictable, unstable, or even unsafe.

Jars come in an ever-increasing variety of sizes (see page 5). Purists will note that the conversions aren't exact—for example, a pint is 470 mL—but will have to accept that this is how the jars are labeled.

Despite the differences in size, you'll find that they tend to cost almost the same price, so I favor recipes that balance economy (i.e., fewer jars) and the amount I'm going to reasonably eat (I don't often have the need for a quart of relish).

The half-gallon size is largely used for fermenting and for storing dried goods. They generally aren't suitable for waterbath canning, unless you're making very thin liquids such as juice.

"STERILIZING" JARS

It is common practice to boil jars for 10 minutes or longer to sterilize them during the canning process. Although boiling jars technically sterilizes them, the natural environment of our kitchens is not fully controlled, and it is impossible to achieve true sterility. When filling jars, work with a small number at a time to keep the jars as clean and sterile as possible.

Adjusting for Altitude

The National Center for Home Food Preservation recommends adjusting processing time (the amount of time your jars are covered by boiling water) for those living at higher elevations. Most readers will be able to use the times specified in the recipes in Part 2, but if you live at higher elevations you'll have to adjust the processing times as follows:

ALTITUDE	ADDITIONAL PROCESSING TIME IN MINUTES
1,001–3,000 ft	5
3,001–6,000 ft	10
6,001 and up	15

Common Problems and How to Solve (or Avoid) Them

JAR BREAKS DURING WATERBATHING. This can happen if you've forgotten to place a rack at the bottom of the canner or if you've placed cold jars in boiling water. This can also happen if a jar had a small crack in it before it was placed in the canner. If the jar is cracked, it should be discarded (along with its contents).

JAR LOSES LIQUID OR BRINE AFTER REMOVAL FROM WATERBATH. This is also called "syphoning." The easiest fix is to carefully remove the canner from the heat source for a few minutes and allow the jars to cool slightly before removing them from the waterbath. This can happen if there were any pieces of food on the rim of the jar before sealing. Lastly, you can have an excess of headspace if you didn't release pockets of trapped air in pickles and other chunky preserves (the pressure would build up and the liquid would be pushed out to release the pressure). These jars should be fine to eat, though they will discolor relatively quickly, so eat them first.

One of the most common preserving questions I get asked is, "How do I stop X from floating in the jar?" My answer is always the same: "Put a seatbelt on it!" Imagine that you are canning long green beans. To seatbelt them, start by filling a standard Mason jar vertically with beans. Pack them as tightly as possible, then wedge a few beans horizontally under the shoulders of the jar, to trap the others underneath. This will work with other veg as well, as long as you have a few long pieces to act as the seatbelt.

JAR DIDN'T SEAL DURING PROCESSING. This could be caused by a piece of food on the rim of the jar or a faulty seal. Always be very careful about cleaning the rims. Process with a new lid or store in the fridge.

YIELD DOESN'T MATCH RECIPE. This is common. The size of vegetables, amount of moisture in fruit, heat of your stove, and cooking time can drastically change the yield of a batch of preserves. I've seen two people in a cooking class end up with totally different yields based on cooking temperature and time alone.

FRUIT OR PICKLES LOSE COLOR. This is caused by storage in direct sunlight or by jars that have lost liquid through **syphoning**. These should be eaten first. A popped lid can also cause this, in which case you'd be best to dispose of the jar.

JELLY OR JAM DOESN'T THICKEN. This is generally caused by undercooking the jelly or not having enough pectin (added or natural). It may continue to set in the jar or after being refrigerated. You can try to reprocess the jam, but I often use these jars to sweeten tea, or add to carbonated water, cocktails, salad dressing, or other cooking.

JELLY OR JAM IS TOO THICK. Generally caused by cooking too long. Once you open the jar, you can add small amounts of boiling water and stir to thin a jam or jelly.

PICKLES ARE TOO SOFT. They can be hardened in the fridge, but vinegar pickles are often softer than people expect. If you want firmer pickles, fermenting will yield the best results (try the fermented dill pickles on page 194).

UNEVEN SPICING OF PICKLES. When spooning brine into pickles it's difficult to get an even amount of dill, mustard, or other spices in each jar. I like to divide my spices in advance and add them to each jar individually.

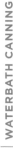

Do's and Don'ts of Waterbath Canning

DO check out the National Center for Home Food Preservation (http://nchfp.uga.edu/) to learn more about up-to-date safety procedures and standards and download the *USDA Complete Guide to Home Canning*.

DO consult trusted books, authors, and websites to find fantastic recipes.

DO remember that you can make small batches. This doesn't have to be an epic, endurance-testing marathon!

DO use caution when choosing to waterbath low-acid foods.

DO check out different foods and styles of waterbathing. Many people think of jam, jelly, and pickles when they think of waterbathing. But there are so many other options!

DON'T be intimidated. There's a lot of scary information about the worst-case scenarios, but the odds are minuscule—and avoidable.

DON'T get creative with the recipes. You could easily change the acid balance and create an unsafe environment for preserving.

DON'T use Grandma or Grandpa's recipes or techniques. Modern agriculture has changed our food—many tomatoes are less acidic, a lot of pork has less fat—and our understanding of food safety has grown. My grandparents used to preserve clams by using a waterbath, and I know people who use wax, invert jars, and wrap them in towels. Neither of these approaches is considered safe today.

DON'T use freshly squeezed lemon juice when a recipe calls for bottled lemon juice. Bottled lemon juice has consistent acidity while different lemons' acid levels vary. When a recipe calls for bottled lemon juice, it is generally added for safety—fresh lemon juice is specified when flavor is the only consideration.

Pressure Canning

How We Got Hooked

I fell in love with pressure canning by accident. I actually bought my pressure canner on impulse. I had been walking through a big hardware store when I saw it sitting on a shelf. It was a large canner, and it was deeply discounted.

I used the canner for a while before finding bags of shucked peas at a local farm stand. I bought the entire lot. They were canned in half-pint jars and put away until winter.

When we opened the peas, they were soft from processing but had retained their summer flavor. And the liquid was just as useful. We added it to stir-fries, rice, soups, and gravy. It was awesome!

Pressure canning allows us to preserve vegetables without adding large amounts of vinegar or sugar. This means that you can make the equivalent of store-bought canned veggies (such as beans and mushrooms), soup, stock, and more—and all of it can sit on your shelf and are nearly ready-to-eat from the jar!

Like waterbath canning, pressure canning isn't difficult and any initial fears will soon be overcome!

What Is Pressure Canning?

Pressure canning processes low-acid foods at higher heat than waterbath, resulting in a safer product. Each pressure canner has its own instructions, but the fundamentals are below.

The Basic Process for Mason Jars with Two-Piece Lids:

1 PREP THE JARS AND PRESSURE CANNER

Place the jars in the large pot to be sterilized. Cover them in water and boil for at least 10 minutes (leave the jars in the water until step 4). Place the rack or towel on the bottom of the pressure canner and add a few inches of water. With pressure canning, you do not want to cover the jars, as the pressurized heat of the steam is what preserves them.

2 PREP YOUR PRESERVE

Follow the prepping instructions in the recipe you're using. Some recipes involve cooking the vegetables (called "hot packing"); others involve only cooking the liquid and then packing raw vegetables into the jars with the liquid (called "cold packing").

3 PREP LIDS

Place the lids in a clean bowl and cover with very hot or boiling water 5–10 minutes before canning.

4 FILL THE JARS AND PLACE LIDS ON TOP.

Remove the jars from the pot, drain well, and set them aside on a bread rack. Turn the pressure canner to high to boil the water again. Fill the jars with the ingredients. Use a spoon to press between the food and the wall of the jar to remove any air bubbles, and take care to wipe the rims clean. The recipe should specify how much headspace (air) to leave. Screw the jar ring in place, finger-tight only.

5 VENT THE CANNER

After filling the jars, place them in the canner and ensure they are not fully submerged. Secure the canner lid in position while leaving the vents open. With the canner still on high heat, allow steam to vent steadily for 10 minutes.

6 PRESSURIZE

Place the proper weight (specified by the recipe as a number of pounds of pressure) on the canner or seal the petcock. The canner will begin to increase pressure and will be ready in 3–10 minutes. Read the number on a dial-gauge canner or listen for a steady jiggle on a weighted canner.

7 START TIMING AND PROCESS

The recipe will specify the processing time. Always start timing after the canner has reached the required pressure. If you live at high altitudes (1,000 feet above sea level or higher), you will need to lengthen the processing time. See the chart on page 25 for more details.

8 COOL

Turn the heat off, leave the lid in place, and allow the canner to cool down. If you force the lid open, you will often cause syphoning. Most canners take about an hour to cool enough to open easily (if I'm canning late at night, I leave jars in the canner overnight and skip the cooling in the next step).

Batch-It I do most of my pressure canning in the fall and winter months. I prepare full meals in advance, such as soups or baked beans, or preserve stock from chicken carcasses that we freeze in the heat of summer to process later. I also preserve a lot of vegetables via pressure canning so it becomes a natural companion to freezing or fermenting.

9 REMOVE FROM THE CANNER

I place the jars on a cutting board overnight, or for 8 hours, to cool.

10 CHECK THE SEALS

Remove the rings (use them for other preserves) and check for any unsealed
jars, which should be stored in the fridge or reprocessed. Wipe clean, label,
and store on a shelf for a year or more, depending on the ingredients.

Common Equipment and Costs

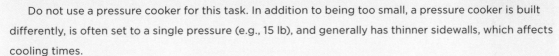

MY MUST-HAVES

A PRESSURE CANNER ($100–$700). My canner was around $150; you don't
have to buy the most expensive one. I do recommend, though, that you buy a
large one (20+ quarts) as it will save time and reduce the number of batches that
you'll have to make—and it doubles as your waterbath canner!

The biggest influence on cost will come down to the material of the canner.
Stainless steel will be more expensive than polished aluminum, for example.

Do not use a pressure cooker for this task. In addition to being too small, a pressure cooker is built
differently, is often set to a single pressure (e.g., 15 lb), and generally has thinner sidewalls, which affects
cooling times.

When buying a canner, you have two choices:

- **A DIAL GAUGE CANNER.** This has a dial (like a speedometer) on top that can be easily
  read. Many people new to pressure canning prefer these because they seem to be more
  accurate/familiar but there are a few drawbacks: they are typically more costly and need
  to be inspected annually to ensure the reading on the gauge is right!
- **A WEIGHTED GAUGE CANNER.** These often come with three
  weights (5, 10, and 15 lb), are more affordable, and require less mainte-
  nance. They tend to be my preference.

The following items are mentioned in the waterbath section (see pages 11–12) and are
equally useful here.

MY MUST-HAVES

- Small rack for bottom of canner ($0–$10)
- Canning funnel ($5–$15)
- Magnetic wand ($5)
- Jar tongs ($10–$15)

MY NICE-TO-HAVES

- Slotted spoon ($5)
- Strainers ($10–$20 each)
- Strong bread rack ($10)
- A good rasp and/or peeler ($10–$15)
- High-speed blender or food processor
  ($100–$800)

Filling Your Pantry

If you're still trying to wrap your head around pressure canning, take a walk down the middle aisles of your grocery store. Most of the canned goods can be recreated—in fact, improved upon—by pressure canning.

STOCKS

Vegetable, meat, and fish stocks can all be pressure canned. We tend to eat a lot of meat in March and April (when very little other local food is available) and can make stock every week or two until we have enough to get through summer.

SOUPS

The general rule of pressure canning is to process the food according to the longest-cooking ingredient (meat takes longer to process than vegetables so if you're using both in a soup, for example, you'd need to process as if it was a jar full of meat).

STEWS

Most stews can be pressure canned (the notable exceptions include recipes that use flour, rice, pasta, or dairy).

MEAT

Many hunters pressure can meat in Mason jars. Although the idea of canned meat may sound less than inviting, I've spoken to numerous people who were shocked at how much they liked it once they tried it. It seems funny to me that canned fish is commonly accepted but canned meat is not!

SAUCES

Many people will pressure can tomato sauce. They do this to avoid adding citric acid or because they want to add other ingredients (such as herbs or other vegetables) which would lower the overall acidity of the recipe and make it unsafe to preserve in a waterbath.

Fundamentals of Pressure Canning

Refer to the notes in Fundamentals of Waterbath Canning for information on seatbelting, safety, and types of jars for much of this content (pages 14–17); pressure canning and waterbath canning are closely related.

RAW/COLD PACKING

Uncooked vegetables are packed tightly into jars before hot brine is poured over them. Although this is done occasionally in waterbath preserving (e.g., pickles), it is most common in pressure canning.

GASKETS

Every pressure canner has a set of gaskets that keep it sealed. Inspect them regularly and order replacements if the gaskets are worn. I like to have an extra set in my house so I'm not left in a bind if I find a problem. Gaskets generally last a year or longer, but each manufacturer will likely recommend a lifespan.

INSPECTING DIAL GAUGE CANNERS

Dial gauge canners should be tested and calibrated yearly. This can be difficult if you don't have access to local testing—my understanding is that testing is far easier to access in the USA than Canada—so check on this before buying one.

Adjusting for Altitude

The National Center for Home Food Preservation recommends adjusting the weight/PSI of your pressure canner based on your elevation. Most readers will be able to use the times specified in the recipes in Part 2, but if you live at higher elevations, you'll have to adjust the processing times as follows:

Weights for a Dial-Gauge Canner Based on Altitude from the National Center for Home Food Preservation:

ALTITUDE	PSI (DIAL GAUGE CANNER)
0–2,000 ft	11
2,001–4,000 ft	12
4,001–6,000 ft	13
6,001–8,000 ft	14

	PSI (WEIGHTED GAUGE)
0–1,000 ft	10
Above 1,000 ft	15

Advantages and Disadvantages

ADVANTAGES

- The flavors are preserved intact.
- Works without adding salt, vinegar, or other ingredients.
- Long shelf life.
- Easy storage.

DISADVANTAGES

- Requires an investment in equipment.
- The high heat kills many of the nutrients in the food.
- Uses a lot of energy, creates a lot of heat, and can make your kitchen uncomfortable to work in.

Storing

Follow the same instructions for storing water-bath canned goods (see page 15).

Common Problems and How to Solve (and Avoid) Them

Refer to the notes on waterbath canning on pages 17–18.

Do's and Don'ts of Pressure Canning

DO read the manual for your pressure canner. It has instructions specific to its use.

DO be careful about your headspace. If a jar is too full, it may begin to syphon, and once it starts, it will drain a lot of liquid.

DO make sure you use the water that's in the jar with your preserve. It has almost infinite uses! I use it to deglaze a pan or add it to a stir-fry at the end of cooking.

DON'T forget to check about what you can and can't add. The National Center for Home Food Preservation recommends that you "do not add noodles or other pasta, rice, flour, cream, milk or other thickening agents to home canned soups. If dried beans or peas are used, they must be fully rehydrated first." (See http://nchfp.uga.edu/how/can_04/soups.html)

DON'T forget to inspect your canner every year as described in the instructions that come with your canner.

DON'T force the lid of the canner open. Opening the pressure canner too soon will cause rapid cooling and result in syphoning from your jars. Be patient and allow the canner to cool naturally.

DON'T use an old canner or pressure cooker in place of a modern pressure canner.

Dehydrating

How We Got Hooked

Dana smirked as she told me, "It's the ugliest gift I've ever given to anyone!"

Within moments I was smiling from ear to ear. Santa had brought me a dehydrator. A big dehydrator.

Although I'm sure I had mentioned dehydrating food to Dana, I don't remember talking about it often. There were so many reasons not to get a dehydrator. We didn't have any place to store it, and I wasn't sure what to do with it.

When I first got my dehydrator, I was sure that I would dry slices of apples and banana. I was also curious about the idea of dehydrating tomato sauce, something I had heard of years ago from a friend who was an avid hiker. I liked the idea of a piece of equipment that made my kitchen feel like a science lab.

In a matter of weeks, my curiosity about dehydration had turned into an obsession. Furthermore, drying food changed my relationship with preserving.

What got me so excited?

1   It was easy.
2   It didn't involve a lot of sugar or vinegar; flavors remained largely unchanged in the process.
3   I could experiment without any safety fears.

Dehydrating taught me that I could do more than make condiments. I could actually make ingredients. I quickly began dreaming of building a pantry and moving preserves to the center of the plate.

What Is Dehydrating?

Drying food is one of the oldest known forms of preserving. It is also remarkably simple. Food is generally cut, sometimes cooked, blanched, or pierced, and dried via relatively gentle heat and/or air circulation.

There are all sorts of ways to dry food, but there are three main points to be aware of:

- **AIR CIRCULATION IS CRITICAL.** A bowl of mushrooms will turn moldy but the same mushrooms spread out on a small rack will dry naturally.

- **TEMPERATURE IS IMPORTANT,** as enzymes in food are killed at high temperatures. It's generally believed that this occurs when food reaches 115°F–120°F, as suggested by Dr. Edward Howell in his book *Food Enzymes for Health and Longevity.* If you're trying to retain maximum nutrition from your preserved foods, temperature is important. See "Raw and Living Food," page 34.
- **HUMIDITY CHANGES THE TIME IT TAKES.** Drying times can change significantly depending on the amount of moisture that's in the air. Food will dry faster when it is less humid. If you are dehydrating a huge amount of food (we once dehydrated for seventeen consecutive days), the process of drying the food can increase the humidity in your kitchen and further slow down the process.

The Basic Process for Dehydrating Food:

To dry food, either use a dehydrator or expose it to air. Air-drying is often done by tying food in bunches or laying it across racks to dry. Both processes remove moisture, thereby reducing bacteria which can lead to spoilage, while allowing good enzymes to remain living. For this reason, dried food is a common element of a raw-food diet. In most cases, the food is ready when it's brittle and breaks. Dried food can be eaten as is, reconstituted in warm liquid, or turned into powder to add to cooking.

Batch-It I often dry food scraps when I'm preparing other preserves. Some of my favorites are mushroom stems for powder; apple skins for smoking food on the BBQ; strawberry hulls for tea; and the tips of strawberries I'm using to make jam (the ends are too tricky to cut with a mandolin).

Common Equipment and Costs

You'll soon see that you can dry food with almost no equipment at all, so none of this is really required. But the following equipment speeds things up, adds efficiencies (such as decreasing the amount of space you'd need to dry food without a dehydrator), and increases the consistency of results.

MY MUST-HAVES

DEHYDRATOR ($50–$600). Although you can dry food without a machine, this is an investment I highly recommend. It's also one worth saving for, although you might get  lucky if you keep your eye on the classifieds. Look for a large rectangular unit that pushes the heated air from the side and back. This removes the need to circulate the trays (as you need to do in the circular units) and allows you to preserve many different flavors without cross-contamination. I also believe it's important to buy a unit that allows you to change the temperature. Most are energy-efficient—ours takes the equivalent energy of a light bulb. Some people will pay big bucks for a stainless steel unit to avoid preserving food using heated plastic, but just as many are comfortable with the material used in most units. We have a large nine-tray unit that cost around $300.

MANDOLIN/FOOD SLICER ($15–$200). I love my kitchen knives, but a slicer is a big help when drying food. A slice of apple that's 1 mm thick will dry 30% faster than a slice that's 1.5 mm thick. We love our $15 slicer.

VEGETABLE PEELER ($6). Our favorite peeler is an all-metal bow peeler. Once you try it, you'll never use another!

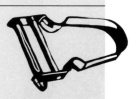

MASON JARS AND LIDS ($1 EACH OR LESS). We like to use vintage jars to store our dried food in because they look so neat and can't be used for canning.

STRING OR TWINE ($3–$5). Some food can be dried by hanging in the kitchen or a dark closet.

MY NICE-TO-HAVES

COFFEE GRINDER OR HIGH-SPEED BLENDER ($50–$100+). This will allow you to transform your dried food into powder—a helpful ingredient in the pantry.

SILPAT MATS ($10–$20) OR PARCHMENT PAPER ($4). Useful when making fruit leather or working with sticky products.

WIRE RACKS ($10–$15). You can air-dry food by laying it on racks.

KITCHEN SCALE ($20–$200). I am a geek. I prefer to weigh an ingredient before and after drying to see what percentage of moisture it lost. This also helps me gauge when a batch is done and learn about the technique in general.

Filling Your Pantry

The most common types of dehydrated foods are dried fruits and vegetables, though candied goods like ginger, orange peel, cherries, and bananas are popular, too. Here are a few other ideas to play around with.

POWDER

Dried vegetables can be blended into powder and used in cooking. Onion and garlic powder are common, although many others are just as flavorful (some of my favorites are mushroom, beet, and celeriac powders). Powder adds flavor to rice, pasta, stir-fries, dry rubs, dough and it's a natural thickener for soups, stews, gravies, and sauces.

LEATHER

Dana and I were raised in the 1970s and remember the first appearance of Fruit Roll-ups! Fruit leather is the homemade, and far superior, version. It's made by spreading sauce or pureed fruits onto parchment paper and letting it dry in sheets. It's generally eaten as is but could be dissolved into tea or mulled cocktails, incorporated into desserts, or used as a cone for a fruit salad.

JERKY

Fish or lean meat, such as game or pork, is cut into strips and marinated or brined before being dried. Careful control of the temperature is required in order to ensure that the meat is properly preserved while avoiding the "danger zone" of cooking it at low temperatures. (See page 55.) Popular examples include beef, salmon, and deer jerky. It can be eaten as is or rehydrated in warm water or sauce or added to pizza, sandwiches, omelets, and more.

RE-DEHYDRATING

This is a term that we invented. It involves drying food, rehydrating it in warm liquid (that isn't water), and dehydrating it again. This allows you to infuse a flavor into the food that you're drying. Strawberries and balsamic vinegar, rhubarb and maple syrup, and mushrooms in stock are common examples.

PARTIALLY-DRIED FOOD

Dehydrating reduces the amount of water in an ingredient, which increases the intensity of flavor in the resulting dried food. Although it's somewhat ineffective for preserving, I love to cook with food that's been partially dried (¼ to ½ the total time of the dried product) as a way to boost the flavors of my cooking. Partially-dried tomatoes, mushrooms, and onions are all great on pizza or sandwiches.

Advantages and Disadvantages

ADVANTAGES

- Easy to do.
- Storage is easy if making powder.
- Taste often remains unaltered or is intensified.
- Can keep enzymes alive.

DISADVANTAGES

- Equipment can be expensive.
- The product can be bulky to store if left whole.

Fundamentals of Dehydrating

COMMERCIALLY-DRIED FOODS

Many people buy dried food as a healthy snack and alternative to fresh fruit, which can rot or bruise. However, commercially-dried food often includes chemical pre-treatments that are omitted on the labels. For example, sulfur dioxide is commonly used on tomatoes before sun-drying them. Other surprises lurking in mass-produced dried food include large additions of sugar and unexpected cooking techniques (many banana chips are actually deep-fried).

SUN-DRYING

Although it's possible to dry food in the sun, it's not practical for most of us as food must be protected from animals, dust, and rain. Many commercial products labeled "sun-dried" are often partially dried indoors or with chemicals. It is possible to dry vegetables and fruit in the sun by spreading them on racks and leaving them in the sun, but you should take them in at night.

AIR-DRYING

This is a great alternative to sun-drying. Food is chopped or left whole and exposed to the air to dry. You can dry hot peppers by tying them with string and hanging them in your window. Herbs can be dried in your closet or another dark space, and mushrooms can be spread on a rack. I leave several racks on top of the kitchen cupboard where they are out of the way but easily accessible when needed.

OVEN-DRYING

Possible but not recommended. The most common problem with oven-drying is the temperature. Most ovens are too hot to dry food without destroying enzymes. And if your oven has only two racks instead of three, minimal food can be preserved.

Storing

Most dried foods are best stored in a closed container such as a freezer bag or Mason jar, and a dark, dry environment. Large chunks of food (such as whole mushrooms or hot peppers) will retain their flavors longer than small bits of the same product (such as chili powder). This is because larger chunks of dried food have less exposure to air than the same weight of smaller pieces or powders. Use care when handling dried food—if moisture enters the jar through wet hands, humidity, or partially-dried food, it will be absorbed and the chance of spoilage will increase.

SOLAR DEHYDRATORS

A solar dehydrator is generally a box with a transparent cover (often made of glass or Plexiglas) that contains multiple sliding trays for drying foods. Because your food is dried inside a box, you don't have to worry about bugs, dust, animals, or rain. The top is built on an angle to make the most of the sun's hours and to encourage air circulation (hot air rises, after all). It can be built right next to your garden and be part of an awesome outdoor preservation kitchen.

Most solar dehydrators are built by hand. The Internet is full of DIY plans and videos on how to make them. Before running off to the hardware store, though, know that many of these designs have two significant problems you'll want to avoid (both can be overcome):

- **LACK OF AIR.** Ensure the plan you use includes a fan or method of air circulation.
- **LACK OF TEMPERATURE CONTROL.** If you don't have the ability to automatically control the temperature, your solar dehydrator will likely dry the food but also kill the enzymes.

Raw Food and Living Foods

Food dried at lower temperatures with the intent of maintaining beneficial enzymes is often referred to as "living foods." While there is nearly absolute agreement that food that is dehydrated with too much heat will lose enzymes, there is a lot of disagreement, misinformation, and discussion about the definition of "too hot." Many proponents claim that food will lose its enzymes or raw qualities at 118°F. Given that, here are a few things to consider:

- If your dehydrator does not have a thermostat, you will not be able to control the temperature and may or may not be losing enzymes.
- The temperature of the food will vary from that of the ambient temperature in the dehydrator. Food placed in a 100°F chamber will not reach 100°F as it dries. This isn't that different from your oven (the temperature of the oven is always higher than that of the food that is being cooked in it), but some claim that the evaporation that occurs during dehydration also cools the food as it dries.
- Many dehydrators will promote drying by varying the temperature through the drying process. The air can be 20 degrees (or more) above or below the setting you have chosen at any given time.

If you try to adjust for the three factors above by drying food at lower temperatures, you may find that the process is painfully slow or doesn't completely dry the food. For optimal results when making living foods, start the dehydrator closer to the peak (e.g., 120°F) for two to three hours before lowering it by 10 to 20 degrees for the remainder of the process. The enzymes should then remain intact, as evaporation will not allow the food to come close to 120°F during the initial drying time.

For optimal preservation of dry foods, it is best to read the manual of your dehydrator to know exactly how it works.

Other Considerations When Buying a Dehydrator

I am in love with large rectangular box dehydrators. Here are some of the common features and things to think about when considering investing in a box dehydrator:

- **TIMERS.** I've never used a timer, though I can see the benefits, especially when drying food overnight or when you're going to be out of the house. You could also buy a power bar with a timer if you don't have this feature.
- **THERMOSTATS.** As mentioned above, the thermostat measures the temperature of the food as opposed to the ambient temperature of the chamber. Take this into consideration when dehydrating.
- **VARIABLE HEAT.** This is a little geeky and probably too much information for most of us, but there is some evidence that drying food at varying temperatures (i.e., changing the temperature through a single batch of preserving) can help maximize the benefits gained by drying food. Most box dehydrators do this automatically.
- **DURABILITY.** I've used our dehydrator for more than two weeks without turning it off once. It's a workhorse! But I have several friends who have found melted parts on circular driers after prolonged use.
- **DITCHING PLASTIC.** If you're avoiding plastic for environmental or health reasons, you can buy a rectangular stainless steel drier. But note that these are much more expensive.

Common Problems and How to Solve (and Avoid) Them

DRIED FOOD TURNS MOLDY IN STORAGE. The food wasn't dry enough when it was placed inside the container, or moisture entered the container. Discard the food and dry it for longer next time, or check the storage area for humidity.

FOOD IS TOO HARD, OR YOU DON'T KNOW WHEN TO REMOVE IT. The food was dried too quickly (i.e., the temperature was too high) or for too long. Dried food will harden as it cools, so read the recipe carefully for when to check the texture by removing a piece of food and letting it rest for at least 10 minutes to verify the final texture. Most recipes will advise on the final texture to look for.

INCONSISTENT RESULTS WITHIN ONE BATCH (SOME FOOD DRYING FASTER THAN OTHERS). There are two main reasons this happens: the food was cut into different widths, or improper circulation made the temperature inconsistent. Try using a mandolin for consistency when slicing and choose a dehydrator with good circulation.

CROSS-CONTAMINATION OF TASTE (APPLES TASTE LIKE HOT PEPPERS THAT WERE DRIED AT THE SAME TIME). There are three ways this might happen: different foods are stored together, different products touched each other during the drying process, or a heat source came only from the bottom or the top of a unit. When heat comes across or from behind the food, the flavor transfer is limited. And keep different foods on separate racks.

DRIED FOOD LOSES COLOR. This is common in dehydrated food stored in a bright area. Move your dried goods to a darker location, or store them in a dark or shaded jar.

Do's and Don'ts of Dehydrating

Drying food is liberating, and the risk of failure is low!

DO feel free to experiment, unless you're using meat or fish, which need greater care.

DO look for recipes that include the expected texture of the finished product. This will help you familiarize yourself with the process.

DON'T touch dried food with wet hands. It's easy to get other pieces damp and contaminate the jar.

DON'T pack food tightly on trays or racks. The key to drying food is air circulation, so your goal is to ensure that as much air as possible is in contact with your food.

Slow-Cooker Kimchi Pulled Pork, page 150

Fermenting

How We Got Hooked

I had been fermenting for a while before I really got it. "Getting it" happened in the blink of an eye.

Dana and I used to refer to fermenting as controlled rotting. We would laugh about it in public, but those words would quietly gnaw at my confidence when I would stare at a jar of fermenting sauerkraut or when measuring the salt for a new hot sauce. I kept on fermenting, but I could feel those words holding me back and stopping me from really exploring the process.

I wrote an email to a friend named Tigress. She had two great preserving blogs (*Tigress in a Jam* and *Tigress in a Pickle*) and she played a pivotal role in revitalizing preserving in 2010 when she hosted a twelve-month preserving challenge called the Can Jam. The email to my feline friend was brief and included the question, "Does it ever bother you to think that we eat food that's kind of rotten?"

Her reply was warm and playful, and full of the conviction I needed to build my own confidence. I don't have her exact words but remember her sentiment. "No. In fact, it kind of freaks me out that we can preserve jam and pickles and that we can kill them so dead that they don't rot after many years in a jar. Ferments are ALIVE." I felt better immediately, and dove into fermenting with gusto.

This method of preserving is ridiculously easy. As long as you have patience and follow a few simple guidelines, you'll be good to go!

What Is Fermenting?

Fermentation is one of the world's oldest techniques of food preservation. Cheese, wine, beer, sauerkraut, sourdough, kimchi, pickles, and many other foods are fermented. There are many different styles of the preserve and three general considerations when fermenting:

- **STARTERS.** Some ferments, such as kombucha, kefir, and sourdough, have different types of "starters" that you need to have in order to make them. Some starters are made, while others are bought, traded, or shared.

- **OXYGEN.** Some ferments thrive with oxygen and open-air fermenting—some forms of honey wine and mead even rely on it—while other ferments treat oxygen as the enemy. It's important to use special containers or airlocks for fermenting when you wish to reduce contact with oxygen, such as when you make alcohol. These airlocks also allow carbon dioxide produced by fermenting to escape without building dangerous levels of pressure in a container.

- **LIQUID/BRINE.** Many ferments, such as pickles, need to be covered by a liquid (often produced by salt pulling water from the item being fermented). It is important that this liquid submerge all ingredients completely. You can use a weight, such as a plate or a rock, to ensure nothing floats. Check the liquid often to remove the first sign of mold or scum (more on this shortly).

Common Equipment and Costs

You don't need all of this equipment for every ferment you'll make. Each style of fermenting uses different tools, but the following list will help you get set up for most types.

MY MUST-HAVES

FOOD SCALE ($20-$200).
Fermenting often works through ratios, which work by weight. Most of my hot sauce uses about 2.5% non-iodized coarse salt measured as a percentage of the weight of the hot peppers.

NON-IODIZED COARSE SALT ($3-$10). I prefer gray salt and am especially fond of any brand that has flakes of salt that vary in size or color. Iodized salt can prohibit fermentation, so steer clear of that.

FILTERED WATER. If you plan to use tap water (I do), it's important to know if there is anything added to it. Chlorine and chloramine are common additions to city water that inhibit fermentation—if you're struggling with fermenting, this may be the cause. Water with chlorine can be left overnight and the chlorine will evaporate. To remove chloramine you will need a water filter (it will also work to remove chlorine). Filtering systems range from jugs you fill with water and store in your fridge ($20+) through in-line systems that filter the water before it comes through your faucet ($80+).

AIRLOCKS ($8-$12). Buy these at a home-brew or wine-supply store. They come in many varieties but all are inserted into stoppers that you can also buy there. A size 12/13 stopper (often used for 6.5-gallon carboys) will fit a regular Mason jar. Smaller stoppers are available for 1-gallon jugs. Airlocks need to be checked through the fermentation process and topped up with water if it begins to evaporate (the airlocks use water as the seal—if it evaporates the airlock will not be functional). Using airlocks is a sure way to eliminate flies and often helps control or stop mold.

ONE CROCK (OR SEVERAL) ($15–$200).

These are usually ceramic and are made specifically for preserving, though they are sometimes sold as planters in antique stores. I like to have at least one large crock in case I want to make a large batch of hot sauce, pickles, or the like. I'm partial to special crocks that feature a v-shaped trough that the lid fits into. The trough is designed to be filled with a small amount of water, which acts as an airlock. These tend to be more expensive and harder to find. Be cautious of old crocks that may be affordable but could have lead in their glaze.

MASON JARS ($1).

I ferment in 1-quart and ½-gallon Mason jars. If I'm using a wide-mouthed jar, I will use a ½-cup Mason jar as a fermenting weight. If I'm using a standard-mouth jar, I use an airlock and seatbelt the ingredients below the surface of the water (see page 18).

WEIGHTS ($0–$60).

You can purchase ceramic weights of multiple sizes (they fit the smallest Mason jars and the largest crocks), which allow you to easily keep everything submerged. You can also use a plate or a small jar to sit on top of your ferments.

JARS OF VARIOUS SIZES.

I collect all sorts of odd jars and jugs for fermenting. Corks for airlocks are tapered, so they will fit a wide variety of jars which allows you to get really creative with using cool glass jars and jugs from vintage stores. Vegetables generally need wider containers to fit weights, while alcohol does better in jars with a thinner neck which reduces air contact and the chances of accidentally creating vinegar. The sizes I commonly use are:

- **½-GALLON WIDE-MOUTH MASON JAR ($3).** You can insert a ½-cup standard jar inside it to weigh the ferment down.
- **1-QUART WIDE-MOUTH MASON JAR ($1).** I use a ½-cup jar the same as above.
- **1-GALLON JUG ($5–$10).** These are handy to make booze in. Filling the jug to where the narrow neck begins will reduce the oxygen in the container. Airlocks with narrow corks (designed specifically for these jugs) will help oxygen escape from the jar during the ferment, which will prevent your booze from turning into vinegar and prevent a build-up of pressure in the jug. These will make five wine-bottles' (26 ounces/750 mL) worth of product.
- **CARBOYS AND DEMIJOHNS ($10–$80).** Most commonly used for wine and beer. These are generally very large glass containers. Browse the classifieds and you may find these widely available and affordable. You can use the same airlock as you use for the 1-gallon jugs but need to buy a wider stopped designed for these containers.

OVERSIZED MEASURING BUCKETS ($15–$25).

These are a cross between a measuring cup and a food-safe bucket. They are great with helping to predict the quantity of liquid and size of container you'll need. Although there are larger sizes, my largest is just over 2 gallons.

ACRYLIC PAINT PENS ($3–$5)

Look for these at an art supply store or a good office supply store. You can write directly on the glass jar, and I frequently label, date, and describe the contents of many jars with their washable ink.

MY NICE-TO-HAVES

WINE/CIDER PRESS ($500–$1,000).

Most of us don't have room for a full-sized wine press in our homes, but they are handy if you have access to a large amount of fruit and want to make your own wine/cider in large quantities.

STEAM JUICER/JUICER ($50–$200). A conventional juicer will work for soft fruit at low volumes. To easily juice large quantities or to extract juice from harder items (such as rhubarb), a steam juicer is an amazing tool. It's a four-part pot that can be filled with gallons of fruit at once. It uses a small amount of steam to extract sediment-free juice. It's also useful for making cordials, jellies, and juice extract for waterbath canning. It's moderately priced, between $120 and $200, but used models can be found in regions where people make fruit wine.

SPECIALTY AIRLOCKS ($15–$30). With the increase of popularity of fermenting, many companies, such as Kraut Source, are designing special airlocks for lactofermentation that make fermenting in a Mason jar incredibly convenient.

GLOVES ($5). If you're working with hot peppers, trying to taste a pickle, or handle a SCOBY, it's nice to have gloves to protect your hands and the good bacteria living in your ferment. Most use latex or reusable dishwashing gloves.

BOTTLING SUPPLIES.
- **BOTTLES ($0–$2 EACH).** Fizzy beverages are safest in plastic (I know that will make many cringe; more on that below), while still beverages can be stored in wine bottles or pop-top bottles. Plastic bottles are best purchased new, while wine and quart bottles from beer can be reused if cleaned and sanitized.
- **LIDS ($1–$2), CORKS ($0.50), AND A BOTTLE CORKER ($20–$200).** Affordable versions can be had at brew-your-own-wine shops or online
- **BOTTLE SANITIZER ($5–$15).** You can get organic varieties online or at a local brew-your-own shop. Each comes with instructions.
- **BOTTLE BRUSH ($10).** Makes it easy to clean the hard-to-reach places.
- **YEAST ($1 PER PACKET).** Look for brewers (ale) or champagne yeast. Champagne yeast will produce a drink with a higher alcohol content. Different types of yeast will provide different taste profiles—don't replace brewers yeast with bread yeast!
- **HYDROMETER ($25).** A device used to measure the amount of alcohol in your product.

WINE FRIDGE ($100+). This is an absolute luxury, though if you keep your eyes open, you'll be surprised at how affordable a near-new wine fridge can be. I have a small fridge that stores many ferments and frees up a lot of room in our main fridge.

Filling Your Pantry

Much like charcuterie, the world of fermenting is full of different styles. This is meant to be a partial list of ideas you may not have thought of so that you can investigate the topic further.

ALCOHOL (MEAD, WINE, COUNTRY/FRUIT WINE, CIDER)

It is almost foolish to describe the basics of fermenting alcohol in a few sentences as people dedicate their lives to the craft of making wine, cider, and more. But I think an introduction to this topic is possible. It is certainly often missing from books or articles on the subject. It took me YEARS to find out how easy it was to make booze like this. Bottling is a simple process as long as you have the basic supplies, which include bottles, corks (or lids), sanitizer, and a tube for syphoning.

DAIRY

Cheese, yogurt, and sour cream are common dairy ferments. Whey (which is full of living bacteria) is often used to kick-start other ferments such as sauerkraut or hot sauce.

LACTO-FERMENTED VEGETABLES (KOSHER/DELI PICKLES, HOT SAUCE, AND MORE)

Vegetables are chopped and often crushed between your hands. Salt is added (generally between 2.5% and 5% of the total volume of ingredients), a weight is placed on top of the vegetables to encourage release of liquids, and everything is left for a few hours or longer (generally two to three days, sometimes a week). Other liquids (generally filtered water) are added to cover the food if needed. Whey or brine from other ferments is sometimes added to increase the amount of living bacteria to start the ferment.

SOUR BEVERAGES (KVASS, KOMBUCHA, WATER KEFIR)

Kefir and kombucha are created with a SCOBY (symbiotic colony of bacteria and yeast). There are different SCOBYs for each beverage and they are not interchangeable. Other types of fermented beverages use salt and/or whey to ferment vegetables and water (such as beet kvass, see page 125) to produce a sour beverage that many credit with health benefits.

WHOLE GRAINS

Sour dough, fermented flour, and other fermented whole grains are thought to be more beneficial than their non-fermented counterparts. It's also believed the process (adding whey or another starter along with liquid to whole grains) allows gluten to be broken down, making it easier to digest. Whole grains are typically fermented for up to a day, though I'm sure some people leave them for longer.

Batch-It Imagine chopping hot peppers, weighing them, and adding 2.5% salt to them. Crush the ingredients with your hands (while wearing gloves) and place them in a wide-mouth Mason jar. Press them in place with a ½-cup jar, leave on the counter for a few weeks, and you've done most of the work of making fermented hot sauce! Because fermenting is so easy to do, it's a natural complement to other styles of preserving.

BEANS, SEEDS, AND NUTS

Many people soak beans in water overnight before cooking them. Leaving them to soak for a day or two will start the fermenting process, which a lot of people believe makes them easier to digest.

BEER, SAKE, AND OTHER GRAIN-BASED FERMENTED BOOZE

These are some of my favorite ferments. The simple steps in making beer are as follows:

- Malted barley is ground and cooked in hot water to release its starch, sugar, and enzymes.
- Flavors are added (hops is a common example).
- The mixture is cooled and yeast is added to begin the fermenting. If it were added when the mixture is hot, it would be killed. An airlock is placed on top of the container and the mixture is fermented to convert the sugar into alcohol.
- The beer is bottled and sometimes aged (though most beers are better drunk fresh).

Despite their history, many home-brew stores have evolved past kit-making, and there are some great places where you can either make beer or buy the equipment to make it at home. I've also found the home-brewing community to be an amazing group of people who are excited to share their knowledge and help someone learn.

I believe home-brewed beer will be one of the biggest areas of growth in the local food/DIY communities in the next few years.

MOLD CULTURES

Tempeh (a soy ferment sold in bricks or logs that is chewier and has more taste, fiber, calories, and protein than tofu), koji (a form of mold most commonly used in the sake brewing process), and amazake (a Japanese fermented rice drink) are all examples of mold cultures. *The Art of Fermentation* by Sandor Katz goes into detail on how to make these.

Advantages and Disadvantages

ADVANTAGES

- Very easy to do with little specialized equipment required.
- There are many styles and methods and room for creativity.
- Many ferments are "living" and can bring benefits like improved gut health.

DISADVANTAGES

- There can be a lot to wrap your head around at first. I recommend reading about the fundamentals and then following a few tested recipes. This will help you learn as you go.

Fundamentals of Fermenting

There are so many styles of fermenting that it becomes difficult to balance the constraints of brevity with ensuring that we're sharing enough information to offer a primer on the topic.

I've picked a few different styles here to show you the basics of each. As you learn more, you'll find there are all sorts of exceptions, some based on tradition and some based on science.

Fermenting is incredibly safe so don't be afraid to experiment—much of what we've learned has been through trial and error.

LACTO FERMENTATION

Most commonly done with vegetables, this is an incredibly easy method for making home preserves. It's used to make sauerkraut, kosher pickles, hot sauce, kimchi, and more.

The general steps are as follows:

1 **VEGETABLES ARE CHOPPED.** When possible, they should also be lightly crushed between your hands to break down the cell structure (this is easy with cabbage but not cucumbers).

2 **NON-IODIZED SALT IS ADDED.** Generally, it's 2%–5% by weight. The vegetables are placed in a non-reactive container. A weight helps press down the vegetables as they begin to release their liquid (which is called a brine). It is imperative that nothing floats to the surface, as "floaters" will almost always create mold. The ferment is left for 12–24 hours and checked according to the recipe requirements.

3 **BRINE.** If the vegetables are fresh, the contents of the jar will often be covered with brine after resting per above. If they are not submerged at this point, add a salt brine to cover all the vegetables, using the same ratio of salt to filtered water as you used for the vegetables originally. The ferment is stored on top of a plate or tray in case it bubbles over and makes a mess. Check daily for any signs of scum or mold. Scum can be removed without tossing the entire ferment, but mold indicates spoilage and I recommend destroying the batch.

4 **FINISHING.** The ferment is complete when the bubbling ceases and you are happy with the taste and texture. The longer it ferments, the sourer and softer it will become. If you wait too long, the product will become unpalatable mush. I recommend newbies start tasting daily after a few days, and continue to taste as the process goes on. The ferment will be unbearably salty at first, but will mellow as time passes. As you gain experience you will taste the ferment less and less as it progresses. It is complete by anywhere from five to thirty days, depending on temperature, salt percentage, and the amount of moisture in the produce you used. The temperature is the

Storing

We are often asked if it's possible to waterbath fermented food. Processing ferments is unsafe due to unknown acidity levels. It will also kill any living bacteria.

The best method of storage is a cold cellar or fridge that can slow, and practically stop, fermentation. I make enough hot sauce in the fall to last a year and it keeps in the fridge without incident.

I've also heard of people freezing sauerkraut and other ferments. While I've never tried it, I wouldn't hesitate to give it a go!

biggest variant (sauerkraut might take five days in my kitchen in the summer and thirty days in the winter).

ALCOHOL

Yeast converts sugar from fruit (and sometimes additional sugar) into alcohol. Different yeasts will produce different flavors and different percentages of alcohol.

The general stages are as follows:

1 **FRUIT IS CRUSHED.** Sometimes it is mixed with water, sugar, or both. Some add a Campden tablet (available at home-brew stores) to kill any natural yeast in the bottle. If you omit this step you will be inviting wild yeasts (from the fruit and the air in your kitchen) which can add interesting but unpredictable flavors.

2 **YEAST IS ADDED.** If you've used a Campden tablet, you must wait 24 hours before this step, or you will kill the added yeast as well the natural yeast.

3 **PRIMARY FERMENT.** An airlock is placed on the fermenting container. This is called the primary ferment, and it can last for days or weeks.

4 **FIRST RACKING AND SECONDARY FERMENT.** Fruit solids and any sediment are removed. Sediment forms as part of the fermenting process and is harmless though it produces a cloudy/gritty beverage and most remove it by syphoning the liquids into a clean jar, leaving the sediment behind. This process is called racking. Some add additional fruit or sugar at this point. It is fermented again with an airlock for a period of weeks or months.

5 **BOTTLING.** This is a simple process as long as you have the basic supplies, which include bottles, corks or lids, sanitizer, and a tube for syphoning. A home-brew or wine-making store will set you up with everything you need, including the instructions for the specific equipment you are using. The mixture is racked again to remove sediment, bottled in sanitized bottles, and sealed. Some add a Campden tablet before aging to prevent fermenting in the bottle, which can cause explosions, though long aging in the secondary ferment will ensure the yeast is dead. See the overview on Bottling on page 48 for more details.

6 **AGING.** The ferment is aged and consumed. Some drinks, such as beer, are best drunk fresh, while others, such as country wine, are aged for one to two years, or even longer.

KITCHEN COUNTER BOOZE

I made this term up. The technique is older than memory but I've modified it a bit for the curious home cook who wants to make 1 quart of booze or less at a time. It's ridiculously fun to make and an important reminder that you don't need to make gallons at a time to have fun and experiment. Check out the Grapes chapter (pages 213–222) or the Pears chapter (pages 267–276) to learn how to make small amounts of booze in a Mason jar.

FERMENTED BEANS

A bit of whey or brine from a fermented pickle is added to dry beans and water and they are left on the counter for 24 hours. See the Beans & Peas chapter (pages 109–118) for more information.

KOMBUCHA

A sweet tea is made and a SCOBY, also called a Mother, is added. SCOBYs can be purchased online, at some farmers' markets, or made from good quality kombucha at home. The SCOBY needs to be handled with care and clean gloves. Other flavors are sometimes added, and the mixture is fermented on your counter until it reaches your desired taste, at which point it is transferred to the fridge. The SCOBY is used in subsequent batches in much the same way as a starter for sourdough bread.

SODA

Fruit, sugar, water, and yeast are combined to make pop. Despite my general aversion to plastic, I use plastic bottles designed for home-brewed beer for this product, as it's a living ferment. Living ferments continue to produce carbon dioxide and build pressure, leading to a dangerous explosion in the most extreme circumstances.

Some people swear by flip-top bottles for this purpose but plastic is safest. We make this so rarely that using plastic doesn't scare me here.

Soda shouldn't be a limb-risking endeavor. You can make it safely and reliably. To minimize the risk:

1 Measure and use yeast sparingly.
2 Use plastic. A slight squeeze on the bottle will tell you how much pressure there is inside. If you don't want to rely on plastic, consider bottling one bottle in plastic and the rest in flip-top bottles, and use your plastic bottle as the tester.
3 "Burp" the bottles by slowly opening them after fermenting has reached the desired state. Unlike commercial products, this is a living ferment and won't go flat once you open it.
4 Open the bottle over the sink or a clean bowl, as our friend and recipe tester Stephanie Hedley recommends.
5 Once the ferment reaches the desired amount of carbonation, transfer the entire batch into the fridge.

Fermenting occurs best in the mid-60s to mid-70s. Lower temperatures will slow fermenting, and higher temperatures will drastically speed up the process, which is why I recommend tasting often when you're learning (with time it becomes possible to gauge the progress of many ferments by eye). This makes guessing the duration of a ferment difficult, and a key to success is tasting and checking often.

Milk is heated to near scalding and cooled to a specific temperature, and then a bacteria starter (often yogurt from a previous batch) is added. The container is kept warm in a dehydrator or oven with the lamp left on to encourage the bacteria to multiply, which creates the density you expect from yogurt.

Overview of Bottling Fermented Beverages

If you've never bottled before, I recommend going to a brew-your-own store where you will be helped with the equipment and can be walked through the process. Each of the recipes that call for bottling in this book are for still (non-carbonated) beverages. Bottling carbonated beverages that you plan to age (like sparkling cider) take more steps and guidance than we can fit into these pages . . .

MY MUST-HAVES:

- Bottles and matching caps. The bottles should be plastic for living ferments, such as ginger beer or soda, or you could have a dangerous explosion.
- Sanitizer
- Bottle brush
- Bottle capper/corker (if not using screw tops)
- A plastic hose

How to Bottle:

1 Soak the bottles with added sanitizer or bleach to clean them.
2 Rinse, wash, and clean your bottles, then sanitize them according to the instructions on the sanitizer. The bottle brush will be your best friend. A bottle rinser, which attaches to your faucet, will power-wash the insides of the bottles and make this a far easier task.
3 Sanitize the caps or lids.
4 Use the plastic hose to syphon liquid into your bottles, ensuring the liquid reaches the neck (you can add filtered water if it doesn't).
5 Secure with a lid and age per instructions. With living ferments, it is important to transfer them to the fridge to slow fermenting and prevent an explosion.

Measuring Alcohol Content

To measure the alcohol in a ferment, use a device called a hydrometer, which you can buy for about $20 from a home-brew store. It will come with instructions and couldn't be easier to use: you start with sanitizing the hydrometer (it looks like an oversized thermometer) and placing your liquid in a sample tube before fermenting. The hydrometer floats and you read the potential alcohol based on how high it floats. When the fermenting is done, you take a second measurement in the same way. Subtract one from the other and you will know the percentage of alcohol in your ferment. This is a bit trickier if you add whole fruit to your ferments, as the solid fruit has additional sugar that dissolves as it breaks down that won't be accounted for in the initial measurement.

Common Problems and How to Solve (and Avoid) Them

Most people's biggest fear is the appearance of mold. I used to be careless with my ferments and would forget to check in on them. If you check your ferments every day, removing scum from lacto-ferments and ensuring airlocks are properly topped up, you'll be virtually guaranteed success.

Do's and Don'ts of Fermenting

DO keep all items submerged under water whenever possible. This will prevent mold.

DO check your ferments daily (when fermenting, not after moving to the fridge). Skim off any mold or scum from the surface at the first sign of it.

DO experiment with different types of ferments and flavors. Experiment with small batches (e.g., 1–2 cups of hot sauce) before moving to large volumes.

DO choose your water carefully. If you are using tap water, make sure to read about Filtered Water in the "Must-Have" equipment list—it is the main reason many people fail at fermenting.

DO place all ferments on a plate, especially early in the process. If the ferment is overly active, it can bubble over and the plate will save a mess.

DO use non-iodized salt, filtered water, and jars that have been well cleaned and rinsed so there are no soap remnants left behind. All of these things can slow or stop fermentation.

DO make sure the fermentation has stopped dead before bottling mead or fruit wines (otherwise you will have a living ferment and pressure can build to disastrous results). See the note in the soda description for more information on living ferments.

DON'T panic. Ferments will taste poor at the beginning (a lacto-fermented vegetable often tastes too salty) but, with time, they will transform.

DON'T eat items with mold. I like to be safe rather than sorry.

DON'T use old fermenting crocks without testing them. Many of the glazes that seal their surfaces were made with lead. Lead-testing kits with complete instructions can be purchased inexpensively online.

DON'T use glass bottles with screw tops (or beer caps) for living ferments like soda. Some people ferment in jars with lids on. Use caution when doing so and burp the jars often or you could end up with an exploding bottle.

How We Got Hooked

People sometimes ask me what one piece of equipment I wish I owned.

My answer is simple. If I had the space in our apartment, I would buy a deep freezer in an instant. It's one piece of equipment that could drastically change our kitchen's productivity: it would let us increase the amount of food we preserve while decreasing our total amount of work.

Tons of people keep food in a fridge or a freezer and don't realize that it's a form of preserving. If you use a fridge or a freezer, you are essentially "cellaring," albeit by using modern techniques. As much as I'd love to explore the magic of a cold room (see below), I think it's incredibly important to learn to use our fridges and freezers better.

According to the David Suzuki Foundation, North Americans waste up to one-third of the food they bring into their homes. I've struggled with basic food management in our house. Like most people, I have occasionally found a bag of mystery ingredients buried within the confines of my fridge and instantly resolved to get better at using the fridge. Beyond looking for frost, I've never been shown how to get the most out of my fridge or freezer. I know the least about the most common preserving techniques in our kitchen!

But I do know that quick pickles and freezer jams take far less time to make than their waterbath equivalents.

What Is Cellaring?

Whether you're using a fridge, cold room, or freezer to preserve food, there are three things to consider:

- **TEMPERATURE.** Colder temperatures will preserve food for longer but will also affect the texture of the food once it has thawed. According to the FDA, your fridge should be above freezing but below 40°F (4°C). Freezer temperature should be below 0°F (-18°C).

- **HUMIDITY.** Too much humidity can lead to mold, while not enough can dry food out.
- **AIR.** "Circulation" might be the better word here. Most food likes to have ample circulation around it, though some foods, especially when frozen, benefit from minimal air exposure. Using narrow jars for sauces and juices creates smaller surface areas (thus limiting oxygen exposure) and can preserve food longer.

Beyond those three things, consider the surrounding environment. Dry food will pull moisture from fresh food, a spoiled apple will help rot the others, and warm food will pull cold from chilled items.

Common Equipment and Costs

MY MUST-HAVES

A FRIDGE ($400+). We recently upgraded to a unit that has the fridge on top of a chest freezer and love it. Because my fridge stores many jars of food I value large door shelves and adjustable inner shelves. When we bought it, we took some Mason jars to the store to see how they'd fit to make sure we had the right one!

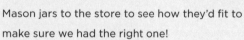

CONTAINERS WITH LIDS ($3+). I prefer investing in glass containers over plastic for many reasons—the main one being they simply last far longer than anything else.

STEAM JUICER OR JUICER ($50–$200+). A juicer allows you to transform fruit (and, depending on their quality, vegetables) into juice that will keep in the fridge or freeze easily.

COOKIE SHEETS/BAKING TRAYS ($10+). Placing fruit and vegetables on trays allows them to freeze separately before being transferred to a container for long-term storage.

PAPER TOWELS OR DISHCLOTHS ($3+). A slightly dampened towel inside a container with food can add moisture while a dry one can help absorb moisture. I often start with a dry one and, as fruit begins to dry, add a slightly dampened piece of towel to the container.

A MARKER PEN, MASKING TAPE, AND LARGE ROLL OF BUTCHERS' PAPER ($30 FOR A LIFETIME SUPPLY). Good-quality freezer paper helps prevent freezer burn. Wrap anything you're freezing with the shiny side of the paper facing the inside. Write the contents and date on the outside of the package, and your food will last longer in your freezer. This is far superior to plastic wrap, and any food purchased wrapped in plastic should be re-wrapped in butchers' paper prior to placement in your freezer.

FRIDGE/FREEZER THERMOMETER ($12). The only way to know for certain if your fridge and freezer are set at the right temperatures.

MY NICE-TO-HAVES

A DEEP FREEZER ($300+). Deep freezers are easy to use and store a large amount of food with little loss of flavor or nutrients, but they take a lot of space. A deep freezer works better than the one attached to your fridge as it stays at a constant temperature and doesn't go through regular defrost cycles like most fridges do.

METAL AND GLASS BOWLS ($3+). Most fruit shouldn't be stored in the fridge until it's fully ripe. Bowls will help you store it in your kitchen until you need to transfer to the fridge or freezer.

SHELF SPACE ($0). Shelves aren't free, but most of us can free some space in our kitchens to store fruits and vegetables. Onions, tomatoes, and bananas should all be stored out of the fridge and apart from any other food (including each other).

S-HOOKS (A.K.A. MEAT HOOKS) ($1–$5). If you don't have shelf space (or even if you do), meat hooks are handy for hanging food in out-of-the-way spaces.

GARAGE/INSULATED SHED ($0 IF YOU ALREADY HAVE ONE). If you happen to have either of these, place a thermometer inside it and check how warm or cold it gets; you may be surprised to find out that it's a great place to store root vegetables in the fall and winter. Just make sure it's wildlife-proofed beforehand!

FREEZER BAGS ($4). Storing food in self-sealing bags is particularly effective, especially if you use a straw to remove as much excess air as possible. I know that many people (including us) try to keep their use of plastic to a minimum, so you'll have to weigh the benefits versus the risks/cost of plastic.

VACUUM PACKERS ($150+). You can buy cheaper models, but the results are generally inferior. I prefer the models which have rolls of plastic sleeves rather than pre-sized bags. These are handy and can extend the life of herbs, jerky, dehydrated products, and cured meats in the fridge or freezer.

Batch-It You can freeze almost anything that you can preserve via another method. People commonly freeze fruit on the hottest days of summer so they can make jam during the colder days of fall. Fermenting, dehydrating, pressure canning, and more can all be done with thawed-out ingredients. Quick pickles and fridge and freezer jams can all be quick ways to preserve food for days, weeks, or months and don't involve the work associated with canning. Many preserves freeze well. The obvious include bacon, stock, jam, and almost anything cooked. The less obvious include living ferments (like sauerkraut), dried herbs (they will keep longer if sealed in bags without air), and fruit leathers.

Filling Your Pantry

Many people don't think too much about using the fridge or freezer; we open the door and throw something inside. But there is so much you can do with these appliances, aside from making frozen veggies, quick pickles, or a quick fruit sauce.

FRIDGE/FREEZER JAM

Add a scant layer of water to a pot to prevent burning, then add 3–4 parts fresh fruit to 1 part sugar and simmer until set. Because you aren't using a waterbath, you can experiment to your heart's content with no safety fears. Pour into a clean container (sterilization is not needed), and when you're done, store the jam in the fridge for up to several weeks or in the freezer for a few months. This was my grandmother's favorite way to make jam.

QUICK PICKLES

Pickles can be made in minutes by submerging any ingredient in sweetened vinegar. I often use 4 parts vinegar to 1 part honey, and I briefly cook onions, carrots, beans, or other vegetables just long enough to absorb the flavors. This is a very common preserving style in many restaurants for its convenience.

JUICE

More than once I've noticed a bag of fruit is starting to get soft when I was short on time to preserve it. An easy technique (if you have the equipment) is to juice the fruit, put it into a narrow-mouthed bottle or jar, and refrigerate it. The juice will often last for a week or longer. Pouring juice up to where the narrow neck begins will minimize the amount of air exposure, and the juice will keep longer. For longer storage, most juices can be canned in a waterbath or frozen in plastic containers (tubs from yogurt and sour cream are my favorites).

THERMOTHERAPY

The legendary Harold McGee researched, and published several articles on, thermotherapy—dipping fruit in hot water before drying it to preserve its life in the fridge. Acting on the findings of various scientists and research teams, he found that 125°F was best for thinner-skinned fruits (like raspberries and strawberries) and 140°F for thicker-skinned fruit (like blueberries or cherries). In both cases he immersed the fruit for 30 seconds before drying them on towels then transferring them to the fridge to store without them going moldy.

VINEGAR RINSE

When I come home from the market with fresh berries, I drizzle a bit of cider or white vinegar over them. A quick rinse of the berries before using will chase away any taste of the vinegar. This will often extend the life of local strawberries by three or four days.

Advantages and Disadvantages

ADVANTAGES

- Most of us have access to a fridge and at least a small freezer. If you learn how to store your food in them properly, you'll reap the benefits daily.
- Food stays nutrient-rich and maintains much of its flavor and nutritional benefits.

DISADVANTAGES

- Moving beyond the basics to a cold room or a deep freezer requires an investment and significant space.
- Some textures change when food is frozen.
- It's easy to lose track of items hidden in a crisper or deep freezer.

Fundamentals of Cellaring

Here are some tips on getting the most out of your fridge and freezer, and a few ideas for other places to store food.

THE FRIDGE

The most common "cellar" most of us have access to today is the fridge. Here are a few things to bear in mind to get the most out of it:

- **AIR/CIRCULATION.** It's important that air is able to circulate in your fridge to keep temperatures as even as possible.
- **CLEANLINESS.** Clean fridges minimize bacterial growth.
- **DANGER ZONE.** Bacteria flourish between 40°F and 140°F. Food should spend as little time as possible at these temperatures.
- **THE DOOR OF THE FRIDGE.** The door of the fridge (and the area of the shelf nearest to it) is often the warmest part of the fridge.
- **EGG CARTONS.** Storing fruit so that it doesn't crush or touch other fruit can extend its life in the fridge. Use egg cartons to divide plums, pears, or groups of smaller fruit.
- **LABELING.** Label food before it goes in the fridge.
- **TURNOVER.** Food that has started to dry, wilt, or rot will affect other food. Remove it as soon as possible.
- **WASH FOOD JUST BEFORE USING.** A lot of food will deteriorate if it's washed in water before being placed in the fridge.

THE FREEZER

Whether using a deep freezer or the one currently in your kitchen, the most important task here is to minimize the amount of air surrounding the ingredients you place inside your freezer. However, if freezing small items like berries, it's best to freeze them in a flat layer on a baking tray before transferring to a bag with minimal air contact.

Storing

Keep fruits and vegetables separate from each other as much as possible, wherever you store them, and you'll be on your way!

- **THAWING.** Frozen food should be thawed out in the fridge; leaving it on the counter will put it in the danger zone (see page 55). It takes a bit more planning but it's worth the effort.
- **LABELING.** Writing the date, contents, and source of the items in your freezer will let you to know what's in there and how long it's been there.
- **ROTATION.** My parents have a system for their freezer. The oldest items are easiest to reach while the newer items are more difficult. It's a clever way to make sure they work their way through the freezer contents.
- **WRAPPING.** Many items, such as meat, are already wrapped or frozen when you get them. Wrapping them in a layer of butchers' paper will add protection and insulation, and increase the life of the product. The shiny side (which prevents air from entering) should face your food and the dull side can be written on easily with a marker.

OTHER COMMON SPACES

Many of us have other places we can use to store food, but don't think of it as cellaring. Here are a few tricks of the trade:

- **COOLER.** To get the most out of a cooler, use ice blocks instead of cubes, place the coolest items at the bottom, and keep the cooler out of direct sunlight or the heat of your car where possible. Check out our hints on traveling with frozen fish (page 206).
- **DRAFTY PLACES.** If you live in a colder climate, you likely have a few drafty places in your house. Perhaps a windowsill, near a door, or, in our case, the space between our screen door and the door to our fire escape. These can be great places to hang vegetables and resilient fruit for longer-term storage during the fall or spring.
- **YOUR GARAGE.** If you live in a cold climate, you may be surprised to find that your garage isn't as cold as the outside—especially nearest to the wall of the house. My father routinely stores root vegetables and apples in his garage, even in the coldest parts of winter.

SPECIAL PLACES

Let's move on from the readily available places to some of the more specialized locations.

- **COLD CELLAR/COLD ROOM.** These don't have to be rooms built for this specific purpose. My parents have a regular room that they use as a cold room. During the winter, they block the vent into this room. They've insulated it to prevent it from cooling the house. In the summer, they open the vent and keep the door closed. The room stays around 55°F–60°F year-round.

    At our hunting camp we have insulated an unused room apart from the rest of the cabin. During hunts, we simply open the window (with the door left shut) and the entire room turns into a fridge!

- **THE GARDEN.** Do not pick vegetables until just before you're ready to use them. Vegetables will start to break down and lose their flavor within hours of being picked, so storing them in the garden is a great place to start.

  For less than $20 you can create a hoop house from flexible PVC, plastic wrap, and twist ties that will act like a greenhouse and trap heat in your garden so that things continue to live well into the fall.

  Some ingredients, including kale and spinach, will taste sweeter after a frost. Harvesting them on a day that's above freezing will ensure they last the longest in your kitchen.
- **SANDBOXES.** Many root vegetables can be stored in boxes of sand. Start by removing the tops from the veggies and placing a layer of sand or sawdust in a box. Place a layer of carrots down, taking care not to let them touch one another, and cover with a thick layer of sand. Repeat and store in the garage or root cellar for several months.
- **STRAW BALE CELLAR.** Stick a 5-gallon pail below ground level, place root vegetables in it, and cover the whole thing with a bale of hay to create a bucket-sized root cellar that will store root vegetables during the cold days of winter.

Common Problems and How to Solve (and Avoid) Them

The most common problems with this method of preserving all come back to understanding how best to store ingredients so that you get the longest shelf life possible. For more detail, we've included ideas on the best way to store the 25 main ingredients within each of their chapters.

Do's and Don'ts of Cellaring

DO read each ingredient chapter for storage instructions.

DO learn about alternative methods of cellaring, including some of the ideas mentioned here. You may have many more options available to you than you ever thought!

DO avoid storing food and wine in the trunk of your car. People often do this at farmers' markets and are surprised to see how quickly their food degrades.

DON'T blindly trust "best before dates." Use them as guidelines (especially if the product hasn't been opened).

DON'T leave meat or produce on the counter for extended periods of time.

DON'T randomly fill your freezer with unlabeled packages. "Mystery items" will almost always eventually make their way into your waste or compost bin.

Salted & Smoked

How We Got Hooked

This group of foods has many different definitions and can be difficult to label. Most consider it to be a set of preserving techniques such as salting, drying, or smoking for meat or other ingredients, such as vegetables, fruit, or tobacco. To complicate things, drying is its own method, and then we begin to split hairs when deciding if salt cod is cured by salt (it is), dehydrated (it is), or both (it is).

Techniques are often combined and fused. Many sausages are fermented in their casings, while smoked products, such as dried chipotles, are dehydrated during or after the curing process. And we can split even more hairs when we consider that salt-cured bacon is often smoked before being stored in the fridge. At what point is a smoked pepper that is also dehydrated considered to be preserved by smoke and at what point does it become a dehydrated ingredient?

My loose definition for salted-preserved (often, but not always, called "cured") or smoke-preserved food is simple: any preserved food that derives its primary flavors from salt or smoke. A smoked jalapeño (a.k.a. a chipotle or morita pepper) that was later dehydrated would, according to my definition, be classified as smoked. Fermented sauerkraut that uses salt but develops its main flavors via lacto-fermentation would not. Smoked food is generally preserved with another technique for longer storage.

In the process of writing this book, I made the conscious decision to focus on cures that could be made in the average home kitchen without costly special equipment, such as a curing chamber, or special ingredients, such as pink salt. I do mention these things in the next chapter, but only to let you know what they're all about. If you're looking to take your knowledge to the next level, check out *Charcuterie* by Michael Ruhlman and Brian Poleyn. If you want to be a real wizard, check out *Charcuterie* (same name, different book) by Fritz Sonnenschmidt.

What Is Salting and Smoking?

The following is an oversimplification of some of the common forms of curing (more on individual styles on pages 62–63).

CURING

The term "curing" can have several uses in preserving. Some use it to describe the overall process by which they preserve food, while others use it to describe almost all preserved meats, and others use it for a smaller sub-category or type of preserved food (most commonly meat).

To cure meat, a relatively large amount of salt is applied and is then left to sit for several days. Some moisture is pulled from the meat while the salt, seasonings, and, on occasion, curing salt are pulled into it. Generally, the meat is then removed from the salt and hung or smoked to dry and finish curing.

DRYING

Meat can be dehydrated (jerky is the most common type), though care must be taken to remove all the moisture. An easy way to do this is by cooking it at 160°F for 10 minutes after drying.

MAKING SAUSAGES

Ground meat is combined with fat and other ingredients and formed into tubes by filling casings (which are made from intestines or, more often, synthetic materials). The sausages are sometimes smoked, hung to cure, and then frozen without any other preservation technique being used.

FERMENTING SAUSAGES

This is a similar process to making sausages except that curing salt (see page 65) is added and humidity is controlled. The process works by lowering the amount of water, decreasing the pH, and adding nitrites/nitrates, which all help promote healthy bacteria while creating conditions likely to inhibit the growth of bad ones.

SMOKING

There is nothing better for me than sipping on a beer and watching smoke slowly coil upwards from my smoker or BBQ. While the addition of smoke is thought to help preserve food, it is rarely used without also curing, drying, or preserving in some other fashion. Smoke alone can alter taste beyond recognition. With the exception of peppers, I generally use smoke as an accent flavor.

Batch-It Curing meat is something I do in isolation, but I use smoke and salt to preserve ingredients like herbs, lemon, chili and conventional peppers, rhubarb, and more. Learning to cure meat is an extremely handy skill for the winter when local ingredients are less available and you have some extra time on your hands for kitchen projects.

Common Equipment and Costs

MY MUST-HAVES

WIRE RACK SHELVING OR HORIZONTAL TOWEL RACK ($15+). We have an entire wire shelf (similar to what you'd find in a commercial kitchen) that makes hanging meat and strands of food easy (and out of reach of Schaefer, our all-consuming pup).

S-HOOKS ($3–$5). Also handy for dehydrating. These come in a variety of sizes and two general varieties: ones with pointy ends for penetrating meat and ones without.

BUTCHERS' TWINE ($5). Twine is used to hang meat or bind it into form for curing.

CHEESECLOTH OR MUSLIN ($5). This is used to wrap meat to keep flies and direct sunlight off the surface.

A-MAZE-N SMOKE MAZE/PELLET TRAY ($35). My friend Pat Weir, who is a competitive BBQ cook, introduced me to these. They come in a variety of sizes and shapes but all will transform your BBQ (or any container) into an affordable smoker. Find more details in "Use Your BBQ as a Cold Smoker" on page 66.

PELLETS/CHIPS/SHAVINGS ($20–$25 FOR 20 LB). I keep several types of chips on hand (hickory, oak, cherry, and apple are the most common) and often trade partial bags with other friends so I have plenty of options. Your specific type of smoker will determine if you use pellets or chips.

KITCHEN SCALE ($30–$200). You'll use a scale to measure ingredients, salt, curing salt, and fat/meat when making sausages. If you're going to get serious about curing, you'll want to start measuring your recipes by weight.

MY NICE-TO-HAVES

CURING CHAMBER ($250+). Homemade versions can be made for $250 or less, but you can spend hundreds or thousands of dollars if you're really extreme. The chamber controls humidity, temperature, and airflow. Homemade versions are often made from abandoned fridges or coolers.

SMOKER OR BBQ WITH SMOKER UNIT ($50–$1,200+). I'd advise saving your money for a unit that will last you a long time rather than buying an entry-level model. My preferred models are electrically controlled, have a thermostat, and feed the wood as needed.

MEAT SLICER ($20–$800). We lucked out and bought an old-fashioned hand-crank meat slicer at a thrift store. If you keep your eyes open, you can find a good deal on a used model.

MEAT GRINDER/SAUSAGE STUFFER/CASINGS ($100–$400+). If you have a stand mixer or a good tomato squeezer, you should investigate attachments for those, which may make this very affordable. A good butcher will often grind your meat for you, so if you need to make sausages now, start with a stuffer. Some models require two hands (and two people) to operate; vertical stuffers tend to be the easiest to operate for one person. This can be a good item to split with family or friends.

VACUUM PACKER ($150+). See the notes in the Cellaring chapter (page 53) for more info.

Filling Your Pantry

Preserving food using salt and smoke is an ancient practice. Almost every culture from around the world has recipes and techniques for curing that have been passed down from generation to generation. Studying curing techniques is a great way to explore the food from around the planet.

BRINING

Many people are familiar with corned beef or brisket, which are often brined in a mixture of salt, water, and seasoning and transformed into succulent ingredients. Salt-cured pork is still commonly purchased in 1-gallon buckets for "boiled dinner" in many places.

CHARCUTERIE

If you decided to host a dinner party and invited one person from each of Italy's twenty regions, you'd be in fine form until you asked them to create a list of the best cured meat in the country. Each region would fiercely defend definitions of what is and isn't valid, worthy, or authentic. Trying to summarize styles of charcuterie from around the planet only compounds that problem.

I've compiled the following list to try to demystify the world of charcuterie. There is NOTHING below that won't be disputed by someone. This isn't meant as a definitive guide but as a starting point from which to launch your learning and exploring.

CURED. Meat that is left (mostly) intact from its original form. It is cured whole.
- **BACON/SPEK.** Most often made from pork belly, this can be made in your fridge. Fatty meat is cured with salt and other flavors to become firmer. Nitrites and/or nitrate are often added to make it pink and crispy. It is often smoked.
- **BRESAOLA.** Air-dried salted beef that is cured without nitrites/nitrates and without a curing chamber. Other countries have variations of air-dried beef (such as the pastrima recipe you'll find on page 240).
- **COPPA (A.K.A. CAPICOLA OR CAPACOLLO)/PROSCIUTTO/JAMÓN SERRANO.** Dry-cured ham that is often served uncooked after being thinly shaved.
- **HAM.** The upper part of a pig's leg is cured in salt or brine to become ham. It's sometimes smoked and sometimes not.
- **JAMÓN IBÉRICO.** This is considered by many to be the best ham in the world. Entire legs of pasture-raised black pigs are cured and thinly shaved (or decadently served as hamsteak). A crucial ingredient in the pigs' diet is acorns, often credited for the ham's amazing taste.
- **LARDO.** Generally this refers to back fat from pork that is cured and thinly sliced. It looks like bacon (though it has very little, if any, meat) and is served without cooking.

SAUSAGE. Ground meat, often mixed with fat, that is generally formed into shapes by filling casings made from intestines (or, just as often, a synthetic substitute). Some forms of sausage require cooking before serving while others do not.

- **BOUDIN/BLOOD SAUSAGE.** Sausage with a healthy dose of fresh or dried blood. Often served on a charcuterie tray or warm at breakfast.
- **CHORIZO.** A spicy pork sausage that gets its traditional color from smoked red pimento peppers (paprika is a common substitute). It is served fresh or fermented. It has such a strong flavor that it's often used as an ingredient rather than eaten alone.
- **FORCEMEAT.** Raw meat that is emulsified with fat and often pressed into a form, such as a terrine or a hot dog.

- **GALANTINES.** Stuffed meat, often poultry or fish, that is poached and sealed and/or topped with an aspic (a jelly made from clarified stock or consommé).
- **MORTADELLA.** An unfermented heat-cured tube of meat that combines lean protein and chunks of fat and generally incorporates other ingredients (pistachios and black pepper are common). It is part of the bologna family and served in uncooked slices.

- **SAUCISSON.** A dry-cured, hard sausage from France that's often made with pork and herbs. It's served without cooking.

SAUSAGE, FERMENTED. Air-dried sausage that's generally preserved in a curing chamber or other device to control humidity. The drying process often ferments the meat, which helps preserve it and further develops unique flavors.

- **SALAMI/SALUMI.** Air-dried meat that is also fermented. This hard sausage is served sliced and without cooking.
- **SOPPRESSATA.** This is a great illustration of the complexity of categorizing cured meats. In southern Italy, soppressata refers to a cured, dry sausage. If you head north, you'll find a different version which is uncured and commonly called Sopressa. Soppressata is often distinguishable by its large diameter (traditional recipes use 3½-inch casings).
- **SUMMER SAUSAGE.** An air-dried sausage that is generally heavily smoked after curing. It's often made with multiple forms of meat (although pork is central to it).

SPREADS

- **HEAD CHEESE.** I have vivid memories of my Pepe (grandfather) making head cheese from scratch. It was one of my favorite things to eat! Despite its name, this is a dairy-free pork preserve made from slow-cooking parts of the pig's head (and often includes the heart, feet, and/ or tongue).

- **PÂTÉS AND MOUSSE.** These are pastes made of cooked meat and fat combined into a uniform consistency. They often include liberal additions of other flavors, including herbs, vegetables, and a touch of alcohol. I was introduced to liverwurst as a child by my Japanese-German babysitters, and it became one of my favorite snacks.
- **RILLETTES.** This is similar to pâté, although it looks more like pulled pork and is often covered by a layer of soft fat to preserve the moisture.
- **TERRINE.** This is a spread made of coarsely chopped ingredients. It is generally shaped into a rectangular loaf and sometimes wrapped in pastry before baking. It is cooled before being served.

SALTED FISH

In this case, salt is a method as well as an ingredient. Salt cod was traditionally made by covering layers of fish heavily in salt before drying them in the sun. Salt cod is usually soaked to rehydrate it and reduce the amount of sodium prior to eating. In addition to drying food, enough salt can create an environment that is hostile to some microorganisms.

SMOKED FISH AND MEATS: COLD VS. HOT

Much like the term "curing," the difference between "hot" and "cold" smoking is a topic of debate among many. Some argue that cold smoking only happens when the temperature is below 100°F while others argue that the temperature should be below 120°F. Harold McGee, one of my absolute food heroes, adds an additional requirement: that the smoke for cold smoking be created in a different chamber than the one in which the food is smoked. I veer toward pragmatic and loose: hot smoking occurs when you smoke and cook something at the same time; cold smoking adds flavor without cooking.

OTHER

- **CONFIT.** Meat (often duck) cooked slowly (not fried) in its own fat.
- **PEPPERETTES.** A favorite among hunters and truck drivers in North America. Generally heavily salted, they look like mini-pepperoni, but are often consumed in the same way you'd eat a chocolate bar—whole. The flavors vary drastically and include plain, BBQ, teriyaki, spicy, and more.

Advantages and Disadvantages

ADVANTAGES

- Cured products tend to have a long shelf life and many can be stored without refrigeration, though you may want to refrigerate if your area is prone to flies or extreme temperatures and humidity.
- Once you've learned the basics, curing allows for many flavor experiments with minimal work involved.
- Although you can learn about world cuisine from every style of preserving, it is worth mentioning that curing offers some of the most diverse types of preserves and is present in almost every country in the world.

DISADVANTAGES

- Cured products have more salt, nitrites, and nitrates than any other preserves. They can also be some of the fattiest preserves.
- Curing is a loose term for many different subtypes of preserving; there's a lot to learn, and although the basics are easy, the learning curve can come as a bit of a shock.
- Believe it or not, the terminology of curing is heavily regionalized. Throw in the cultural and tradition factors that come with many preserved foods, and you'll soon find that the lingo can be tricky.
- Setting yourself up with a smoker, curing chamber, meat grinder, and sausage stuffer can play havoc with your bank account.
- Meat and fish are the most commonly cured ingredients. They also happen to be some of the most expensive items for many of us.

Fundamentals of Salting and Smoking

CURING SALT/PINK SALT/NITRITES AND NITRATES. Nitrites and nitrates are found in most preserved meats and, in lower quantities, in many root vegetables and green leafy vegetables. Small amounts of either (such as the amounts naturally found naturally on vegetables) are seen as relatively harmless while larger amounts can be detrimental to your health.

Nitrites help kill bacteria, turn meat "redder," and can affect flavor. If you are looking to make many types of charcuterie you will likely need to learn much more about them.

The most common forms of curing salts are labeled as:

- **INSTA CURE #1.** A mixture of sodium nitrite and sodium chloride, most often used for preserves that will be cooked before serving (such as bacon or ham).
- **INSTA CURE #2.** A combination of sodium nitrite, sodium nitrate, and sodium chloride, used for long-cured meats that are generally served at room temperature (these meats shouldn't be cooked on high heat).

The two biggest criticisms of curing salt are: it is potentially deadly (22 milligrams per kilogram of your weight can be lethal), and some research seems to indicate that it is potentially carcinogenic. It is generally dyed pink, which is why it's known as pink salt (not to be confused with Himalayan pink salt).

You can buy curing salt online, at many European grocery stores, and at outdoor/hunting stores.

HUMIDITY. This plays a vital role in curing. If you have too much humidity, your product will mold. Too little of it will lead to a dehydrated product. Curing chambers control the humidity, generally keeping it around 65%–70%.

PURE DRIED VACUUM SALT (PDV). The River Cottage Handbooks are amazing reference tools that focus on a single topic. No. 13 (*Curing & Smoking*) introduced me to PDV as an alternative to nitrates and nitrites. The biggest disadvantage for home cooks is that it is typically sold in bulk (50-pound bags seem to be the most common size).

TEMPERATURE. Most curing chambers keep the temperature between 50°F and 55°F.

WOOD. Comes in many forms: chips, pellets, and shavings are the most common. Larger pieces will burn slower than smaller pieces. Many people soak wood before lighting it to lengthen the drying time. If you ever find yourself with a bit of leftover wine that's just past its prime, consider soaking your wood chips in it before smoking for added flavor!

Using Your BBQ as a Cold Smoker

As mentioned in the list of Must-Haves, I'm a big fan of the A-Maze-N Smoke Maze or other similar smoking trays. For less than $40, you can convert your BBQ into a reliable cold smoker by doing this:

1 Fill the tray with pellets or chips (different units are built specifically for both).
2 Light the tray with a blowtorch; it takes about 30 seconds. Once lit, let it burn for 2–3 minutes before blowing it out. This will ensure there's enough smoldering wood to stay lit. You can light one side for a light smoke, both sides for heavy smoke (my usual preference) or even light it in the middle. With both sides lit, it burns for 4–5 hours.
3 Place the smoker on one side of your BBQ. Use care; the metal will be hot where you lit it.

4 Place items you want smoked on the rack above it or beside it. Items directly over the tray will cook slightly from the heat of the coals even though the BBQ isn't on.

5 Close the lid.

Professional smokers will better control the temperature and airflow, produce a precise amount of smoke, and allow for a greater quantity of food, but if you're short on space or budget, this is a great way to add smoke to your toolkit at a minimal cost.

Common Problems and How to Solve (and Avoid) Them

Curing can be the simplest form of preserving, as many of the techniques were invented before the comforts of the modern kitchen.

Do's and Don'ts of Salting and Smoking

The biggest "do" when it comes to curing is to simply do your research.

DO follow recipes. You can play with seasonings but don't invent techniques. For example, bresaola can be cured without curing salts, but that's not true of everything.

DO learn about pink salt. It's not the devil, but it's important to know how to use it properly.

DO experiment with smoke and be aware that you can have too much of a good thing!

DON'T be intimidated. While there's a nearly endless journey of knowledge when studying curing, don't confuse that with its being overly technical.

DON'T start with massive projects that are costly and might fail.

DON'T be afraid to look into building your own curing chamber. They can be made affordably and instantly hugely expand your preserving repertoire.

Fermented Pancakes with Maple Syrup
with Dried Blueberries, page 140

Infusing

How We Got Hooked

Infusing is often overlooked as a preservation technique and many don't think of it as a method of preserving at all. I love infusing because you can make a recipe in seconds or minutes and it's easily done while doing other preserving. By learning to infuse you can easily add 15–30 items to your pantry per year in less than an hour!

I didn't spend a lot of time thinking about infusing until March 2, 2010. Dana and I were attending Terroir (a conference for the hospitality industry), and I had the chance to sit in on a cocktail demonstration by two of Toronto's best: Jen Agg and Dave Mitton.

Dave poured a drink called a Ronald Clayton. It was named in honor of his grandfather, and the ingredients, which included tobacco syrup and vanilla-infused Canadian whisky, told a sensory story about the man. Jen later got talking about alcohol and infusing. A few months later I visited her restaurant. I stared behind the counter at various jars of infused booze and fell madly in love with the idea of having a liquor cabinet made of small-batch infusions that were one-of-a-kind.

Infusing isn't limited to alcohol, though. Tea and coffee are common infusions, though are rarely thought of as such. The high acidity in vinegar makes it a natural medium for preserving flavors by infusion. Less acidic liquids like water, milk, stock, or juice can all be infused with flavors, though their lifespan will be limited unless frozen or canned.

What Is Infusing?

In a nutshell: Something solid (generally food that's fresh or dried) is covered in liquid and left for minutes, hours, days, or months. The flavors are passed into the liquid, which is strained, and the solids are discarded or consumed separately.

If you can make tea...

Batch-It

Because infusing is so simple, it's easy to make a batch of something while preserving almost anything. Fermenting hot sauce? Throw some peppers in vodka. Dehydrating cherries? Add them to a jar with bourbon while you're at it. Strawberry jam? Infuse white wine vinegar with some berries at the same time. Infusing can also be mixed with other techniques with interesting results. Blueberries strained from infused gin could be dehydrated into a powder; dried apples could be added to cider vinegar to increase the apple flavors in it.

Common Equipment and Costs

MY MUST-HAVES

JARS (WITH LIDS) OF MULTIPLE SIZES ($0–$5). Most of my infusions range from ½ cup to 4 cups. I like to have a variety of jars on hand. Tinted Mason jars are ideal to protect your infusion from light, but you can use any pretty jar that's easy to clean.

STRAINERS ($5–$15 EACH). I own four or five strainers. Each has different-sized holes that make straining easy. I start by using a strainer with wide holes and get progressively smaller. This helps avoid clogging and makes the process quick and easy.

PAINT PEN OR JAR LABELS (<$1). I like to write the ingredients, date, and time on my infusions. A paint pen is washable and writes on glass.

VINEGARS ($2–$10). Mirin, rice wine, sherry, white, and red wine vinegar are the common types we use. Cheaper vinegar is usually perfectly fine for infusing.

ALCOHOL (COST VARIES). As with vinegar, I like to have a few extra bottles of booze around the house in the spring in case I decide to infuse spontaneously. Grain alcohol and vodka are the most common since they are flavor-neutral. Rum (white and dark), gin, brandy, and bourbon are commonly used for fruit infusions. Wine can be used for shorter infusions such as sangria.

MY NICE-TO-HAVES

INFUSION BALLS/WANDS ($5–$15). These are common with loose-leaf tea and allow you to avoid straining since the infused item is contained inside a vessel. These are useful for short infusions, typically involving heated liquids.

CHEESECLOTH ($3–$5). This can be used to strain infusions or to make a jelly sack or tea bag to add to ferments.

FUNNELS ($5–$12). These make filling and straining easy.

SPICES ($3–$10). We have a significant spice collection locked away in a drawer. Adding a jelly sack of peppercorns, cloves, cinnamon, or other spices into an infusion can add an extra twist. They will lose flavor over time but will retain their flavors best if stored an airtight container, such as a Mason jar.

AIRLOCKS ($8–$12). They aren't absolutely necessary, but I've used them for longer infusions, such as the year-long raspberry brandy (page 303).

Filling Your Pantry

Infusions generally take moments to make and are some of the most versatile cooking ingredients in the pantry. I stock my pantry with a wide selection of vinegar (and a smaller selection of booze) in the early spring so that I can spontaneously infuse when making other preserves.

INFUSED OIL

Oil, unlike vinegar or alcohol, provides an oxygen-free environment that can create botulism. Infused oils should be kept in the fridge and generally eaten within ten days of their creation. Using dried foods for the infusion reduces the amount of moisture (from the water contained in the food) and can further reduce the risk of botulism in these.

INFUSED HONEY

Honey is more acidic than oil and is safer to infuse; its typical pH level is 3.4–6.1. I generally infuse only with dried herbs (recipe on page 229) or hops, but have done a few infusions with fresh ingredients, which I refrigerated and consumed within ten days.

BITTERS

Bitters are strongly flavored liquor that is used in small quantities to flavor cocktails and in non-alcoholic drinks as a digestive aid. Contrary to their name, bitters don't have to be bitter, though their flavors are intense. They're usually created with high-percentage alcohol (such as grain alcohol) or lightly flavored booze (such as vodka).

TINCTURE

Traditionally this was a medicinal mix of a drug and alcohol. As infusing has become more popular, this term has been hijacked and is now used for many different infusions. Use tinctures in small quantities to add flavors to cocktails or cooking.

UNCOMMON LIQUIDS

Any liquid can be infused. My friend Chef Carlene Besai made "tea" with cream and Earl Grey tea leaves (and no water) that she then mixed with solid chocolate for a fondue almost ten years ago. This remains the most imaginative type of infusion I've ever experienced.

UNCOMMON FLAVORS

Bacon, jerky, gummy worms, and wood chips (as you'll find in out the hot sauce chapter) can all be interesting ingredients to infuse with.

Advantages and Disadvantages

ADVANTAGES

- This is one of the easiest ways to preserve food.
- Batches can be incredibly small.
- There's no need for special equipment.

• DISADVANTAGES

- Small batches = small volumes, so your store of these will be limited by volume.
- The flavor and texture of the original product are changed significantly.

Fundamentals of Infusing

There are very few rules when it comes to infusing, but there are a few things to keep in mind.

MIX 'N' MATCH

There are two schools of thought when it comes to infusing with flavor combinations (e.g., apple-cinnamon vodka). Some do the infusion with all the ingredients in a single jar and others keep them separate. My general preference is to infuse the liquids separately (i.e., cinnamon vodka and apple vodka) and then mix the infusions together. This allows for better control over the balance of flavors while also producing multiple infusions (apple, cinnamon, and apple-cinnamon) instead of just one. See the strawberry hops bitters on page 322 for another example.

GO FOR BROKE

Looking to make spicy vinegar? Don't wimp out—add as many hot peppers as you have to impart the maximum possible flavor. If it's too intense, you can always add additional vinegar to mellow it out, but you can never make it more intense!

TEMPERATURE MATTERS

Hot liquids pull flavors out of dried food quickly—think of steeping tea. Subtler flavors can be transferred with cold liquid, such as cold-brewed coffee. If you heat the food you are submerging (e.g., toasting peppercorns) before you pour the liquid over it, the heated food will pull the flavors inside of it and better infuse the liquid into the solid.

POUR SOME SUGAR ON ME

Sugar is sometimes added to infused liquids to make a liqueur, but it can inhibit the flavor transfer and is generally better added after the infusing is complete.

BEGIN WITH THE END IN MIND

Planning to make a Bloody Mary? Infuse your vodka with a hot pepper, fresh thyme, and garlic. Opting for an oil and vinegar salad dressing? Infuse white wine vinegar with peppercorns, fruit, or herbs.

BUT KEEP A FEW CONSIDERATIONS IN MIND TOO

Alcohol and high-acid liquids will preserve the food and flavor the longest. Using fresh fruit is fine, but the fruit can lose its texture over time and result in a sediment-filled infusion that needs to be filtered several times. And make sure to keep the food under the liquid's surface to prevent mold growth.

DON'T BE AFRAID TO GO SMALL

Some of my infusions are ½ cup or less. This allows you to be very experimental with little risk—just remember to take notes in case you want to repeat your successes!

Common Problems and How to Solve (and Avoid) Them

OVER-INFUSION. I've made a few infusions that sucked. I once left pears and apples in vodka for too long and the mixture became overly bitter and unpleasant. If this happens, don't despair! Strain the solids (if you haven't already) and allow the infusion to sit for a few months. It will mellow. You can also infuse softer flavors like vanilla into these mixtures to balance them out while you wait for the taste to calm down.

MOLD. Mold is the enemy—if it appears at any stage of the process, destroy the product. Mold most commonly appears during the first few days of an infusion. Watch the process carefully; if a small bit of scum appears on the surface, you can remove it with a clean spoon, wiping the neck of the jar as well, and continue to monitor. The primary way to prevent mold is to make sure that nothing is floating on the surface of your infusion. Seatbelt your ingredients (see page 18) or weigh them down with a weight or smaller jar to prevent them from floating. Although airlocks aren't used often, I find them to be the easiest way to control mold so you may want to experiment with them. Once your infusion is complete, there's a small chance that mold could appear. If this concerns you, lessen the chances by straining the solids from the infused liquid and storing the infusion in the fridge or cellar.

FERMENTING. Sometimes you'll notice bubbles in the liquid, which is a sign that the infusion has begun to ferment. This is especially true when adding fruit and sugar to alcohol; the wild yeast can begin to ferment before the liquid is absorbed by the fruit. This isn't a bad thing, but it's worth noting so you don't panic at the sign of bubbles and needlessly toss out your work.

Storing

Infusions are more delicate than other preserves. They should be stored in dark and cool places. Vinegar or alcohol infusions can be stored on a shelf, especially if any added flavor ingredients are submerged. Floating ingredients increase the likelihood of spoilage. We often use tinted jars for additional protection from the light of the room. We store all other infusions in the fridge.

LOST COLOR. Some loss of color is unavoidable, especially with ingredients such as fruit or chili peppers, but it can be minimized by your choice of storage location. Keep your infusions out of direct sunlight, or try using colored glass that will minimize light getting in.

TEXTURE. Fresh fruit such as peaches or plums can break down when infused. Strain the solids to remove them, or infuse with dried fruit to prevent sediment.

WEAK FLAVORS. Use more of your chosen ingredient to increase the flavor. I prefer to infuse with too much flavor rather than too little, as it's easy to dilute afterwards.

STRONG FLAVORS. If you've gone too far, strain the solids and dilute with more liquid, then allow the infusion to age and mellow. In extreme cases, you can do a second round of infusing with an ingredient like vanilla, which is great at smoothing flavors.

Do's and Don'ts of Infusing

DO use care and do your research before infusing oil or honey.

DO taste your infusion often, especially at the start.

DO keep extra jars, vinegar, and alcohol on hand at all times to allow for spontaneous infusing experiments.

DO keep notes of what's in the jar so you can repeat the results!

DON'T be afraid to experiment.

DON'T consume any infusions that have developed mold.

DON'T store infused oil on the counter or for long periods of time.

a trip to the Market
in 25
INGREDIENTS

Apples

When I was eight or nine years old, my mother took my best friend and me to the local museum for a fall heritage day celebration. The museum was a sprawling property with multiple buildings, including an old blacksmith's store, schoolhouse, church, and train station (complete with train).

Near the General Store, we discovered several "settlers" stirring a brown paste over a propane stove. I watched as they poured spoonfuls of dense liquid into jars and then offered me a taste. The liquid was apple butter—sweet yet savory, and unlike anything I had ever tasted before. I spent my allowance on a jar to bring home.

I'm sure that day planted a meaningful seed, although I now prefer applesauce to apple butter. The smells of slow-simmering applesauce warm any space on the coldest of days. I often cook it a little longer than necessary, wrap myself in a sweater and a blanket, and allow the vapors to envelop our house as I sip on a Scotch or brandy and try to stay awake.

PRESERVING NOSE-TO-TAIL

- **FLESH** Typically the sweetest part. Infinitely useful and can be preserved as sauce, jelly, or cider, or dehydrated.
- **JUICE** Separated from the flesh by pressing or using, for example, a steam juicer. Can be waterbathed or frozen.
- **SKIN** Can be bitter. Can be pureed into a sauce, dried for teas, or used for smoking.
- **CORE (INCLUDING SEEDS)** Generally discarded but can be fermented into vinegar, pressed for cider, added to mead, or cooked down and strained for a sauce.

TIPS FOR STORING

Apples are best stored in a cold location. We store them on the counter for a few weeks—if we're worried about some turning soft we transfer them to the fridge where they will last for up to six months.

For longer-term storage, apples can be chilled almost to their freezing point. If you live in a cold climate, you can do this through the winter by wrapping them individually in ink-free newsprint, stacking them in a box or a bushel basket, and keeping them in a cold room or garage. They will last for months!

You can also set them by a drafty windowsill or hang them in a mesh bag in a closed-off porch.

FILLING THE PANTRY

CANNED
Applesauce, chutney, juice, or slices in light syrup.

DEHYDRATED
Slices, leather.

FERMENTED
Vinegar, hard cider. Also an ingredient in weinkraut (page 144).

INFUSED
Dried or fresh, often used to infuse vodka.

1 Homemade Pectin
2 Applescrap Vinegar
3 Quick Sauce
4 Shriveled Apple Skins
5 Applesauce
6 Dried Apple Slices

Batch-It

Applesauce

WATERBATH

LEVEL: ● ○ ○

YIELD: 7–8 PINT JARS

EFFORT: 1 HOUR

ELAPSED: 2½ HOURS

EAT: WITHIN 1–2 YEARS

12 lb apples, different types
   if possible

3 cinnamon sticks

12 whole cloves

1 cup honey

¼ cup fresh lemon juice

YOU WILL NEED

2 pieces of cheesecloth

Applescrap Vinegar

FERMENT

LEVEL: ● ● ○

YIELD: 1½–2 QUARTS

EFFORT: 10 MINUTES

ELAPSED: 4–6 WEEKS

EAT: WITHIN 1–2 YEARS

1 cup apple wood chips

½ cup honey

4 cups filtered water, plus extra

Peels and cores from the
   applesauce apples

YOU WILL NEED

1½-gallon wide-mouth jar

1½-cup Mason jar to use as a
   fermenting weight

3 pieces of cheesecloth

If you don't have a half-gallon jar,
use a food-safe bucket and a plate
to weigh down the scraps in step 8

When I first learned how to make applesauce, I was bothered by the amount of scraps that were thrown into the compost. Batching out homemade applesauce (a longtime favorite of my Meme's (grandmother) with homemade cider vinegar is an easy way to repurpose the scraps! Because the amount of acidity in homemade vinegar is inconsistent, it should not be used for other canning projects.

START THE SAUCE:

1 Core and peel the apples, setting the scraps aside for the vinegar.

2 In a high-speed blender, pulse the apples until the pieces are very small. The smaller the pieces, the faster they will cook.

3 Wrap the cinnamon sticks in one piece of the cheesecloth. Wrap the cloves in the second piece of cheesecloth and set the cloves aside.

4 Place the apple pieces in a large pot, add the honey and the wrapped cinnamon sticks, and bring to a simmer. Simmer uncovered for 30 minutes, stirring occasionally.

ASSEMBLE THE VINEGAR:

5 While the applesauce is simmering, toast the wood chips in a large frying pan over high heat, moving the pan frequently until the wood just begins to smoke.

6 Tie the wood chips inside a cheesecloth sack. Make sure all the wood is secure so none of it escapes into your vinegar.

7 Dissolve the honey in the water.

8 Fill the ½-gallon jar (or wide-mouth jars) with apple scraps. Place the wood chip bag on top to prevent the apple scraps from floating. Pour in the honey water, adding more water to fully submerge the apples if necessary. Place the ½-cup Mason jar on top to keep the scraps submerged.

9 Cover with a clean cloth and place in a warm spot in kitchen.

PROCESS THE SAUCE:

10 Prepare your canning pot and rack, and sterilize your jars and lids (see page 17).

11 Add the wrapped cloves to the applesauce and continue to simmer uncovered for 30 minutes more.

12 Remove the cloves and cinnamon. Add the honey and lemon juice and mix to combine.

13 Remove the sterilized jars from the canner and turn the heat to high. Fill the jars, leaving ½ inch of headspace. Gently jostle the jars or use the handle of a spoon to release any air bubbles. Wipe the rims of the jars, apply the lids, and process for 15 minutes (if you live higher than 1,000 feet above sea level, refer to the Adjust for Altitude chart on page 17 for additional processing times). Remove the jars and allow them to cool.

RETURN TO THE VINEGAR:

14 Skim off any residue that appears daily. Taste after 1 month and ferment for up to four weeks more. It's done when you like the taste. Store in the fridge for maximum life.

Quick Sauce

Don't worry about apples rotting on your shelf ever again! Peel and core two or three apples and toss with 1 Tbsp of honey and 1 tsp of lemon juice. Blend the ingredients add honey and lemon to taste and store in an airtight container in the fridge for weeks. Cook to thicken if desired. If you use a high-speed blender you can de-stem and quarter the apples and puree with skin and cores intact.

Homemade Pectin

WATERBATH

LEVEL: ● ● ●

YIELD: 2 1-CUP JARS

EFFORT: 1 HOUR

ELAPSED: 2 DAYS

EAT: WITHIN 2 YEARS

4 lb green, unripe apples

Rubbing or grain alcohol for testing

Use thick-skinned apples that are unripe if possible. This is a great ingredient for thickening jams and jellies because it doesn't have the extreme bitterness that most commercial pectin has. Just add a few tablespoons to any jam as it cooks.

1 Quarter the apples, leaving the skin and seeds intact.

2 Place the apple quarters in a large pot and cover them with water. Bring to a boil on high heat, then turn down to a low simmer uncovered until the apples are soft, 3–4 hours.

3 Place the dish towel inside the colander and carefully spoon the soft apple flesh into it. Cover loosely with a clean towel and allow it to strain for 24 hours on the counter (the longer, the better). Resist the urge to squeeze it!

4 After the mixture has strained, transfer it to a pot over medium heat until it has reduced by half, about 20 minutes.

5 To test it, put a spoonful of the pectin in a glass and chill it in the freezer for 15 minutes. Pour a small amount of rubbing or grain alcohol into the glass. If it coagulates enough that you can remove it with a fork, you're done. If not, reduce the pectin further.

6 Prepare your canning pot and rack, and sterilize your jars and lids (see page 17).

7 Fill the jars, leaving ¼ inch of headspace. Gently jostle the jars or use the handle of a spoon to release any air bubbles. Wipe the rims of the jars, apply the lids, and process for 10 minutes (if you live higher than 1,000 feet above sea level, refer to the Adjust for Altitude chart on page 17 for additional processing time). Remove the jars and allow them to cool before storing.

VARIATIONS: You can make this with red apples, though you'll get red pectin. You can also use citrus pith to make pectin.

CENTER OF THE PLATE: This is used only for jam making. Whenever you have a jam that's not setting, you can add a few tablespoons to help thicken it during cooking.

> **TIP: A FREE RACK FOR THE WATERBATH**
>
> Don't have a rack that will fit on the bottom of your waterbath? Don't fret! You can place a clean dishcloth on the bottom or make one by connecting extra jar rings together with twist ties!

10 Minutes or less

Dried Apple Slices

DEHYDRATE

LEVEL: ● ○ ○

YIELD: 4 HALF-PINT JARS

EAT: WITHIN 1 YEAR

4 lb apples

¼ cup brown sugar, lightly packed (optional)

2 Tbsp fresh lemon juice

YOU WILL NEED

Dehydrator

Mandolin (optional)

You can dehydrate apples with or without their peels. I prefer to peel and core them. Dried apple slices are common snacks. They can be rehydrated in water or added to baking or salads.

Peel and core the apples. Slice them in ¼-inch slices, transfer to a bowl, and toss with the brown sugar and lemon juice. Lay the slices on dehydrator trays, leaving space between them. Dry at 125°F until the chips are dry in the center but soft and bendable, 4–6 hours. Test for dryness by allowing one to cool—it should be flexible but dry inside when broken in two. Store in airtight jars on a shelf for up to two years.

Shriveled Apple Skins

DEHYDRATE

LEVEL: ● ○ ○

YIELD: 1–2 CUPS

EAT: WITHIN 1 YEAR

Skins from 4 lb apples

YOU WILL NEED

Dehydrator

When making applesauce or chips don't discard the skins. You can dry them. Cover ¼ cup dried apple skin with boiling water for an alternative to tea. Apple skins can also be added to herbal tea or hot toddies, pulverized and used as part of a rub, or tossed into the BBQ for smoke.

Scatter the skins on dehydrator trays, leaving space between them. Dry at 125°F until brittle, 4–6 hours. Periodically scatter by tossing your fingers through them and continue until the skins are dry and brittle. Store in airtight jars or a freezer bag on a shelf.

Broiled Scallops with Apple Gastrique

SERVINGS: 4

EFFORT: 15 MINUTES

ELAPSED: 30 MINUTES

GASTRIQUE:

¼ cup loosely packed dried apple slices (page 85)

Zest of 1 lemon

¼ cup honey

½ cup apple cider vinegar (page 82) or store-bought

Coarse salt

Black pepper

SCALLOPS:

1½ lb bay scallops

1 Tbsp coarse salt

2 Tbsp unsalted butter, chilled

1½ Tbsp fresh lemon juice (about ½ lemon)

¼ Tbsp chopped flat-leaf parsley, for garnish

Black pepper

My mother's Maritime roots meant that scallops were an occasional midweek meal. As an adult, I would struggle with cooking scallops until our friend Chef Matt Demille set me straight. His instructions were simple: "Brine them for a few minutes in salt water." This removes the guesswork from cooking them and makes them easier to sear without overcooking.

MAKE THE GASTRIQUE:

1 Roughly chop the dried apples and place them in a pot.

2 Add the lemon zest and honey and cook over medium-high heat, stirring until the honey darkens.

3 Add the vinegar and a pinch of salt and black pepper to taste. Lightly simmer, uncovered, until it has thickened into syrup, 15–20 minutes.

MAKE THE SCALLOPS:

4 Preheat the oven broiler to 500°F.

5 Sprinkle the salt over the scallops and add just enough cold water to barely cover them. Refrigerate for at least 10 minutes, and no more than 20 minutes.

6 While the scallops brine, melt the butter with the lemon juice in a small pot over medium-low heat.

7 Strain the scallops and rinse them well.

8 Gently toss the scallops in the melted butter. Place them on a baking tray, leaving space between them so they don't touch.

9 Broil for 3 minutes, then gently shake the pan to toss them. You can flip them individually, but I don't think it's worth the effort. Broil for 3 more minutes and remove from the heat. Loosely tent with aluminum foil and let rest for 4 minutes.

10 Spread the gastrique on a serving plate and put the scallops on top.

PANTRY RAID: The gastrique can be made with 2 Tbsp of any jam instead of apple slices, or you may wish to add a bit of infused booze (such as the raspberry brandy on page 303) for more flavor. Both would be added in step 2.

Chicken Stuffed with Apple, Walnuts, and Cheddar

SERVINGS: 2

EFFORT: 20 MINUTES

ELAPSED: 45 MINUTES

1 piece of stale bread, chopped
   into small pieces (fresh bread
   can be used in a pinch)

⅓ cup applesauce (page 82)

3 Tbsp grated cheddar cheese,
   preferably aged

1½ Tbsp chopped walnuts

2 boneless chicken breasts,
   skin on

1 Tbsp unsalted butter, chilled

1 garlic clove, minced

½ medium onion, diced

Coarse salt

1 small carrot, diced

½ stalk celery, diced

1 Tbsp peanut or vegetable oil

1 cup chicken stock

2 tsp white wine vinegar
   or ¼ cup dry white wine

2 bay leaves

Black pepper

Once you've learned to debone a chicken, you'll find that it takes only 5 or 10 minutes, and the carcass can be frozen or instantly used for stock. Don't get too hung up on adding back the chicken skin. It's a nice touch, but it's not essential.

STUFF THE CHICKEN (THIS CAN BE DONE IN ADVANCE):

1 Combine the bread with the applesauce, cheese, and walnuts in a bowl.

2 Using your fingers, remove the skin from the chicken.

3 Place the breasts between sheets of parchment paper and, using a meat mallet, gently flatten until they are ½ inch thick.

4 Scoop the stuffing into the middle of the breasts. Roll them into long cylinders, wrap them with chicken skin as best you can, and secure in place with toothpicks.

COOK THE CHICKEN:

5 Heat a frying pan on medium-high and melt the butter. Add the garlic, onion, and a pinch of salt, and cook until translucent, about 5 minutes.

6 Add the carrot and celery. Cook for 2 minutes, until soft.

7 Remove the vegetables from the pan, add the oil, and heat until the oil just begins to smoke.

8 Sear the chicken on all sides until brown, 3–4 minutes per side. Add the cooked veg, stock, vinegar, and bay leaves. Season to taste with salt and pepper, cover, and simmer for 20 minutes.

9 Remove the chicken from the pan and set on a serving plate. Loosely tent with aluminum foil and set aside.

10 Discard the bay leaves. Transfer the remaining ingredients from the pan to a blender and blend until smooth. Return to the pan and reduce by half over medium heat, about 5 minutes.

11 To serve, spread the sauce on a platter and place the chicken on top. Season to taste with salt and pepper.

PANTRY RAID: Add rehydrated dried apples, salt from preserved lemons (page 185), or 1–2 tsp of lemon powder made by grinding dehydrated shaved citrus slices (page 187).

Apricots

Apricots are not something I grew up with. I didn't avoid them; they just didn't really feature in my life until I was much older. I sometimes still struggle to understand them as a fruit. I shared this confession with my friend Joshna Maharaj, who smiled and said, "Apricots have more perfume than flavor." That single sentence changed my relationship with them—and with food in general. I had never previously considered that an ingredient could have a characteristic more dominant than its taste.

I think preserved apricots are better than fresh. Our friend Tara Besignano-Lee, a Toronto chef, recently served a cheese tray complete with dried apricots that she had rehydrated in boiling water. The concentrated taste and rich texture elevated the fruit way beyond its fresh counterpart. Biting into one of those rehydrated apricots created an explosion of apricot flavor in my mouth. It was as if she had captured the smell of the fruit and transferred it to my tongue.

Preserving isn't just a form of storing food; it can raise it to new heights. In my mind there are few fruits that demonstrate this better than the humble apricot.

PRESERVING NOSE-TO-TAIL

- **SKIN** You can peel apricots by blanching as you would a peach, but most people don't. Dry for a powder and add to rubs or fish.
- **FLESH** The flesh (often with the skin attached) is processed into jam or butter, dried, or fermented into fruit wine.
- **PIT** Apricots have a pit that can be cracked to reveal a kernel that looks like an almond. Some claim it is a natural cancer fighter, but it also contains cyanide. If you want to use the kernel, you should do some serious research first.

TIPS FOR STORING

Ripen apricots on the counter before chilling. To refrigerate apricots, place them in a wide-mouth Mason jar with a small sheet of parchment paper between layers and make sure there is plenty of air around them.

If you're in danger of losing apricots, remove their pits and puree them. Transfer the puree to an ice cube tray and add them to smoothies; thaw them and use to glaze meat or add to salad dressing; or thaw and warm with maple syrup for pancakes or French toast.

FILLING THE PANTRY

CELLARED
Frozen in halves or quarters.

CANNED
Jams, jellies, fruit butter.

DEHYDRATED
Dried as slices or candied.

INFUSED
The delicate flavors work better with alcohol than vinegar.

1 Apricot-Infused Granola
2 Apricot-Infused Kirsch
3 Candied Brandied Apricots
4 Apricot Butter
5 Roasted Apricot Vanilla Jam

Batch-It

Roasted Apricot Vanilla Jam

WATERBATH

LEVEL: ◉ ◉ ○

YIELD: 2–3 PINT JARS

EFFORT: 1 HOUR

ELAPSED: 1½ HOURS

EAT: WITHIN 2 YEARS

3 lb apricots

1 lemon

4 cups brown sugar, lightly packed

Ground cinnamon

Seeds from 2 vanilla pods or 1 Tbsp natural vanilla extract

Apricot-Infused Granola

DEHYDRATE

LEVEL: ◉ ○ ○

YIELD: 6 CUPS

EFFORT: 10 MINUTES

ELAPSED: 1 HOUR

EAT: WITHIN 1 YEAR

4 cups rolled oats

½ cup almonds (chopped or slivered, which is my preference)

½ cup combined of roasted apricot vanilla jam and reserved jam foam

¼ cup fresh lemon juice

¼ cup + 1 Tbsp olive oil

2 Tbsp honey

1 Tbsp Kirsch or pure vanilla extract

Salt

Jam making often means that you're left with a small amount of extra jam (a combination of the foam you've skimmed while cooking and not quite enough jam to fill the last bottle). You can leave it in your fridge, but I much prefer to whip up a quick batch of granola while the jam is in the waterbath.

MAKE THE JAM:

1 Preheat the oven to 350°F.

2 Cut the apricots in half and place them skin side down on a rimmed baking tray.

3 Squeeze the lemon over the apricots and sprinkle them with 1 tsp of brown sugar and cinnamon to lightly season.

4 Bake for 30 minutes, checking after 15 minutes and every 5 minutes thereafter. Although some color is desired, you don't want to completely blacken the tops, so remove the apricots when they begin to darken. Remove from oven and allow to cool.

5 Turn down the oven temperature to 300°F (this is for the granola).

6 Place the roasted apricots in a bowl with the remaining sugar and mix well to combine. Don't worry if the skins loosen.

7 Prepare your canning pot and rack, and sterilize the jars and lids (see page 17). Place a small plate in the freezer.

8 Place the apricots in a large pot with the water and vanilla. Bring to a simmer, uncovered, on medium-high heat. Stir frequently and skim the jam to remove any foam or bubbles from the top. Keep the foam in a bowl to use for the granola.

9 Cook until the jam is glossy, about 10–12 minutes. Test it by placing a small spoonful on the plate in the freezer. After 2 minutes, remove the plate and run your finger through the jam; if it remains divided, it's done. If not, continue to cook and test again after 2–3 minutes.

10 Remove the jars from the canner and turn the heat to high. Ladle the jam into the jars, leaving ½ inch of headspace. Gently jostle the jars or use the handle of a spoon to release any air bubbles. Wipe the rims of the jars, apply the lids, and

process for 10 minutes (if you live higher than 1,000 feet above sea level, refer to the Adjust for Altitude chart on page 17 for additional processing time). Remove the jars and allow them to cool.

PREP THE GRANOLA:

11 Mix all the granola ingredients together, reserving 1 Tbsp olive oil. If you don't have enough jam, you can puree extra apricots, or even apples, and add them to make up the difference.

12 Spread the remaining 1 Tbsp of olive oil onto a baking tray. Scatter the granola mixture on the tray.

13 Bake for 30–40 minutes, stirring after 15 minutes, until golden.

14 Allow the granola to cool to room temperature, remove with a spatula, and store in a jar.

10 Minutes or less

Apricot Butter

FERMENT

LEVEL: ◉ ○ ○

YIELD: ½ PINT

EAT: WITHIN 2 MONTHS

2 cups dried unsulfured apricots (the sulfur could slow or inhibit fermentation)

2 cups apple cider

¼ cup raw honey

2 Tbsp orange juice

1 tsp fine sea salt

YOU WILL NEED

1 pint standard-mouth Mason jar, sterilized

Airlock with number 13 cork

I first read about fermenting dried fruit in Sally Fallon's *Nourishing Traditions*. My recipe is different in several ways from hers, but both recipes provide an alternative to a typical fruit butter, which is often high in sugar and cooked on high heat, takes more work, and lacks the health benefits obtained by fermenting.

Combine the apricots and cider in a pot, bring to a simmer, and simmer for 3 minutes. Strain off the fruit (reserving the liquid to drink later). Let the fruit cool enough to handle. Add the apricots, honey, orange juice, and salt to a food processor and pulse into a paste. Pour into the sterilized jar, secure with the airlock, and place on your counter, out of direct sunlight, for two to five days. Cover with the lid and refrigerate.

Candied Brandied Apricots

DEHYDRATE

LEVEL: ◉ ◉ ○

YIELD: 1½ CUPS

EFFORT: 30 MINUTES

ELAPSED: 2–2½ DAYS

EAT: WITHIN 1 YEAR

3 lb apricots (peeling them is optional)

½ cup brown sugar, loosely packed

3 Tbsp fresh ginger, chopped then measured

½ cup honey

½ cup water

2 Tbsp brandy (optional)

YOU WILL NEED

Cheesecloth or muslin

Dehydrator

There are easier ways to make candied fruit than this, but this technique is well worth the effort. You'll appreciate this tasty treat in winter.

1 Cut the apricots into quarters and remove the pits.

2 Toss the apricots in the sugar and, using the widest pot or rimmed tray that will fit in your fridge, spread the apricots as thinly as you can. Cover tightly and refrigerate for 24 hours.

3 Strain the fruit, reserving any liquid. Place on a dehydrating tray and dry at 135°F for 6 hours.

4 Tie the chopped ginger in a cheesecloth sack and place it in a pot with the reserved apricot liquid, honey, water, and brandy. Bring to a simmer and reduce, stirring to prevent burning, until ½ cup of liquid remains, about 10 minutes.

5 Remove the ginger sack. Add the dried apricots to the liquid and cook until most of the liquid is absorbed. It may begin to thicken and turn to actual candy. If this happens, move quickly to the next step.

6 Using a spoon (they will be too hot to touch), carefully spread the apricots on a dehydrator tray. Some will stick together, but don't worry if they do. Return to the dehydrator and dry at 135°F for 4–6 hours, until hard.

VARIATIONS: Replace the ginger with cardamom, add 1 Tbsp of lemon juice, or add ½ cup pumpkin seeds with the apricots after you have removed the ginger sack.

CENTER OF THE PLATE: These are candy. Eat them as is, chop them into salad, or bake with them. They are also an interesting addition to your favorite tea (toss some in the tea ball when you infuse your tea).

TIP: SKIM JAM WITH A SLOTTED SPOON

When you cook jam it starts as a frothy mess. Bubbles are removed to make a clearer product and to remove excess air from the jar. Many people use a standard spoon for this, but I've found that a skimmer (it looks like a combination of a spoon and a sieve) or a spatula with holes is better than a normal spoon. The foam sticks to the tool and the liquids pour through. Place the foam in a bowl and spread on hot toast.

Frozen Fruit Paste

LEVEL: ● ○ ○

YIELD: 1 CUP

EFFORT: 45 MINUTES

ELAPSED: 1–2 DAYS

EAT: WITHIN 4–6 MONTHS

4 lb fresh apricots, quartered with
    pits removed

2 tsp + 1 Tbsp fresh lemon juice

2 Tbsp brown sugar

1 Tbsp honey

1 tsp pure vanilla extract

Salt

YOU WILL NEED

Dehydrator

Small baking pan or bread pan
    (10 x 10 inches)

Our friend Sarah Hood introduced me to membrillo (quince paste) a number of years ago at our beloved (and now deceased) local pub, the Avro. It was similar to fruit leather, but thicker and overwhelming in the best of ways. Her treat started a small researching obsession, which led me to apricot paste. This is my non-traditional version. You can use this to make Qamar-el-Deen (a traditional Middle Eastern beverage made from apricot paste).

1   Toss the apricot quarters in 2 tsp lemon juice. Arrange them without touching on a dehydrator tray and dehydrate at 135°F for 8–12 hours, until brittle.

2   Place the dehydrated apricots in a pot and cover with boiling water. Place a tight lid on the pot and leave on the counter for 6 hours or overnight.

3   Add 1½ cups water, the remaining 1 Tbsp lemon juice, brown sugar, honey, vanilla, and a pinch of salt to the apricots. Simmer over medium heat until the fruit is soft, about 20 minutes.

4   Transfer the fruit mixture to a blender, and puree as smooth as possible. If visible chunks remain, strain the mixture.

5   Line the baking pan with parchment paper. Pour in the paste and dehydrate at 135°F for about 6 hours. It is done when it pulls away from the paper easily and holds its form.

6   Wrap tightly and store in fridge for up to one month or in the freezer for three or more months.

VARIATIONS: Add chopped ginger to taste to the apricots before covering with boiling water, or replace the lemon with orange.

CENTER OF THE PLATE: Eat with cheese or cured meats. You can also make a beverage by covering 1 part paste with 3 parts boiling water and allowing it to rest for several hours. Puree or stir, chill, and serve.

Apricot-Infused Kirsch

Wash 4 or 5 apricots, cut them in quarters, and remove the pits and stems. Place them in a large jar and cover with 1 cup of kirsch. Secure with a lid and taste often. Strain when you like the taste (some people like to wait for days while others wait for months). Eat the boozy fruit or add it to baking, jam, or granola. Kirsch can be stored on a shelf indefinitely.

Curry Baked Acorn Squash with Apricot Vanilla Preserves

SERVINGS: 4–6 AS A SIDE DISH

EFFORT: 10 MINUTES

ELAPSED: 1½ HOURS

2 medium acorn squash, cut in half and seeds removed

2 Tbsp unsalted butter, chilled, or herb butter (page 227)

3 cloves garlic, minced

½ inch piece ginger, minced

⅔ cup apricot jam or apricot butter (pages 92–93)

1 tsp yellow curry powder

Dried chili powder or flakes

Salt

Black pepper

As a child, I always associated squash with Thanksgiving or Christmas. The holidays weren't complete without a piece of roasted squash caramelized with brown sugar and butter. But you don't have to wait for a special occasion to make this recipe!

1 Preheat the oven to 400°F.

2 Place about ½ inch of water in the bottom of a roasting pan to help steam the squash and keep it moist as it cooks.

3 Score the squash by cutting a grid pattern into the flesh. Cut as deeply as possible without cutting through the skin.

4 In a small pot, melt the butter over medium heat and cook the garlic and ginger until soft but not brown, about 3 minutes.

5 Remove the pot from the heat, add the apricot jam, curry powder, a pinch of chili powder, and salt and pepper to taste and mix well.

6 Pour this sauce evenly into the hollowed-out center of each piece of squash. Bake uncovered for 15 minutes, then baste the squash with the cooking juices that have collect in its center and check the water level, adding more if needed. Repeat 15 minutes later.

7 The squash should be cooked through after 40–45 minutes. Baste it one final time, if any liquid remains in the pan, and place it under the broiler for 1–2 minutes, until golden brown. Serve on its own or with wild rice.

PANTRY RAID: Try adding herb-infused honey, a dash of limoncello (page 187), or flavored salt (pages 167, 185, and 229).

Apricot Triangles

SERVINGS: 12 (ABOUT 24 TRIANGLES)

EFFORT: 45 MINUTES

ELAPSED: 1½ HOURS

1 cup unsalted, shelled pistachios

¾ cup dried apricots or ¼ cup apricot paste (page 95)

¾ cup honey

Zest of 1 medium orange, chopped fine (or ¼ tsp orange bitters)

½ inch piece ginger, minced

½ tsp freshly grated nutmeg

1 lb ricotta cheese

1 lb phyllo dough, thawed and covered with a damp towel

½ cup unsalted butter, measured then melted

3 eggs, lightly beaten

This recipe is influenced by baklava, though it's not as sweet. It's also a lot less messy to eat since it's not covered with the traditional honey-sugar syrup. These triangles can be frozen and eaten cold, or warmed in the oven when you're ready to feast.

1 Preheat the oven to 350°F.

2 Roughly chop the pistachios and apricots to the same size.

3 Combine the honey, orange zest, ginger, and nutmeg in a pot over medium-high heat, until the honey reaches a simmer, which should take about 2 minutes. Stir constantly.

4 Remove the honey mixture from the heat, add the apricots and pistachios and mix to combine. Let cool enough to handle, about 2 minutes.

5 Fold in the ricotta.

6 Keep the phyllo covered with a damp towel except for the piece you are actually working with.

7 Spread a single sheet of phyllo onto a large cutting board. Cut it in half lengthwise and then fold one piece in half lengthwise so that you have a long rectangle. (Put the other piece under the damp towel for now.) Brush the uppermost side of the phyllo with melted butter.

8 Lay the phyllo lengthwise in front of you. Place a spoonful of filling on the phyllo kitty-corner to the corner closest to your body. Carefully fold the corner closest to you diagonally, up and over to cover the filling and to make a triangle. Fold the pastry down on itself to continue making a triangle shape, as if you were folding a flag.

9 Gently push down on the filling to move it into the corners of the pastry. Place on a baking tray and repeat with the remaining phyllo and filling.

10 Lightly brush the triangles with the egg wash.

11 Bake for 30–35 minutes, or until golden brown.

PANTRY RAID: Add ¼ cup of any jam in stage 3 or replace dried apricots with same volume of any dried fruit.

Asparagus

My first experience with eating locally came from the book *The 100-Mile Diet*. Before reading the book I didn't realize that buying local was a "thing."

The majority of the food we eat is local and in season. We didn't make a conscious decision to be locavores, it just kind of happened. As we spent more time at farmers' markets, we began consuming more locally grown food. We made a significant change by accident when a farmer sold me three giant bags of asparagus for $20 at the end of a market day. I was buried in asparagus and dug myself out the only way I knew how: I pickled and pressure canned more asparagus than we could eat in a year. As a result, we didn't have to buy any that winter, and asparagus became the first ingredient we didn't buy out of season.

When we finally bought fresh asparagus the following spring, the taste of the first bite exploded in my mouth like fireworks across the night sky. I was shocked, but decided immediately to stop buying ingredients out of season. These days, we buy most of our food in season and preserve it to eat for the rest of the year. The preserves extend the season and allow us to enjoy the fresh product when it's at its most intense.

PRESERVING NOSE-TO-TAIL

- **WOODY ENDS** Generally tossed aside as being too coarse. They have lots of flavor and can be frozen and used to make stock, added to rice as it cooks, or dried and pulverized into asparagus powder.
- **STALKS** Great for pickling but equally beautiful as a relish, soup, or dried. These freeze better than the tips.
- **TIPS** Equally pretty and delicious, especially when pickled.

TIPS FOR STORING

Asparagus dries out quickly, so you'll often see it stored in water. Store it in a coffee mug or Mason jar in your fridge. Cover the bottom of the stems with light sugar water (1 Tbsp of sugar per 1 cup of water).

If it starts to dry out, cut 1 inch off the ends and replace the sweetened water in the jar. It will rehydrate in this liqueur.

FILLING THE PANTRY

CHILLED
Freeze after blanching.

CANNED
Relish or pickled.

PRESSURE CANNED
Pressure canned whole or as a soup.

1 Asparagus Relish
2 Pickled Asparagus Spears
3 Asparagus Soup Concentrate
4 Dehydrated Asparagus Stalks
5 Fermented Asparagus Pickles

Batch-It

Pickled Asparagus Spears

WATERBATH

LEVEL: ● ○ ○

YIELD: 3 PINT JARS

EFFORT: 30 MINUTES

ELAPSED: 1½ HOURS

EAT: AFTER 6 WEEKS AND WITHIN 2
    YEARS

Tops of 5 lb asparagus, cleaned and
    cut to the length of the jar

3 cups white wine vinegar (must be
    5% acidity or more)

2½ cups water

½ cup lime juice (4–5 limes)

3 Tbsp honey

6 cloves garlic, peeled and slightly
    smashed

24 whole peppercorns

1½ tsp cayenne pepper

VARIATION

Replace the cayenne with 3 Tbsp
    dill seeds.

Asparagus spears are more beautiful than the stalks.
I pickle them while I'm using the bottoms to make relish.
The pickles have a bite that cuts through the acidity of the
brine. The brine is an awesome cooking ingredient that
you can add to stir-fries, salads, and fish. The relish is
savory enough to be used on a hamburger but subtle
enough to use for white fish, seafood, or cured ham.
The relish is very tart, so I remove it from the jar with a
fork and leave the brine (which is the most acidic) behind.

MAKE THE PICKLED SPEARS:

1   Prepare your canning pot and rack, and sterilize your jars
    and lids (see page 17). Prepare a bowl of ice-cold water.

2   In a pot of boiling water, blanch the asparagus for 10 sec-
    onds; remove and place in the cold water.

3   Make a brine by placing the vinegar, water, lime juice, and
    honey in a pot and mixing them well. Bring to a simmer over
    medium heat for 3 minutes.

4   Remove the jars from the canner and turn the heat to high.

5   Place 2 cloves garlic, 8 peppercorns, and ½ tsp cayenne in
    each jar.

PACK THE JARS AND PROCESS:

6   Pack the jars with asparagus as tightly as you can; they will
    shrink as they cook. If you want to ensure they don't float,
    seatbelt them (see page 18), though I usually don't because I
    prefer the aesthetics of vertical spears alone.

7   Fill each jar with brine, leaving ½ inch of headspace. Gently
    jostle the jars or use the handle of a spoon to release any air
    bubbles. Wipe the rims of the jars, apply the lids, and pro-
    cess for 10 minutes (if you live higher than 1,000 feet above
    sea level, refer to the Adjust for Altitude chart on page 17 for
    additional processing time). Remove the jars and allow them
    to cool.

Asparagus Relish

WATERBATH

LEVEL: ● ● ○

YIELD: 4 HALF-PINT JARS

EFFORT: 30 MINUTES

ELAPSED: 2 HOURS

EAT: WITHIN 1–2 YEARS

4 cups finely chopped asparagus
    stalks

1 cup onion, minced (measure after
    cutting)

2 cups white vinegar (5% or higher),
    divided

½ cup water

½ cup honey

2 Tbsp mustard seeds

1 Tbsp dill seeds

2 tsp kosher salt

1 tsp celery seeds

1 tsp red chili flakes

VARIATIONS

Add up to an additional ⅓ cup of
    honey, replace the white vinegar
    with 1 cup of white and 1 cup of
    white wine vinegar.

MAKE THE RELISH:

8   In a large pot, combine the asparagus, onion, and 1 cup of
    the vinegar over medium heat. Bring to a simmer for 3 min-
    utes, stirring and watching that it doesn't dry. If it does,
    remove it from the heat.

9   Drain the vegetables and discard the liquid. Rinse the veg-
    etables in cold water.

10 Return the cooked asparagus and onion to the pot and add
    the remaining 1 cup vinegar, the water, honey, mustard
    seeds, dill seeds, salt, celery seeds, and chili flakes. Simmer
    for 5 minutes.

11 Remove the jars from the canner and turn the heat to high.

12 Spoon the relish into the jars, wipe the rims, apply the lids,
    and process for 10 minutes (if you live higher than 1,000
    feet above sea level, refer to the Adjust for Altitude chart on
    page 17 for additional processing time). Remove the jars and
    allow them to cool.

> **TIP: MEASURE TWICE, CUT ONCE?**
> I used to struggle to cut asparagus and other long
> vegetables to the right length for the jars I was
> using. I now have a special cutting board dedicated
> to preserving. Once I found the perfect
> length of a vegetable for a jar, I used it as a
> guide and made two marks with a marker pen
> on the side of the cutting board. Now I just
> look for my marks and can quickly cut each
> vegetable perfectly!

Asparagus Soup Concentrate

PRESSURE CAN

LEVEL: ● ● ○

YIELD: 4–5 QUART JARS (6–8 QUARTS
    WHEN SERVING)

EFFORT: 1 HOUR

ELAPSED: 2½ HOURS

EAT: WITHIN 6 MONTHS

FOR PRESERVING

2 Tbsp cooking oil or lard

3 medium onions, cut into thin rings

4–6 medium peeled potatoes, cut
    into 1-inch cubes

Salt

Black pepper

12 cups vegetable or chicken stock
    (+ more if needed)

4 bunches of asparagus, broken into
    pieces

¼ cup flat-leaf parsley

5 sprigs thyme

FOR SERVING

⅔ cup heavy (35%) cream

1–2 Tbsp unsalted butter, chilled

2–3 tsp sherry

Salt

Black pepper

1–2 cups stock per jar

YOU WILL NEED

Blender (high-speed or immersion
    recommended)

Cheesecloth

This isn't your traditional soup-in-a-can. Chunks of onions, potatoes, and asparagus are seasoned and preserved in stock. When you are ready to eat the soup, you blend all the basic ingredients together and add a few more.

MAKE THE SOUP:

1 Warm the fat in a heavy frying pan over medium-high heat and cook the onions and potatoes (in batches if necessary) until slightly brown. Season with salt and pepper as they cook, adding more fat if needed.

2 Place the onions, potatoes, and stock in a large pot over medium-high heat and bring to a bare simmer.

3 Fry the asparagus in the frying pan you used for the onions and potatoes until slightly softened, about 5 minutes.

4 Add the asparagus and parsley to the pot. Tie the thyme in a cheesecloth sack, season the soup with salt and pepper, and simmer uncovered for 30 minutes.

5 Remove the thyme and discard. Add more stock if desired.

PRESERVE THE SOUP:

6 Prepare the pressure canner and jars and lids. (See pages 21–23.)

7 Distribute the soup between 4 or 5 jars, leaving 1 inch of headspace. Gently jostle the jars or use the handle of a spoon to release any air bubbles. Secure the lids and process at 10 lb of pressure for 75 minutes at sea level (if you live higher than 1,000 feet above sea level, refer to the Adjust for Altitude Chart on page 25 for additional processing times). Store on a shelf out of direct sunlight.

SERVE THE SOUP:

8 Pour the soup into a blender and puree until smooth.

9 Add the cream, butter, sherry, and salt and pepper to taste. Add 1–2 cups additional stock per jar to extend the soup.

10 Warm the soup to serving temperature.

VARIATIONS: You can add parmesan cheese, strained yogurt, aged cheddar cheese, or strips of prosciutto or bacon before serving to make this a meal in its own right.

10 Minutes or less

Frozen Asparagus

CELLAR

LEVEL: ● ○ ○

YIELD: 2 LB

EAT: WITHIN 6 MONTHS

2 lb asparagus

Salt

Steaming asparagus will preserve its color and texture when it's frozen. If you don't have a steamer, you can blanch them for about 3 minutes. We freeze asparagus in two steps to stop the spears from sticking together, but you could freeze them directly from the ice bath if that doesn't concern you.

Prepare a bowl of ice-cold water. Trim the asparagus and blanch in a large pot of boiling salt water (it should taste like the ocean) for 30 seconds before cooling in the ice water. Dry with a towel, spread on a tray (not touching), and freeze for 90 minutes. Transfer to a container or freezer bag and freeze for three to six months.

Fermented Asparagus Pickles

FERMENT

LEVEL: ● ○ ○

YIELD: 1 QUART

EAT: WITHIN 3 MONTHS

1½–2 lb asparagus (I use the stalks)

1½ tsp coarse salt

2 green onions

1–2 thick orange slices

Filtered water

Fermenting asparagus is slightly more complicated than fermenting carrots (page 155), but the outcome is more dependable than pickling cucumbers (page 194). It's a great preserve to develop your skills with. To ensure success, you need only to keep a close eye on them and taste often.

Cut the stalks so that they stand ¾–1 inch below where the jar neck begins to narrow. Pack the jar tightly with asparagus, then add the salt. Add water to barely cover the contents. Lay green onion on top of the asparagus. "Seatbelt" the ingredients into place by wedging an orange slice across the top to prevent floating. Add additional water so that all ingredients are completely submerged and place it on a small plate. Loosely cover with a clean cloth and allow to ferment until you like the sourness (two to four days is typical) before securing with a lid and storing in fridge.

Dehydrated Asparagus Stalks

Blanch asparagus stalks for 15 seconds in boiling water before transferring them to an ice bath. Dry at 125°F until brittle, 8–10 hours. They will resemble grass but pack a full-on asparagus punch that's great crumbled onto salad or fried fish!

ASPARAGUS

Pickled Aioli and Pickled Poached Eggs

SERVINGS: 2

EFFORT: 40 MINUTES

ELAPSED: 40 MINUTES

PICKLED AIOLI:

2 garlic cloves, minced

1 large egg yolk

2 tsp pickling brine from the pickled
   asparagus (page 102)

½ tsp Dijon mustard

¼ cup olive oil

3 Tbsp grapeseed (or other lightly
   flavored) oil

Salt

PICKLED POACHED EGGS:

¼ cup asparagus pickle brine
   (page 102)

Salt

4 eggs

SANDWICH:

2 (6-inch) pieces of baguette, cut
   lengthwise (like a submarine)

1 Tbsp unsalted butter, chilled

8 slices aged cheddar

2–3 healthy handfuls of arugula

16 (or more) pieces of pickled
   asparagus (page 102)

1 piece of garlic from the pickle
   brine, chopped thin (page 102)

Salt

Pepper

Smoked paprika

YOU WILL NEED

If you're new to poaching eggs,
   you may find a large ladle to be
   helpful!

Restaurants commonly add vinegar to the poaching liquid in order to poach many eggs at once. Although it's possible to add a small amount of vinegar without changing the flavor, a chef with a heavy hand can turn the eggs slightly acidic. I realized that we can partially flavor an egg while poaching it. Instead of using conventional vinegar, I like to go all-in with asparagus pickle brine.

MAKE THE AIOLI:

1 Combine the garlic, egg yolk, brine, and mustard in a blender.

2 With the blender running, slowly drizzle in the oils. If the mixture separates, stop adding oil and blend until it self-corrects.

3 Continue blending until all the oil is added and the mixture is thick. Season with salt, place in an airtight container, and store in the fridge. This aioli will keep for about 1 week.

POACH THE EGGS:

4 Add 1 inch of water to a wide saucepan.

5 Season the water with the brine and a healthy pinch of salt. Bring the liquid to a simmer without letting it boil.

6 Turn the broiler on (you'll toast the bread while you cook the eggs).

7 Partially fill a ladle with water from the pot. Crack an egg into the ladle. Hold the ladle with the egg inside the pot for a few seconds (this will help the egg set) before gently releasing the egg into the water. Continue with the other eggs. Cook for 3½–4½ minutes.

MAKE THE SANDWICHES:

8 Butter the cut side of the bread and toast it under the broiler.

9 Coat each slice of toast with aioli then add a layer of cheese, arugula, and pickled asparagus.

10 Place a poached egg on top of each piece of bread, garnish with slices of pickled garlic and season with salt, pepper, and smoked paprika.

PANTRY RAID: Herb butter (page 227) or beet or mushroom powder (pages 122 and 251) could all be added to the toast.

Ricotta Gnocchi, Pistachios, Brown Butter, and Asparagus Relish

SERVINGS: 4 SIDES OR 2 MAINS

EFFORT: 1 HOUR

ELAPSED: 1½ HOURS

½ cup unsalted butter, chilled

½ tsp salt

1 cup all-purpose flour

⅛ tsp dried sage, ground

1 egg, lightly beaten

1 cup ricotta cheese

¾ cup fresh Parmesan cheese, finely grated

¾ cup cold butter

¼ cup asparagus relish (or more to taste) (page 103)

¼ cup whole shelled pistachios, roughly chopped

Honey (optional)

This is a calorie-rich meal that's ideal for the depths of winter. The gnocchi can be made hours in advance as long as you have room in your fridge to store them, covered, without stacking them. You can double this recipe.

MAKE THE GNOCCHI:

1 In a large pot, bring 1 cup water to a boil with the butter and salt.

2 Turn down the heat to medium, add the flour and sage, and whisk to incorporate. Cook until the mixture thickens and darkens slightly, stirring often, 5–7 minutes.

3 Separate the dough into small piles and allow it to cool enough to handle.

4 Roll the dough into one large ball and add the egg and both cheeses. Fold until the dough is a consistent texture.

5 Toss some flour on a cutting board. Roll the dough in the flour and form long cylinders, ¾ inch in diameter. Cut the cylinders into ¾-inch pieces and roll each piece in flour. Place on a plate without stacking them.

MAKE THE SAUCE:

6 Dice the butter and place it in a pan.

7 Cook on medium heat, stirring and watching it closely once it begins to simmer. Watch for the solids to appear on the bottom of the pan and turn just past golden brown. Transfer the butter immediately to a cool bowl. If the solids turn black, you've burned it and will have to start again.

8 Add the asparagus relish and chopped pistachios to the bowl with the butter and stir well. Add honey to taste.

COMPLETE THE DISH:

9 Place a large pot of heavily salted water on high heat.

10 As the water nears a boil, gently reheat your sauce in a pan.

11 Drop the gnocchi into the boiling water, stirring as you go. Once they start to float, they are done. Drain well and toss in the brown butter sauce. Season with salt and pepper and serve.

PANTRY RAID: A touch of infused honey (page 229), herbes salées (page 229), or dried herbs (page 227).

Beans & Peas

One day, after Dana and I had been visiting my parents, instead of heading straight home, we decided to visit a local apple orchard and hobby farm that had a petting zoo and corn maze.

As we walked through the farm store, I reflected on the difficulties of operating a farm in southern Ontario. And then I saw eight bags of shucked peas. Each bag was about a quart. I knew that the store would be closed for the next three days, and I realized that this was a last-ditch effort to salvage what they had harvested.

We pressure canned peas for the first time that night. I placed them on the shelf and forgot about them until later in the winter when I tossed some into a pan of fried rice just before serving. The peas were like little flavor bombs and instantly brought me back to the best tastes of spring and summer!

PRESERVING NOSE-TO-TAIL

I break beans, legumes, and peas into three categories based on the shells:

- **EDIBLE SHELLS** Pressure can or dry whole or in pieces.
- **NON-EDIBLE SHELLS WITH THICK WALLS** Shuck and dehydrate, or freeze to use in stock or in rice or pasta.
- **NON-EDIBLE SHELLS WITH THIN WALLS (E.G., ROMANO BEANS)** You could dry them and toss them into the BBQ for added smoke, but I generally dry these beans in the shells.

TIPS FOR STORING

If you buy beans or peas in plastic bags, remove them from the plastic as soon as you get home. Beans like to be dry. Store them in an airtight container with a sheet of paper towel to absorb any extra moisture. If you're in a pinch, see page 115 for how to air-dry beans. I dehydrated beans four or five times by accident before I started doing it intentionally.

FILLING THE PANTRY

CHILLED
Blanch and freeze on trays.

CANNED
Pickles such as dilly beans.

PRESSURE CANNED
Canned as soup or in water.

DEHYDRATED
They dry perfectly and keep nearly indefinitely.

1 Smoke-Dried Beans
2 Dried Green and Yellow Beans
3 Air-Dried Beans
4 Fermented Beans
5 Masala Pickled Yellow Beans
6 Canned Maple Bacon Beans

Batch-It

Fermented Beans

FERMENT

LEVEL: ● ○ ○

YIELD: 8 CUPS (2 QUARTS)

EFFORT: 3 MINUTES

ELAPSED: 2–5 DAYS

EAT: WITHIN A WEEK

6 cups dried beans (any type will
   do; I use garbanzo and kidney
   most often)

4 Tbsp whey

Filtered water to cover
   (approx. 4–5 cups)

YOU WILL NEED

Container (I use 2 1-quart
   Mason jars)

Smoke-Dried Beans

SMOKE

LEVEL: ● ● ○

YIELD: 1 CUP

EFFORT: 30 MINUTES

ELAPSED: 8–10 HOURS

EAT: WITHIN 6 MONTHS

4 cups (1 pint) fermented beans

YOU WILL NEED

Cold smoker

Dehydrator

Mark Trealout is a local farmer and a friend who first told me about cooking dried beans after fermenting them—apparently this makes them easier for many people to digest. I've also found that it makes them absorb smoke well, so I grind them into a powder and use them as a finishing salt right before serving!

FERMENT THE BEANS:

1   Split the beans, whey, and water between the 2 Mason jars and stir to combine. Cover loosely with a clean towel. Store in a warm location, tasting and stirring every 12 hours. The longer they sit, the more they will soften. Wait 24–36 hours before transferring them to the fridge or cooking them in plenty of boiling salt water.

SMOKE THE BEANS:

2   Spread 4 cups of fermented beans on a rimmed baking tray and cold-smoke for 5 hours. See page 66 for instructions on how to turn your BBQ into a cold smoker.

3   Transfer to a dehydrator at 125°F for about 4 hours, until completely dry (they will dry much faster than fresh beans). Store on a shelf in an airtight Mason jar.

Masala Pickled Yellow Beans

WATERBATH

LEVEL: ◉ ◉ ○

YIELD: 5 2-CUP JARS (DON'T USE
    WIDE-MOUTH JARS)

EFFORT: 35 MINUTES

ELAPSED: 1 HOUR

EAT: AFTER 6 WEEKS
    AND WITHIN 1–2 YEARS

2½ cups white vinegar (5% or
    higher)

2½ Tbsp honey

¼ cup pickling salt

5 medium cloves garlic, finely
    chopped

5 pieces of ginger (each the size of
    a garlic clove), finely chopped

5 Tbsp garam masala

2½–5 tsp cayenne pepper
    (according to taste)

Zest of 1 lemon

3 lb yellow beans, cut ¾ inch shorter
    than the jars you are using

Thin slices of lemon (cut as thinly as
    possible), seeds removed

5 bay leaves

Dilly beans (beans pickled like dill pickles) are a favorite snack at our house and were the inspiration for this pickle. This recipe is a fusion of the flavors of Indian pickles and the vinegar pickles that are more common to North America. I've been playing with curry as a pickling ingredient for years and love the unexpected twist it brings.

1 Prepare your canning pot and rack, and sterilize your jars and lids (see page 17).

2 Place the vinegar, 2½ cups of water, honey, and salt in a large saucepan and bring to a near a simmer.

3 Remove the jars from the canner and turn the heat to high.

4 Divide the garlic, ginger, curry, cayenne, and lemon zest evenly among the five jars as the brine heats.

5 Carefully place the beans vertically inside the jar. When each jar is about half full, place a few slices of lemon and a bay leaf between the beans and the glass. These are largely decorative but will also add flavor. Pack tightly and seatbelt (see page 18) to prevent floating. Add the brine, leaving ½ inch of headspace and jostling the ingredients to remove the air bubbles.

6 Wipe the rims, apply the lids, and process for 10 minutes (if you live higher than 1,000 feet above sea level, refer to the Adjust for Altitude chart on page 17 for additional processing time).

7 Remove the jars from the canner and allow to cool.

VARIATIONS: Adding hot peppers (red ones) will make this even prettier. And you could substitute lime for the lemon.

CENTER OF THE PLATE: Use this in almost any dish where you'd use beans. I love these on a sandwich, where they add a touch of heat and are complemented by grainy mustard.

Canned Maple Bacon Beans

PRESSURE CAN

LEVEL: ◉ ◉ ◯
YIELD: 5+ QUART JARS
EFFORT: 45 MINUTES
ELAPSED: 5–6 HOURS
EAT: WITHIN 1 YEAR

4 lb dried navy beans
Salt
1 lb pork belly, cut into
    bite-sized bits
2 onions, chopped into large
    chunks
1 tsp powdered mustard
3 Tbsp maple syrup
1 Tbsp cider vinegar

We make meals like this on quiet winter afternoons. This recipe makes 20 portions of food (10 meals for us).

1   Sort and wash the beans. Place them in a large stock pot and cover with lots of heavily salted cold water. Boil for 5 minutes, partially covered. Remove from the heat, and allow the beans to rest in the cooking liquid for 1 hour.

2   Drain the beans and discard the water. Return the beans to the pot and cover with at least 12 cups of heavily salted cold water. Bring to a boil over high heat and boil for 2 minutes. Remove from the heat and let the beans sit in the water.

3   Preheat the oven to 350°F.

4   Heat a large oven-safe pot (we use a 5½-quart Dutch oven) with a lid on medium-high heat. This pot will have to hold both the pork and the beans.

5   Once the pan is hot, brown the pork on all sides, about 10 minutes. The pork will have enough fat so don't add extra.

6   Add the onion, mustard, and salt, and cook until the onion is translucent, about 2 minutes.

7   Add the beans and 4 cups of their cooking liquid to the pork. Add the maple syrup and vinegar.

8   Cover and place in the oven. Stir every hour for 4–5 hours, adding more cooking liquid from the beans if necessary. The beans are ready when still slightly firm.

9   Before canning, add salt or additional maple syrup to taste.

10 Prepare your canning equipment and pressure canner (see pages 21–23). Hot-pack in sterilized jars, leaving 1 inch headspace, and process for 65 minutes at sea level (if you live higher than 1,000 feet above sea level, refer to the Adjust for Altitude Chart on page 25 for additional processing time).

VARIATIONS: Replace the maple syrup with the same volume of molasses or honey. Use a different type of bean or add smoke-dried peppers just before baking.

CENTER OF THE PLATE: All you need to do with this recipe is warm it up in a pot, but you can add freshly chopped onions, stock, or canned beans before serving.

10 Minutes or less

Dried Green and Yellow Beans

DEHYDRATE

LEVEL: ◉ ○ ○

YIELD: 4 CUPS (1 QUART)

EAT: WITHIN 1 YEAR

4–5 lb green and yellow beans

YOU WILL NEED
Dehydrator

Beans with edible shells are dense and best dried in a dehydrator. They are easily rehydrated and an interesting ingredient to add to stews or rice as it cooks, as they will absorb liquid while also infusing their flavors across the dish. This will also work with shelled peas.

Fill a large pot with salted water, leaving enough room to add the beans without overflow. I recommend using a pasta pot with a matching colander that will make it easy to remove the beans at one time. Bring the water to a hard boil over high heat. Place the beans in the pot, cover with a lid, and blanch for 4 minutes, filling the sink with cold water as they boil. Remove the beans from the pot and transfer to the cold water. Chop into ½-inch pieces and spread on drying racks. Dehydrate at 125°F for 8–10 hours, until brittle. Store in a jar with a lid that will prevent moisture from entering.

Air-Dried Beans (or Peas)

Air circulation is the key to dehydrating food. Spread the shelled peas or beans on drying racks. Thin-shelled beans can be tied into strands, like you would with hot peppers. Place the veggies out of direct sunlight in a dry spot in your kitchen (I often use the top of a cabinet). They are done when bone dry.

Bloody Mary with Brine and Pickled Beans

SERVINGS: 1

EFFORT: 5 MINUTES

ELAPSED: 5 MINUTES

1–2 tsp fresh lemon juice plus a
lemon wedge

1 Tbsp celery powder

12 oz tomato juice

2 oz vodka or hot pepper-infused
vodka (page 175)

1 Tbsp pickle brine, storebought or
homemade (page 113)

1½ tsp jarred horseradish or 1 tsp
fresh horseradish

1 tsp HP sauce, Marmite,
or BBQ sauce

¼ tsp Worcestershire sauce or hot
sauce, to taste

Salt

Black pepper

A pile of ice

Pickled beans (page 113) and
fermented pepper slices
(page 177), for garnish

A Bloody Mary is an excuse to empty the fridge and pantry of any remaining pickles or vegetable powders. Don't be shy with your ice—you should add so much that it crests the glass by at least 2 fingers in height. Contrary to popular belief, this will not water your drink down. The ice will melt more slowly and the contents of the glass will remain colder. I like to serve this in a pint glass or jar that's been rinsed in water and chilled in the freezer for at least an hour.

1 Make a slit the lemon wedge to separate the flesh from the peel and run it around the rim of the glass, squeezing as you go. Dip the rim of the glass in the celery powder.

2 In a separate glass, combine the tomato juice, vodka, brine, horseradish, HP, Worcestershire or hot sauce, salt, and pepper to taste. Stir well.

3 Fill your serving glass with ice. Fill with the drink mix and garnish with beans.

PANTRY RAID: Add mushroom powder (page 251) with the celery powder to rim the drink, add a splash of mushroom stock or brine from kimchi (page 147).

TIP: FIRMER PICKLES AND THICKER JELLY

Most pickles will become crisper when chilled. If you want firmer pickles, it's often as easy as throwing the jar in the fridge before serving them. Jam and jelly will become thinner when heated, so if you want thinner jam after opening a jar, heat it slightly. You can also add a light simple syrup (1 tsp honey mixed with 1 tsp water) to jam to thin it after opening.

Rice Pilaf with Dried Green and Yellow Beans and Dried Mushrooms

SERVINGS: 4

EFFORT: 5 MINUTES

ELAPSED: ½ HOUR

4 cups water or any type of stock

Salt

1 cup dried whole mushrooms (page 252)

⅓ cup dried yellow or green beans (page 115)

1 Tbsp unsalted butter, chilled

1 cup long-grain white rice

1 Tbsp tomato paste or tomato powder

2–3 bay leaves

Rice used to intimidate me. I always messed up cooking it. It was too wet or too dry or not cooked enough. I even bought a rice cooker, hoping that would solve my problems! Then I took a cooking class with Chef Jeff Dueck, who changed my approach to cooking it (he used the oven), and I've never failed since.

1 Preheat the oven to 325°F.

2 In a large pot, bring the water to a boil on high heat and add a healthy pinch of salt.

3 Add the mushrooms and beans, and simmer, uncovered, until softened, 4–6 minutes.

4 Drain the mushrooms and beans, reserving the liquid. Set aside.

5 Melt the butter in an oven-safe pot with a lid (I use a 3-quart pot) on medium-high heat. Add the rice, season with salt and cook, stirring, for 3–4 minutes.

6 Add the tomato paste, bay leaves, and 2 cups of the reserved cooking water.

7 Cover the pot with its lid and bring to a boil on high heat. Once boiling, transfer to the oven and cook for 17 minutes, without opening the oven door.

8 Test the rice. Once it is cooked, remove the pot from the oven. If any liquid remains, reserve it for other cooking. Discard the bay leaves, and add the mushrooms and beans to the rice. Stir, and allow it to rest for a few minutes. Stir everything together again before serving.

PANTRY RAID: Hot peppers, stock (page 236), or brine from pressure canned vegetables (pages 122 and 250) or a few tablespoonfuls of mushroom, onion, or carrot powder when frying the rice in step 5 for a makeshift mirepoix.

Beets

When I was 33, a 20-year-old man approached me at my day job and asked me a question. I answered as best I could and then an awkward silence developed. I then decided to ask an innocent question: "What are you up to this weekend?"

He looked at his desk-mate, and their faces lit up. "Me and him—we're getting together and making some beats!" I was so excited to hear that the next generation was canning! My geeky inner self was pumped! "Pickled or dried?" I asked. The moment between the words leaving my mouth and reaching his ears was one of the longest in my life. I realized too late that my colleagues were talking about music, not canning. I immediately made things worse: "You're spinning records?"

Now they were laughing, but in a kind-hearted manner that let me laugh with them. I shared the story with my team and they called me "DJ Pickled Beets" for several months. I still can't pickle beets without laughing at myself.

PRESERVING NOSE-TO-TAIL

- **ROOTS** Can be dried and added as a garnish for a delicate, earthy crunch.
- **SKIN** If you're pickling a large amount of beets you may find yourself with a LOT of skin on your hands. Use it to ferment a kvass (page 125) or dry it into powder.
- **FLESH** Pickled and powdered.
- **STALK** A great ingredient for a fridge pickle; it's almost a cross between chard and celery.
- **GREENS** Cook and freeze as you would with spinach. Also used in vegetable stock.

TIPS FOR STORING

Beets like dark, humid places, so avoid the crisper unless it has a humidity setting. Line an airtight container with a damp paper towel or cloth, add the beets, top with another layer of towel, and seal. A cold cellar is perfect; if you're adventurous, you'll likely find success with the sandbox technique described on page 57.

Regardless of which technique you choose (cellar or fridge), beets are best stored in layers separated by parchment or newsprint paper (but not newspaper).

FILLING THE PANTRY

CHILLED
Store in the fridge, cold room, or garage.

CANNED
Pickled beets are practically a universal truth!

PRESSURE CANNED
Pressure canned as an ingredient in soup, such as borscht (page 146).

DEHYDRATED
Beet chips and pulverized beet powder (used as a garnish on thick winter soups) are both great.

FERMENTED
Commonly used in kvass (see below).

1 Beet and Ginger Kvass
2 Turnip Beet Pickles
3 Dehydrated Beets and Powder
4 Canned Orange Beets
5 Quick Pickled Beet Stalks and Walnuts
6 Charred Pickled Beets

Batch-It

Canned Orange Beets

PRESSURE CAN

LEVEL: ● ● ○

YIELD: 5–6 QUART JARS

EFFORT: 25 MINUTES

ELAPSED: 1¼ HOURS

EAT: WITHIN 2 YEARS

10 lb small (1½–2½ inches
diameter) orange beets

Salt (optional though
recommended)

Water

Dehydrated Beets and Powder

DEHYDRATE

LEVEL: ● ○ ○

EFFORT: 10 MINUTES

ELAPSED: 8–10 HOURS

YIELD: ¼–½ CUP

EAT: WITHIN 1 YEAR

5 lb beets and/or the skins from
the beets you canned

Beets are messy work, which is why I like to pressure can them. I get all the messy work out of the way in a single day and then I can use beets in my cooking without making a mess. Instead of tossing the skins, we dehydrate them (I add a few whole beets to increase the quantity) and turn them into an intense powder that makes an awesome soup garnish.

CAN THE BEETS:

1 Wash the beets, keeping the roots and stems attached, and simmer in a large pot of water for 20–25 minutes, until you can easily slip the skins off with a gloved hand. Place the skins in a bowl.

2 Prepare the canner and sterilize your jars and lids.

3 Strain the beets, allow them to cool enough to handle, peel, and trim off the stems and roots. Beets larger than 2½ inches in diameter should be chopped smaller to match the others (this will also ensure better texture after preserving).

4 Heat the water for filling the jars to a simmer.

5 Place 1 tsp salt in each jar, add the beets, and then add enough water to cover them. Leave 1 inch of headspace. Gently jostle the jars or use the handle of a spoon to release any air bubbles.

6 Process at 10 lb of pressure for 35 minutes at sea level (if you live higher than 1,000 feet above sea level, refer to the Adjust for Altitude Chart on page 25 for additional processing time).

DEHYDRATE THE SKINS:

7 Weigh the skins. If you have less than 5 lb of skins, chop the missing weight of fresh beets, cleaned and with roots and stem removed, into ½-inch slices. Boil until tender, 1–2 minutes, and add to the skins.

8 Spread the beet slices and skins on a tray and dehydrate at 125°F for 8–10 hours, until brittle.

9 To make powder, pulverize the dehydrated beets and skins using a high-speed blender or spice grinder. Store the skins and powder on a shelf in a clean, dry, airtight jar.

VARIATIONS: Think of this preserve as a ready-to-use ingredient. It's best not to add extra to this one; the more things you add to it, the fewer uses you'll have for it.

CENTER OF THE PLATE: Beet hummus, beet slices, or chopped beet with roasted veg. The brine can be used to darken stocks, soups, pasta sauce, noodles, and rice, or it can be chilled and sipped. You can also use the brine in other ferments (such as the turnip quick preserve below).

TIP: OPENING DIFFICULT SEALS
Sometimes lids seal so tight that they are tough to pry from a jar after you've removed the ring. Open these jars by carefully prying the lid with a beer bottle opener.

Turnip Beet Pickles

If you've ever eaten shawarma, you'll be familiar with the pinkish-purple pickled turnip that comes with it. Traditionally, the color often comes from beets. To make your own version, chop a medium-sized beet into thick strips and place the strips in a 1-quart Mason jar. Cut a medium-sized turnip into thick strips, place on top of the beets, add 2 Tbsp of non-iodized salt, and top with water. Cover loosely with a clean cloth and ferment for two to seven days, skimming any scum that might appear. It is ready when you like the taste—the longer it ferments the sourer and softer it will become. Store it in an airtight container where it will keep for months. It will darken with time.

Charred Pickled Beets

LEVEL: ● ○ ○

YIELD: 8–9 PINT JARS

EFFORT: 45 MINUTES

ELAPSED: 1½ HOURS

EAT: AFTER 6 WEEKS AND
   WITHIN 2 YEARS

10 lb beets

2 cups white vinegar (5% or higher)

1 cup balsamic vinegar (5% acidity
   or greater)

½ cup honey or 1¼ cups white sugar

1 tsp pickling salt

12 sprigs thyme

12 shallots, peeled with ends
   removed but kept whole

6 tsp caraway seeds

YOU WILL NEED

BBQ (optional)

Kitchen gloves (they'll be dyed
   permanently)

Pickled beets were a staple of my childhood, but I've always had a strained relationship with them. I have never really disliked them, I just forget that I enjoy them as much as I do. This recipe makes them memorable; the use of fire deepens their flavors and the heat also enhances the natural sweetness.

1 Preheat the BBQ (or a baking sheet under a broiler) to maximum heat while you clean the beets and remove any greens. Place the beets on the BBQ rack and close the lid. Open the lid every 2–3 minutes to rotate the beets; once the skin is completely charred, after 15–25 minutes, transfer the beets to a large pot and cover with a lid. When the beets are cool enough to handle, pop on your gloves and peel the beets by pushing against the skin.

2 Chop the beets so they are the same size as the shallots.

3 Prepare your canning pot and rack, and sterilize your jars and lids (see page 17).

4 Prepare a brine by placing both vinegars, the honey, and the salt in a medium-sized pot. Mix to combine and bring to a simmer over medium heat.

5 Remove the jars from the canner and turn the heat to high.

6 Divide the thyme, shallots, caraway seeds, and beets between the jars. Cover with brine, leaving ½ inch of headspace. Gently jostle the jars to release any air bubbles.

7 Wipe the rims of the jars, apply the lids, and process for 30 minutes (if you live higher than 1,000 feet above sea level, refer to the Adjust for Altitude chart on page 17 for additional processing time). Remove the jars from the canner and allow them to cool.

VARIATIONS: Replace the balsamic vinegar with sherry vinegar or white wine vinegar, and add 1–2 cloves of garlic or 2 tsp of dill in each jar.

CENTER OF THE PLATE: Try a beet sandwich with pickled beets, goat cheese, pistachios, fresh greens, and a touch of honey. The brine is a fun addition to rice, which will assume its color. This is also great with white fish.

10 Minutes or less

Beet and Ginger Kvass

FERMENT

LEVEL: ● ○ ○

YIELD: 2 QUARTS

EAT: WITHIN 1 MONTH

4–5 small beets, diced

2 Tbsp minced ginger

2 Tbsp whey

2 tsp non-iodized coarse salt

Filtered water

Kvass is a fermented beverage that's common in Russia and Ukraine. If you drink kombucha, think of this as its cousin. Kvass can be an acquired taste, but I've fallen madly in love with it. The flavors are salty and sour, but it can be sweetened according to taste when serving.

Toss the beets with the ginger, whey, and salt. Place in the sterilized jar, cover loosely with a cloth or coffee filter, and leave on the counter overnight. The next day, add filtered water to cover the contents, leaving 1 inch of headspace. Replace the cover and check daily, removing any film that appears. Taste after two or three days; it's ready when you are happy with the taste. It starts off salty and becomes more sour/earthy with time (I have left it for ten or more days). Strain and refrigerate in an airtight jar.

Quick Pickled Beet Stalks and Walnuts

CELLAR

LEVEL: ● ○ ○

YIELD: 1 PINT

EAT: WITHIN 2 MONTHS

BRINE:

½ cup rice wine vinegar

¼ cup freshly squeezed orange juice

2 Tbsp honey

Salt

PICKLE:

1 cup beet stems

1 stalk celery

1 medium carrot

2 green onions

¼ cup walnuts

The stem (or stalk) of a beet is as edible as its root or leaves. It tastes like a combination of chard and celery. Many people toss it out either because they don't know what to do with it or because it takes up so much space in the fridge. If you're going to make this pickle, use fresh stems.

Simmer the brine ingredients in a pot for 3 minutes over medium heat. Place the dry ingredients in a Mason jar. Add the boiling brine, cover with a lid, and shake well. Allow the jar to cool until it can be comfortably handled, then transfer to the fridge. Over the next few days, carefully shake the contents a few times to distribute the brine. It will continue to develop its flavors in the first 24–48 hours.

Beet Hummus

SERVINGS: 2-3

EFFORT: 10 MINUTES

ELAPSED: 30 MINUTES

3 cloves garlic, peeled

¼ cup tahini

2 tsp ground cumin

2 tsp sesame oil (or an additional 1 Tbsp tahini)

2 Tbsp fresh lemon juice (add more if you wish)

1 quart jar of pressure canned beets (page 122)

¼ cup beet stock (the liquid the beets were preserved in)

Olive oil (optional)

We often think of hummus as the exclusive domain of the chickpea. When local farmers' markets started selling this bright purple version, it really made some heads spin. I like the added punch of using some of the preserving liquid to make this the "beet-iest" hummus on the block! This is looser than most hummus; you can cut back on the beet stock (or reduce it by half) to make it thicker. This is great with pita bread or in place of mayo in a sandwich.

1   Place the garlic in a blender, and chop until fine.

2   Add the tahini, cumin, sesame oil, and lemon juice to the blender. Scrape the sides to make sure the garlic is incorporated, and blend for 10 seconds.

3   Add the beets and blend until smooth. Add the beet stock, 1 Tbsp at a time, until the hummus achieves the texture you like (you may not use the whole ¼ cup, or you may have to add more). I prefer to chill the hummus in the freezer for a few minutes before eating, but that's optional. Serve in a bowl and top with a drizzle of olive oil.

PANTRY RAID: Replace the sesame oil with chili oil (page 174), serve under a layer of fermented hot peppers (page 177), or serve with lots of pickles.

Salad with Pickled Beets, Pistachios, and Fried Goat Cheese

SERVINGS: 4 SIDES OR 2 MAINS

EFFORT: 20 MINUTES

ELAPSED: 45 MINUTES

FRIED GOAT CHEESE:

16 oz log of goat cheese

¾ cup all-purpose flour

¼ tsp salt

2 eggs, beaten

1 cup dried bread crumbs or panko

Finely grated zest of 1 lemon

½ tsp dried thyme

2 Tbsp olive oil

SALAD:

2 Tbsp fresh lemon juice
    (about ½ lemon)

2 Tbsp orange juice

2 tsp pickled beet brine

1½ tsp honey

Salt

3 Tbsp peanut or vegetable oil

6 cups arugula

1½–2 cups pickled beets, measured
    then chopped (page 124)

⅓ cup pistachio nuts, measured then
    chopped

Parmesan (or other hard cheese),
    for garnish

YOU WILL NEED

A rasp for the cheese

Beets love oranges and thyme. Because some oranges are sweeter than others, you may find the dressing for this salad too sweet. If that's the case, just add more lemon. The cheese is optional, though I like to add it to make this dish a filling meal. You can top it off with a fried egg if you're really hungry!

PREPARE THE GOAT CHEESE:

1 Slice the cheese into ¾-inch disks. Place them in a single layer on a plate and chill in the freezer for 30 minutes.

2 Arrange three bowls on your working surface: the first should have the flour with the salt, the second should have the eggs, and the third should have the breadcrumbs, lemon zest, and thyme.

ASSEMBLE THE SALAD:

3 Mix the lemon, orange juice, brine, and honey together in a bowl, and season to taste with salt. Whisk in the olive oil.

4 Toss the arugula with the beets, pistachios, and dressing. Allow this to rest for at least 15 minutes while you cook the cheese.

FRY THE CHEESE:

5 Preheat a frying pan over medium-high heat for about 5 minutes.

6 Keeping one hand dry, coat each piece of goat cheese in flour, dip it in egg, and then dip in the bread crumbs. Set each piece on the cold plate until you've dipped all of the cheese.

7 Add the oil to the pan. As it nears the smoking point, which will happen quickly, add the cheese. Cook until golden, 2–3 minutes, flipping once.

8 Plate the salad, add the fried goat cheese, and sprinkle with some Parmesan. Serve immediately.

PANTRY RAID: Add ¼ cup mushroom powder (page 251) to the crust on the cheese, or finely chop the rind of a slice of preserved lemon (page 185) and mix into the flour coating.

the
MOON
STOOD
Still

Blueberries

An airlock is a simple device often used to ferment alcohol. It allows carbon dioxide and air to escape from an active fermentation while preventing oxygen from entering the jar. Gas escapes through a straw-shaped tube that uses water to seal the contents from the outside world. This not only prevents your preserve from turning to vinegar but also prevents the expanding gas from exploding because it can't escape.

In my original recipe for blueberry mead, I added the blueberries during the first (primary) ferment—the most active stage. My first test batch was a little too full and a little too active.

On the second day of fermenting, I found a small bit of blueberry on the table. I found some more in a bowl of apples. And more in the sink. It took 20 minutes before I looked up and saw that there were blueberries actually embedded into our ceiling. The outcome may have been messy, but the airlock had done its job—otherwise it would have been shards of glass, not blueberry, in the apple bowl.

Some investigation revealed that a blueberry had clogged the airlock. Gas couldn't escape and pressure built up until the blueberry (and excess gas) was expunged from the container.

I now recommend adding blueberries to the second stage of fermenting, which is far less volatile and, as a bonus, will produce stronger berry flavor!

PRESERVING NOSE-TO-TAIL

Blueberries are difficult to separate into parts, although you can juice them to remove the pulp. You can (and should) dehydrate the solids that are strained from the blueberry-ginger soda (page 136) and other ferments. Pulse them into a powder and add to granola, yogurt, or baking.

TIPS FOR STORING

If you're going to eat blueberries in one to three days, store them without washing in a vented container. For longer storage, rinse them under cold water and drain them well. Dry them by lightly tossing them in a clean dishcloth. Place a paper towel or dishcloth on the bottom of an airtight container and place the berries on top, leaving ample headspace. Cover and refrigerate for seven to ten days.

FILLING THE PANTRY

CHILLED

Spread across a cookie tray to freeze before transferring to an airtight container.

CANNED

Jam and jelly.

DEHYDRATED

They dry fantastically.

FERMENTED

Blueberry wine and mead.

INFUSED

Infuse well in alcohol or vinegar.

1 Maple Syrup with Dried Blueberries
2 Blueberry-Ginger Mead
3 Blueberry-Ginger Soda
4 Blueberry Gin
5 Blueberry Maple Jam 2.0
6 Dried Berries

Batch-It

Dried Berries

DEHYDRATE

LEVEL: ⬤ ○ ○

YIELD: 2 CUPS DRIED BLUEBERRIES

EFFORT: 30 MINUTES

ELAPSED: 8-10 HOURS

EAT: WITHIN 1 YEAR

8 cups blueberries

YOU WILL NEED

A large needle or old meat
   thermometer small enough to
   pierce the blueberries
Dehydrator

Maple Syrup with Dried Blueberries

INFUSE

LEVEL: ⬤ ○ ○

YIELD: 1½ CUPS

EFFORT: 5 MINUTES

ELAPSED: 10 MINUTES

EAT: WITHIN 10 DAYS

¼ cup dried blueberries
1 cup maple syrup

I like to think of recipes like these recipes as chain reactions. The first recipe becomes a key ingredient in the second. The next time you are about to dry anything, take a few moments to think about what you could also infuse with the dried goods and you'll be creating your own batches easily.

DRY THE BERRIES:

1 Sterilize the pin or meat thermometer by immersing it in boiling water for 2 minutes.
2 Check the berries by piercing them with the needle (see below).
3 Spread the berries on drying racks and dehydrate at 135°F for 6–7 hours. They are done when brittle. Store in a dry jar with a lid out of direct sunlight.

MAKE THE INFUSED MAPLE SYRUP:

4 Place the blueberries in a pot and add the syrup.
5 Cook on medium-high until the mixture begins to boil, stirring to prevent burning. Remove from the heat as soon as the syrup boils.
6 Place in a container, cover loosely, and allow the syrup to cool before securing the lid and transferring to the fridge. The flavor will develop a lot in the first few hours, though the impatient can eat it right away.

TIP: DRYING SMOOTH-SKINNED FRUIT? CHECK IT!
Blueberries, grapes, and cranberries have smooth skin. This protects the fruit and lengthens the dehydrating process by preventing the loss of moisture. In order to dehydrate smooth-skinned fruit, you need to "check" it. You can do this by piercing the fruit with a needle or by plunging it into boiling water for 15–30 seconds and then transferring it to an ice bath.

Blueberry Maple Jam 2.0

WATERBATH

LEVEL: ●●○

YIELD: 4 HALF-PINT JARS

EFFORT: 30 MINUTES

ELAPSED: 1½ HOURS

EAT: WITHIN 2 YEARS

6 cups blueberries

3 cups brown sugar, lightly packed

Peels and cores (seeds included) of
   3 apples

1 cinnamon stick

1 cup maple syrup

⅓ cup bottled lemon juice

1 Tbsp lemon zest, finely grated

YOU WILL NEED

Cheesecloth

Funnel

We've made versions of this recipe for five years, and it is by far the most popular recipe from our blog. Our friend Marisa McClellan, from the blog *Food in Jars*, made her own version of this in her book *Preserving by the Pint*. Since she raised the bar and reinterpreted our original recipe, we thought it would be fun do the same in return with our newest version.

1 Place the berries in a large pot, crush them lightly, and add the sugar. Stir to mix, cover, and rest for 1–4 hours on the counter.

2 Place the apple peels and cores and the cinnamon stick inside the cheesecloth to make a teabag.

3 Place the teabag in a large pot with the blueberries, maple syrup, lemon juice, and lemon zest.

4 Prepare your canning pot and rack, and sterilize your jars and lids (see page 17).

5 Bring the fruit to a simmer over medium heat, skimming off any foam that appears. Cook until set, at least 20 minutes, then make sure the jam passes the freezer test (see page 13). Remove the teabag from the jam.

6 Remove the jars from the canner and turn the heat to high. Using a funnel, pour the jam into the jars. Wipe the rims of the jars, apply the lids, and process for 10 minutes (if you live higher than 1,000 feet above sea level, refer to the Adjust for Altitude chart on page 17 for additional processing time). Remove the jars and allow them to cool.

VARIATIONS: Omit the cinnamon and add 20 peppercorns or a few dried chilies (page 174) to the teabag.

CENTER OF THE PLATE: This is awesome as part of a cheese tray or diluted into warmed maple syrup for an amazing pancake topping. You can also mix 1 part of this jam with 2 parts goat cheese to stuff French toast.

Blueberry-Ginger Mead

FERMENT

LEVEL: ● ● ○

YIELD: 1 GALLON/5 26 OZ (750 ML)
    BOTTLES

EFFORT: 2 HOURS

ELAPSED: 5 MONTHS

DRINK: YOU CAN DRINK RIGHT AWAY BUT
    BEST AFTER 1-2 YEARS OF AGING

3 quarts filtered water

3 cups good-quality honey

4–6 inches ginger, cubed

1 cinnamon stick

1 lemon (juice and zest)

1 lime (juice and zest)

2 tsp pure vanilla extract

1 tsp yeast nutrient

1 packet (5 g) ale or champagne
    yeast

AFTER 2 WEEKS:

2 cups blueberries

½ cup granulated sugar

YOU WILL NEED

Two 1-gallon fermenting vessels
    (jugs, available at home-brew
    stores, are most common)

Funnel that fits the jug

Sanitizer

Airlock

Syphoning hose

5 26 oz (750 mL) wine bottles

Corks and corker

If you haven't bottled before, I
recommend a visit to your local
wine-brewing store which will help
you source what you need and
learn how to use it (see page 48 for
more details).

Many people compare the flavors of blueberry mead to red wine. Blueberry mead also tastes better if you let it age, though you can drink it after bottling, especially if you decant it for a bit. If you're ready to commit to making mead, make a double batch for two years' supply and only drink half of it fresh. Do the same thing in year two. By year three you can make a single batch; as long as you continue making mead, you can drink the oldest stuff first and let the new stuff age.

STEP 1 (DAY 1): START THE FERMENT

1   Combine 4 cups of the water with the honey in a pot and bring to a simmer over medium heat. Stir to dissolve the honey.

2   Add the ginger, cinnamon stick, lemon zest, and lime zest to the pot. Mix to combine. Simmer over medium heat for 10 minutes. Skim off any foam that appears on the surface.

3   Remove the pot from the heat and add the remaining water, lemon juice, lime juice, and vanilla. Stir to combine.

4   When the liquid is cool enough to touch, add the yeast nutrient, stir, and wait for 15 minutes (it will form a froth on the surface).

5   Strain out the solids and discard them, add the yeast to the liquid, and stir until it dissolves.

6   Sanitize one of the 1-gallon jugs.

7   Add honey-yeast water in one of the 1-gallon jugs and top with filtered water if needed to where the neck of the jug begins. Secure with an airlock and place on a plate in case of overflow. Allow the mixture to ferment—it should visibly foam.

STAGE 2 (ABOUT 2 WEEKS LATER): RACK, FLAVOR, AND START THE SECONDARY FERMENTATION

8   Once the fermenting slows (after approximately two weeks), lightly crush the berries in a non-reactive bowl and mix with the ½ cup sugar. Loosely cover with a clean cloth and leave on the counter for at least 1 hour, to a maximum of 24 hours before continuing to the next step.

9 Sanitize the second jug and place the berries and any liquid they've released inside it.

10 Rack the mead from the first jug into the second jug. You do this by syphoning the first jar into the second, leaving as much sediment behind as possible. This will result in a clearer mead.

11 The level of the mead should come to where the neck narrows. If you have extra mead, age it in the fridge. If you don't have enough, add filtered water until you get the right level.

STAGE 3 (ABOUT 3 WEEKS AFTER STAGE 2): RACK AND AGE

12 After three weeks, sanitize the original jug. Rack the mead back into it, removing any solids and sediment. Top with filtered water, secure with an airlock, and age for three months.

13 Check the airlock from time to time and ensure the water is at the fill line. If it evaporates, air will enter the bottle and oxidize your wine, spoiling it or turning it to vinegar.

STAGE 4 (ABOUT 3 MONTHS AFTER STAGE 3): BOTTLE AND AGE FURTHER

14 Make sure the ferment has stopped completely—there should have been no visible signs of bubbles for weeks. Rack, bottle, and age; you can drink immediately, but it will be better after one or two years. See the bottling overview on page 48 for more details.

VARIATIONS: Add 1 oz of hops in step 7, skip the cinnamon, or use maple sugar instead of granulated sugar.

CENTER OF THE PLATE: Serve as is or add to a gin and tonic for something out of this world.

NOTE: Mead (and all fermented alcohol) has some unique language and equipment. Review the Fermenting chapter (pages 39–49) for a quick primer.

Blueberry Gin

When I spoke at TEDxToronto, I planned to finish my speech with a mini preserving course by pouring gin over berries on stage, but the theater wouldn't let me bring glass or booze on stage. I preserved them at home instead and am still enjoying them two years later. To preserve berries in gin, partially drink a bottle of gin, and then add berries to it. Any amount of berries will do, but I like to add at least 15%–20% berries (by volume) to the bottle.

Blueberry-Ginger Soda

FERMENT

LEVEL: ● ● ○

YIELD: 4 QUART JARS

EFFORT: 45 MINUTES

ELAPSED: 1–2 DAYS

DRINK: WITHIN 1 MONTH

2 pints (4 cups) blueberries

¾ cup maple syrup (or 1½ cups of brown sugar, lightly packed)

8-inch piece of unpeeled ginger, or more to taste, chopped into small pieces

Purified filtered water

4–6 Tbsp fresh lemon juice, about 2 lemons

2 Tbsp port

⅛ tsp champagne yeast

Salt

YOU WILL NEED

Cheesecloth

Bottle Sanitizer

4 26 oz (750 mL) plastic bottles, caps and bottling equipment

This combines the concepts behind our blueberry maple jam (page 133) with the infused flavors of cherry ginger beer (page 166) and the technique of our rhubarb soda (page 314). It's a delicious kind of Franken-recipe.

1   Wash the blueberries and lightly crush them.

2   Place the berries, maple syrup, ginger, and 3 cups of the water in a pot. Turn the heat to high and simmer, uncovered, for 20 minutes, mashing the berries as the liquid reduces. Add more water if the mixture thickens.

3   Let the mixture cool, then puree it in a blender or food processor until smooth.

4   Strain the liquid through a fine sieve. (Squeezing it will add flavor but will result in a cloudier product.) When the mixture has cooled to room temperature, add the lemon juice, port, champagne yeast, and a pinch of salt.

5   Divide this blueberry concentrate between the bottles. Add filtered water to each until they are ¾ full. Place the lid on top, and shake the contents to mix. Taste, and add additional maple syrup if desired. Add additional filtered water until 1 inch of headspace remains in each bottle.

6   Place the caps on the bottles and leave in a warm, dark place in your kitchen. Squeeze daily to test for carbonation. When the bottle is difficult to squeeze (12–48 hours), it's done. Store this in the fridge (this will prevent explosions by slowing fermentation). Open the bottles slowly over a bowl as this soda can be a little volatile!

BBQ Salmon with Blueberry-Ginger Sauce

SERVINGS: 4

EFFORT: 25 MINUTES

ELAPSED: 45 MINUTES

SAUCE:

1½ Tbsp unsalted butter, chilled

¾ cup green onions (greens and
   whites), chopped into small rings
   (reserve 1–2 Tbsp for garnish)

1 garlic clove

½-inch piece ginger, finely chopped

¼ tsp coarse salt

Pinch dried thyme, finely chopped

¼ tsp cinnamon

¾ cup blueberry maple jam 2.0
   (page 133)

2 Tbsp water

2 tsp balsamic vinegar

Black pepper

SALMON:

Four 6-oz salmon fillets,
   about 1 inch thick

Vegetable oil

Salt

Black pepper

Cayenne or chili powder (optional)

Lemon slices with seeds removed

Although this recipe can be made in an oven, I consider the BBQ to be a key component of the recipe (especially if you use charcoal). The smoky flavor creates a contrast to the sauce, which might overpower the salmon if cooked in the oven alone.

Remove the salmon from the fridge 30 minutes before cooking.

PREPARE THE SAUCE (YOU CAN DO THIS IN ADVANCE):

1 Heat the butter over medium heat and add the green onions, garlic, ginger, salt, a pinch of thyme, and cinnamon. Sauté until the garlic is soft and sweet, about 4 minutes.

2 Add the blueberry jam, water, and balsamic, stirring until incorporated. If the sauce is too thick, add small amounts of water until it is the consistency of a thin gravy. If it's too sweet, you may wish to add additional balsamic.

3 Season liberally with black pepper and remove from the heat.

GRILL THE SALMON:

4 Preheat the BBQ to medium-high, or if using the oven, preheat it to 425°F.

5 Dry the salmon with a towel, rub all sides with a light coating of oil, and season liberally with salt, pepper, and cayenne.

6 Once hot, wipe the BBQ grill with oil and immediately place the salmon skin side down. If your BBQ has hot spots, place the thin parts of the salmon farthest from them. Resist the temptation to poke, move, or flip the salmon. The fish is cooked when you see fat starting to release on the surface of the flesh (the white bits that appear when it cooks). If you're using the oven, this should take 8–12 minutes.

7 Serve with warm sauce and garnish with the reserved green onion.

PANTRY RAID: Use peach-bourbon BBQ Sauce (page 262), add 1–2 Tbsp smoked peach powder (page 260) to the rub, or replace your usual amount of salt with the same amount of herbes salées (page 229).

Fermented Pancakes with Maple Syrup with Dried Blueberries

SERVINGS: 4

EFFORT: 30 MINUTES

ELAPSED: 1–2 DAYS

2 cups whole grain flour (gluten-free is fine)

2 cups buttermilk

4 egg whites

2 egg yolks

2 Tbsp melted butter

½ tsp baking soda

½ tsp baking powder

¼ tsp orange bitters or pure vanilla extract (optional)

¼ tsp salt

Cooking oil (coconut oil is good)

2 cups maple syrup with dried blueberries (page 132)

These pancakes are fermented—they emulate the process used to make sourdough. If you eat a lot of pancakes, you can start with 3 cups of flour and buttermilk and reserve one-third of the mixture as a starter for future batches (it will store for several weeks in your fridge).

DAY 1:

1 Mix the flour and buttermilk in a jar, loosely cover with a clean cloth and leave in a warm place for 24–36 hours, shaking carefully from time to time. The longer you leave it, the more sour and savory the pancakes will taste. The mixture sometimes separates slightly; don't be turned off if you find a dark, watery layer before mixing again. This will keep in the fridge for a week or more.

DAY 2:

2 Preheat the oven to 225°F.

3 Beat the egg whites until frothy and lightly set, which will help keep the pancakes airy.

4 In a separate bowl, mix the egg yolks and melted butter with the baking soda, baking powder, bitters, and salt. Stir until combined.

5 Fold the egg whites into the batter, stirring as little as possible to create a uniform mixture.

6 Warm a frying pan over medium-high heat.

7 Pour ¼ inch of oil into the frying pan and let it heat. You can test it by adding a drop of water—it should instantly sizzle and dance across the surface.

8 Add ¼ cup batter per pancake to the frying pan (you'll need to do this in batches). Do not flip until the outsides look dry and new bubbles mark the surface.

9 Flip the pancakes once, cook for a few minutes (test by cutting a pancake), and keep warm in the oven. Add more oil to the pan if needed and continue until the batter has all been used.

10 Serve with warmed maple syrup with dried blueberries.

PANTRY RAID: Replace the maple syrup with a mixture of ¼ cup blueberry-maple jam and ¾ cup maple syrup, or add dried berries to the batter just before cooking.

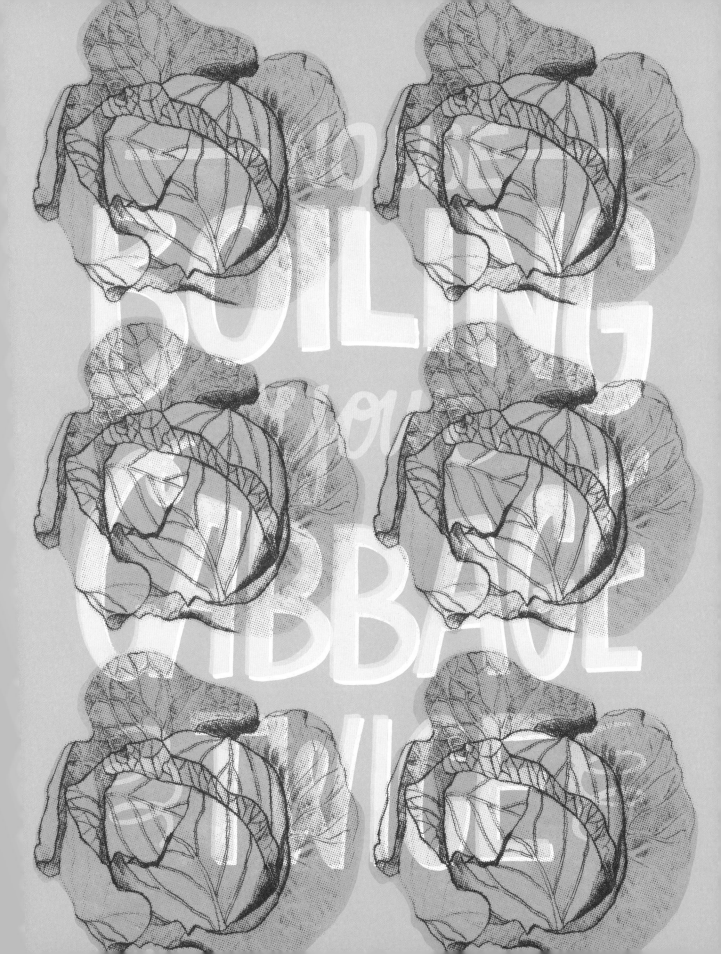

Cabbage

Cabbage is often overlooked by people. I think it is one of those ingredients that really come into their own through preserving. You'll find it my kitchen all through the winter and early spring.

I will always remember the day, almost twenty years ago, when my Uncle John and Aunt Sandra gave us a few packages of home-made perogies that they'd bought at a Ukrainian flea market. Though I was slightly turned off by the description of fermented sauerkraut, I boiled the frozen pucks until they softened and then pan-fried them crisp. I finished them off with sour cream, salt, and too much pepper. The crunch of the fried exterior gave way to the soft dough and then the sour tang of the kraut. The filling was unlike anything I had ever eaten before, and the entire experience was way beyond my expectations.

PRESERVING NOSE-TO-TAIL

Cabbages come in many different forms but have two shared components: leaves and ribs (the thick stem that divides the center of the leaves). Most commonly fermented, they also freeze well. They can be preserved together, but the thickest part of the ribs is often removed from the leaf as it takes longer to ferment, dry, or cook than the thinner bits.

The ribs can be fermented on their own, pickled, added to stock, or dried and powdered for rubs, soup garnishes, or gravy. The leaves can be fermented whole (often done for cabbage rolls) or made into endless varieties of krauts, kimchis, and fermented slaws.

TIPS FOR STORING

Store cabbage whole for as long as possible. If you use only part of a cabbage, wrap the rest tightly in plastic wrap, and ferment or freeze it as soon as possible.

Cabbage stores best in a cold room or fridge but will also last for weeks on a shelf, though some nutrients will likely be lost. When storing cabbage, it's important to check on it every few days and to peel any dry or browned leaves away from the exterior.

If cabbage is going soft, preserve it or shred it, and braise it in tomato sauce or stock—it will last for five to seven more days in the fridge or freezer.

FILLING THE PANTRY

CHILLED

Cabbages keep well in a garage or cold room. Most types freeze very well after blanching, or in recipes such as cabbage rolls.

PRESSURE CANNED

Often pressure canned as part of soup.

FERMENTED

Kraut, kimchi, and whole heads of cabbage can be fermented.

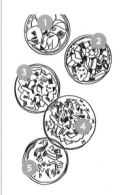

1 Fermented Brussels
  Sprouts
2 Borscht
3 Weinkraut
4 Carrot Sauerkraut with
  Red Cabbage
5 Kimchi

Batch-It

Carrot Sauerkraut with Red Cabbage

FERMENT

LEVEL: ◉ ◉ ○

YIELD: 2 QUART JARS

EFFORT: 15 MINUTES

ELAPSED: 5–30 DAYS

EAT: WITHIN 6 MONTHS

2–2½ lb cabbage, shredded

4–5 medium carrots, shredded

3 cloves garlic, finely chopped

2 Tbsp salt

Filtered water

YOU WILL NEED

1 wide-mouth Mason jar

1½-cup Mason jar to use as a
    fermenting weight

Weinkraut

FERMENT

LEVEL: ◉ ◉ ○

YIELD: 2 QUART JARS

EFFORT: 15 MINUTES

ELAPSED: 5–30 DAYS

EAT: WITHIN 6 MONTHS

2–2½ lb cabbage, shredded

2 tart apples, peeled and julienned

1 Tbsp salt

2 tsp caraway seeds

½–1 cup white wine

YOU WILL NEED

1 wide-mouth Mason jar

1½-cup Mason jar to use as a
    fermenting weight

Why make one kraut when you can make two? Kraut comes in many forms. Sauerkraut is the most common in North America but other varieties include weinkraut (made with white wine), blaukraut, and rotkraut (also known as rotsauerkraut), which are both made with red cabbage and sometimes are cooked instead of fermented. Most large cabbages weigh about 5 lb, so I either halve a cabbage for two different recipes or make one of the sauerkrauts with any uncooked cabbage I have on hand (such as the leftovers from the quick slaw and fish tacos on page 160).

DAY 1: PREP AND INITIAL SALTING

Start by shredding the cabbage for each recipe. I use two large non-reactive bowls to keep the recipes separated.

MAKE THE CARROT SAUERKRAUT:

1 Add the carrots, garlic, and salt to one bowl of cabbage.
2 Squeeze the vegetables in your hands for a few minutes. This will help break down the cell structure, releasing the water more easily.
3 Cover the bowl loosely with a cloth and leave on the counter overnight.

MAKE THE WEINKRAUT:

4 Add the apples, salt, and caraway seeds to the second bowl of cabbage. Squeeze the vegetables in your hands for a few minutes.
5 Cover the bowl loosely with a cloth and leave on the counter overnight.

DAY 2: FILL THE JARS AND START THE FERMENT

6 Clean the jars.
7 Fill one jar with the ingredients from the carrot kraut. Pack the jar tightly by pushing down on the small jar to be used as a weight on top. Add any liquid from the bowl. If the ingredients are not completely submerged, add filtered water to submerge them. Using the small jar as a weight, push down to keep all ingredients under the surface of the brine.

8 Change your focus to the weinkraut. Drain and discard any liquid from the bowl. Fill the empty jar with the ingredients from the weinkraut. Pack the jar tightly by pushing down on the small jars to be used as a weight on top. Add wine to ensure there is enough liquid to completely submerge the vegetables. Place the small jar on top and push down to keep all ingredients under the surface of the brine.

9 Cover both jars loosely with a towel. Place each on a plate and leave in a warm spot in your kitchen. Check daily and skim off any bubbles or light mold from the surface.

DAYS 3–30: TASTING

10 Taste after three or four days. It will be too salty at first but will become more sour with time. It should take five to thirty days (it will take less time in the summer than in the fall or winter) to become suitably sour.

11 Store in the fridge to slow fermenting and eat with everything!

Fermented Brussels Sprouts

I know that Brussels sprouts aren't cabbage but both are part of the brassicaceae/cabbage family. Trim the bottom off each sprout and cut enough sprouts to pack tightly in a 1-quart Mason jar. Add 1½ tsp coarse salt and 1½ Tbsp caraway seeds. Toss well. Submerge with filtered water, then cover loosely with a dishcloth. Place on a plate (in case of any overflow) and store out of direct sunlight in a moderately cool space in your kitchen. Check daily and taste after four days. Continue to taste every few days; they are ready when you like how sour they are, anywhere between five and fifteen days. Cover with a lid and store in fridge for months.

Frozen Cabbage

CELLAR

LEVEL: ● ○ ○

YIELD: 2½ LB

EAT: WITHIN 3–6 MONTHS

½ cabbage

Many cabbages weigh 5 lb or more. Learning to freeze cabbage can make it much more manageable!

Bring a large pot with lots of water to a hard boil. Chop the cabbage into strips or shred it, then blanch it for 90 seconds. Transfer the cabbage to an ice bath (or sink filled with cold water). Drain the cabbage, dry, and place it in an airtight container or freezer bag to freeze. Freezing will soften it, and it is best used for cooking. It is particularly good to add to soup.

Borscht

PRESSURE CAN

9 medium beets, peeled and cut into quarters

6 medium carrots, peeled and cut into thick chunks

9 medium red potatoes, peeled and cut into thick chunks

3 medium onions

3 cloves garlic

1½ Tbsp honey

1 large head cabbage

1 pint canned tomatoes (including liquid) or 1 16 oz can of store-bought tomatoes. Dice either one.

6 quarts (24 cups) water. Use a Mason jar to measure 1 quart at a time.

1 Tbsp white wine vinegar

½-1 Tbsp dill weed

Salt

Black pepper

Granulated sugar (optional)

Borscht warms the house and fills it with comforting smells as it cooks. Once processed, this soup can sit on the shelf and be quickly warmed or even chilled for a complete meal.

1 Preheat the oven to 425°F.

2 Toss the beets, carrots, potatoes, onions, and garlic with the honey and scatter them over a rimmed baking tray. Roast for 40 minutes, flipping a few times to prevent burning.

3 Shred the cabbage with a knife.

4 Drain the tomato liquid into a large stock pot, squeezing the tomatoes to remove as much of their natural juices as possible. Bring the liquid to a boil over high heat and lower to a moderate simmer over medium heat. Reduce it by 75%, about 5–10 minutes.

5 Prepare the pressure canner and rack, and sterilize your jars and lids. (See pages 21–23.)

6 Combine the roasted veggies, water, vinegar, dill, salt, and pepper to the tomato liquid and lightly simmer, uncovered, for 30 minutes.

7 Taste the soup; add more salt and pepper and up to 2 tsp of sugar to taste.

8 Process in the canner at less than 10 lb of pressure for 50 minutes at sea level (if you live higher than 1,000 feet above sea level, refer to the Adjust for Altitude chart on page 25 for additional processing time).

VARIATIONS: Replace the water with stock.

CENTER OF THE PLATE: Serve hot or cold. Top with sour cream or strained yogurt or add additional stock to stretch the recipe.

Kimchi

FERMENT

LEVEL: ◉ ◉ ○

YIELD: ½-GALLON JAR

EFFORT: 20 MINUTES

ELAPSED: 24 HOURS PLUS 5–30 DAYS

EAT: WITHIN 3 MONTHS

1 large Napa cabbage (about 5 lb)

2–3 medium kohlrabi, shredded

1 bunch green onions, sliced lengthwise then chopped into 1-inch pieces

6 Tbsp coarse salt

12 cloves garlic, minced

4 inches ginger, peeled and minced

¼ cup honey

¼ cup cayenne pepper

1½ Tbsp smoked paprika

up to 4 cups filtered water (though none may be required depending on the freshness of your cabbage and how much water it releases)

YOU WILL NEED

½-gallon Mason jar (you can use multiple Mason jars if needed)

Fermenting weights or small jars to ensure the cabbage stays submerged

Kimchi is a seasonal and regional Korean ferment that changes drastically according to who is making it. Some insist that fish sauce is essential, some use fruit rather than vegetables, and some use cucumbers, green onions, or radish instead of cabbage. My recipe is inspired by readily available ingredients.

DAY 1: INITIAL SALTING

1 Remove the thick ribs from the cabbage and chop them into ½-inch squares. Cut the leaves into 1-inch squares.

2 Toss the cabbage, kohlrabi, and green onions with the 6 Tbsp salt, squeezing the cabbage in your hands as you go. Spend a few minutes crunching it up. Be aggressive; crushing the cabbage like this will make it easier for the fermenting to occur and helps release the water trapped in the plant.

3 Place the cabbage in the Mason jar and leave on the counter. Cover loosely with a towel and leave overnight. By morning you'll see the cabbage will have released a lot of its water.

DAY 2: RINSE AND MIX

4 Drain the cabbage, reserving the liquid.

5 Using a large bowl, mix the cabbage with the garlic, ginger, honey, cayenne, and paprika.

6 Pack the vegetables into the Mason jar. Cover with brine (you can discard any extra or add filtered water to ensure cabbage remains under surface of the brine). Place the small jar on top as a weight to hold it under.

DAYS 3–30: FERMENTING

7 Check the ferment every day, removing any foam or mold that appears. Begin tasting after three or four days. Place in fridge when you like the taste, generally after five to thirty days.

VARIATIONS: You can dehydrate kimchi to make an amazing powder. You can also add 2 Tbsp of fish sauce on the second day.

CENTER OF THE PLATE: Add it to pizza, tacos, rice, hot dogs, or jjigae (kimchi soup).

Sauerkraut Perogies

SERVINGS: 30–36 PEROGIES,
ABOUT 6 SERVINGS
EFFORT: 1½ HOURS
ELAPSED: 2 HOURS

DOUGH:

3 cups all-purpose flour

1 tsp salt

1 egg, lightly beaten

2 Tbsp unsalted butter, melted

2 Tbsp vegetable oil

FILLING:

4–6 pieces of smoked bacon
(page 238) or store-bought

1 large shallot, finely chopped

2 cloves garlic, finely chopped

3 cups sauerkraut, drained and
squeezed dry (either recipe on
page 144)

TO SERVE:

Sour cream

Chives

YOU WILL NEED

3- or 3½-inch circular cookie
cutter or sturdy glass with
same diameter

Many people prefer perogies served directly from a boiling pot of water. I'm a sucker for crispy things, though, and so I generally finish these in a frying pan. You will find that larger batches take incrementally less time.

MAKE THE DOUGH:

1 Whisk together the flour and salt. Add ¾ cup water, egg, butter, and oil to make a soft dough. If it is too dry, add more water 1 Tbsp at a time.

2 Scatter flour on a cutting board and knead the dough for 3 minutes. Cover with a damp towel and rest for 30 minutes.

MAKE THE FILLING:

3 Fry the bacon in a frying pan over medium-high heat. When it's crispy, remove from the pan and add the shallot. Cook for 3 minutes and then add the garlic. Cook for an additional 2 minutes, remove from the heat, and strain off the fat.

4 Chop the bacon and sauerkraut into ¼-inch pieces, and mix with the shallots and garlic.

MAKE AND FREEZE THE PEROGIES:

5 Cut the dough into three pieces. Roll each piece into ⅛-inch-thick sheets on a lightly floured surface and cut out 3-inch circles. Place 1½–2 Tbsp of filling onto one half of each circle. Fold over into half-moons and seal by wetting the edges of the dough and pressing down.

6 To freeze, place the perogies in a single layer on a rimmed baking tray. Once frozen, transfer them to an airtight container. You can also cook them from fresh.

TO COOK:

7 Bring a large pot of salted water to a boil over high heat.

8 Place the perogies in the water, stirring gently to prevent them from sticking to the bottom or each other. They will cook in 3–10 minutes depending on their size and if they were frozen or fresh. They are usually done when they float.

9 You can eat them now, or fry them in bacon fat, butter, and olive oil. Serve with sour cream and chives.

PANTRY RAID: Substitute 1 cup of the sauerkraut for 1 cup of kimchi, or try serving with Greek yogurt.

Slow-Cooker Kimchi Pulled Pork

SERVINGS: 6 LARGE SERVINGS

EFFORT: 30 MINUTES

ELAPSED: 1–3 DAYS

3 cups kimchi, tightly packed (page 147)

4 lb pork shoulder roast

Salt

Black pepper

¼ cup lard or cooking oil

1 pint (or an 8 oz can) canned tomatoes (page 333), roughly chopped, including liquid

½ cup chicken broth

¼ cup tomato paste

2 Tbsp apple cider vinegar, homemade (page 82) or store-bought

2 Tbsp brown sugar, lightly packed

2 bay leaves

YOU WILL NEED

Blender

Slow cooker

The classic way to eat pulled pork is as a sandwich, but don't let yourself be trapped by tradition—after all, kimchi isn't a classic ingredient in pulled pork either. It's a great ingredient to top pizza and pretty awesome when served with noodles. If you are a freak (like me) and happen to have dehydrated kimchi powder on hand, use it for a killer topping!

1   Using a food processor or blender, puree the kimchi.

2   Season the pork liberally with salt and pepper and rub with half of the kimchi. Place in an airtight container and marinate overnight, or for up to two days.

3   Heat the lard in a large frying pan over high heat until it just starts to smoke. Sear the pork on all sides.

4   Place the remaining kimchi puree and the tomatoes, broth, tomato paste, vinegar, sugar, and bay leaves in a slow cooker.

5   Cook on low for 8–10 hours, until you can shred the pork easily with a fork. Remove the pork and tent it loosely with aluminum foil.

6   Remove the bay leaves from the liquid, then transfer the liquid to a blender or food processor and puree it into a sauce.

7   Place the puree in a large pot over high heat, and reduce to half its original volume, about 12 minutes.

8   Shred the pork with two forks in a large serving bowl. Season with salt and pepper and add the sauce, ½ cup at a time, until you're happy with the taste.

PANTRY RAID: A few Tbsp of BBQ sauce (page 262), onion powder, or mushroom powder (page 251) can all impart additional flavor when added to the braising liquid in step 4. Serve with pickles, ferments, or quick pickles.

TIP: FINE POWDERS

Any dehydrated food can be changed into a powder by using a blender. For the finest powders, freeze the dried goods for 10 minutes before pulverizing; they will be more brittle and blend more smoothly.

Carrots

Four teaspoons of chili flakes per pint jar seemed like a lot to me but I was sure that's what I read, so I proceeded with full confidence. It was my first batch of pickled carrots and who was I to challenge a recipe I had never made?

A few months later we opened our first jar with friends. By then I had realized that the instructions actually called for 4 teaspoons of chili flakes for the entire eight-jar batch. My first bite was a cautious one. The texture was great and there was a pleasant sweet-and-sour taste as the flavors of the carrots intersected with the heat of the peppers. Our friends dove into the jar and the pickle was gone in minutes. The extra kick was what they liked best.

If you've never tasted pickled carrots, you must give them a try. They are the most underrated pickle that I know of—though you might find that fewer hot peppers makes for a more comfortable experience!

PRESERVING NOSE-TO-TAIL

- **TOPS** The Internet is rife with claims of people experiencing anaphylactic reactions to eating carrot tops. Yet scientists insist that they are safe to eat. I've used organic greens in curing gravlax, but do some research before using them so that you're both informed and comfortable.
- **PEELS** can be fermented or dried and turned into soup.
- **FLESH** Can be preserved in endless ways; peeling carrots allows for faster fermentation and absorption of flavors.

TIPS FOR STORING

If you grow your own carrots you know that the best place to store them is your garden! Cover them with a large pile of straw or mulched leaves and harvest as needed before the ground freezes.

If storing in the fridge, remove the tops by snapping (not cutting) them off. Store the tops as you would herbs—in a container or wrapped in a slightly damp paper towel. You may find that letting carrots air-dry for a few hours will toughen their exterior and extend their fridge life.

Carrots also store well in cold rooms or garages in mesh bags, and keep well using the sandbox technique described on page 57.

FILLING THE PANTRY

CHILLED

Carrot soup or puree can be frozen.

CANNED

Pickled carrots are crunchy, acidic, and sweet.

DEHYDRATED

Carrots dry easily (peel, chop, and blanch them first) and can be tossed into soup, stew, or sauces. They can also be turned into powder.

FERMENTED

Our fridge has a near-constant supply of fermented carrots. They can be eaten out of the jar, served as a side, added to salads or stir-fries, or used as sandwich toppings.

1 Pickled Dilly Carrots
2 Fridge Pickles with Mirin
3 Pickled Carrots with Horseradish
4 Whey-Fermented Carrot Juice
5 Carrot Lime Pickle
6 Air-Dried Carrots

Batch-It

Whey-Fermented Carrot Juice

FERMENT

LEVEL: ● ○ ○

YIELD: 2 QUARTS

EFFORT: 15 MINUTES

ELAPSED: 2-10 DAYS

EAT: WITHIN 1 MONTH

1½ lb carrots, grated

3 inches ginger, minced

1 Tbsp non-iodized salt

¼ cup whey or brine from
fermented carrot sauerkraut
(page 144)

Filtered water

YOU WILL NEED

1½-gallon Mason jar

Air-Dried Carrots

DEHYDRATE

LEVEL: ● ○ ○

YIELD: 3-4 CUPS DRIED CARROTS

EFFORT: 15 MINUTES

ELAPSED: 8-12 HOURS

EAT: WITHIN 1 YEAR

2½ lb large carrots, grated

Both of these recipes begin with grated carrots, so it makes sense to grate once, preserve twice!

We first made fermented carrot juice for a class we were running for Alison Fryer at the now defunct Cookbook Store in Toronto. This book would not have existed in its current form without her, so it felt natural to include this recipe. More than 30 people attended the event and, to my surprise, almost all raved about the drink. It's salty, sour, and earthy all at the same time.

The dehydrated carrots are more technique than recipe and are great to have on hand for cooking and thickening liquids.

PREP THE CARROTS FOR FERMENTING:

1   Mix the carrots with the ginger and salt in a large non-reactive bowl. Squeeze the carrots in your fists for a few minutes. Transfer the carrots and any liquids into a clean half-gallon jar. Cover loosely with a clean towel and leave overnight. If you are in a rush, though, you can move to step 2, though I think that leaving them overnight allows for stronger flavor development.

2   Add the whey and top with filtered water. Cover loosely with a towel or coffee filter and place in a warm spot in your kitchen, out of direct sunlight.

DRY THE CARROTS:

3   Place a cooling rack inside a large, rimmed baking tray. Spread the grated carrots on top. Some will fall through, others will rest vertically against the rack and many will sit on top—the idea here is to create air circulation between pieces where possible. Using large carrots will help prevent them from sliding through the holes of the rack. Any escapees will be caught by the baking tray. Store on the counter or, for faster results, in an unheated oven with the oven light turned on—this little bit of heat will dry the carrots out faster than the air-drying method.

4   Run your fingers through the carrots after 2 hours to help prevent them sticking to each other and to increase air

circulation. Repeat this a few random times during the drying process. You may also lift the rack on one side to collect any pieces that fell through and scatter them back on top.

5   Drying is complete when carrots are brittle, after 12–36 hours, depending on the humidity and temperature of your kitchen.

6   Place in clean, dry, airtight jars in a dry, dark spot.

MONITOR THE FERMENTING CARROT JUICE:

7   Check the ferment daily and skim off any scum, mold, or foam that appears. Taste after two to three days; it will be bittersweet. The longer it ferments the less salty and more bitter it will become. The taste will be less intense when chilled. Once you are happy with the taste, cover tightly and transfer the juice to the fridge. To serve, you can strain or puree the solids into the juice with a high-speed blender.

10 Minutes or less

Pickled Dilly Carrots

FERMENT

LEVEL: ● ○ ○

YIELD: 1 QUART

EAT: AFTER 1 MONTH AND WITHIN 1 YEAR

6–8 medium carrots,
   peeled and cut into disks

¼ cup dill weed or
   1 Tbsp dried dill seed

3 cloves garlic, peeled

2 Tbsp coarse salt

Filtered water

YOU WILL NEED

1 quart standard Mason jar

Airlock (not required but will
   yield best results)

Peel the carrots and chop them into ½-inch chunks. Add the dill and garlic to the jar and top with carrots (they won't float so don't be worried about packing them in). Add the salt, cover tightly with a lid, and shake to distribute. Top with enough water to make sure everything is submerged. Cover loosely with a clean towel or coffee filter and let sit on your counter overnight. Taste on day three (and every one or two days after). As with any ferment, check daily and remove any sign of foam or mold. This generally takes five to ten days depending on your taste preference. Keep in mind that this will take less time in a warm room.

10 Minutes or less

Carrot Lime Pickle

FERMENT

LEVEL: ◉ ◉ ○

YIELD: 1–1½ PINTS

EAT: AFTER 2 MONTHS AND
    WITHIN 1 YEAR

STAGE 1 (THE FIRST 4–5 WEEKS):

2 Tbsp chili flakes

1 Tbsp garam masala

2 tsp ground turmeric

9 organic limes, cut in 12 pieces
    each with any visible seeds
    removed

6 Tbsp organic lime juice, about 3
    limes

3 Tbsp honey

2 Tbsp coarse salt

1 Tbsp minced ginger

1 Tbsp minced garlic

STAGE 2 (THE NEXT 5–30 DAYS):

8–10 medium carrots, shredded
    (about 1½–2 cups after shredding)

1 Tbsp coarse salt

YOU WILL NEED

1-quart Mason jar

This is a hybrid pickle. It's almost a pickle-in-a-pickle. We start by making a fairly typical Indian lime pickle and, after a few weeks, add carrot to finish the ferment. Some people like to use large pieces of carrot and lime for this, but I chop them small and use them in place of a chutney or hot sauce.

For stage 1, toast the chili flakes, garam masala, and turmeric for a few minutes in a frying pan over medium-high heat, stirring constantly. Place the toasted spices in the 1-quart Mason jar with the limes, lime juice, honey, salt, ginger, and garlic. Secure the jar with the lid and place it in a warm location in your house; I use a sunny spot in my living room. Shake or flip the jar every day before opening and closing the container to release any pressure that has built up. The goal is to ferment the limes without them becoming mushy, which generally takes four to five weeks. Taste periodically to see how the flavors are changing.

For stage 2, toss the shredded carrots with the coarse salt. Cover loosely with a clean towel and leave on the counter overnight. The next day, mix the carrots and their liquid into the jar with the fermented limes (if you have extra carrots, cover them with filtered water and ferment them on their own). Continue to shake daily and taste every few days as they ferment. They are done when you are happy with the flavor. Let the carrots and limes ferment together for five to thirty days, depending on how sour you would like them and how warm your house is, before transferring to the fridge.

> ### TIP: SPEED VS. SOUR
>
> Typically, the longer something ferments, the more sour it becomes. Small pieces of vegetables will ferment faster than larger pieces. If you want to ferment something fast, cut it small; if you want it to be really sour, cut it in larger chunks.

Pickled Carrots with Horseradish

WATERBATH

LEVEL: ◉ ◉ ○

YIELD: 4 PINT JARS

EFFORT: 45 MINUTES

ELAPSED: 1½ HOURS

EAT: AFTER 6 WEEKS

   AND WITHIN 1–2 YEARS

2¾ lb peeled carrots,
   about 3½ lb as purchased

5½ cups white distilled (5%) vinegar

1 cup water

2 cups granulated sugar

2 tsp canning salt

1 large onion, cut into strips

12 cloves garlic

4 Tbsp grated fresh horseradish

4 tsp dill seed

2 tsp celery seeds

Chili peppers aren't the only source of heat in the kitchen. Fresh horseradish has a flavor like nothing else. If you don't have access to horseradish root, replace it with 2 tsp chili flakes per jar.

1   Prepare your canning pot and rack, and sterilize your jars and lids (see page 17).

2   Cut the peeled carrots in quarters and wash them again.

3   Combine the vinegar and water in a large saucepan with the sugar and salt and bring to a boil on high heat. Reduce the heat but maintain the boil, and add the onions and boil for 10 minutes.

4   Remove the jars from the canner and turn the heat to high.

5   Place the garlic, horseradish, dill, and celery seeds in the bottom of the sterilized jars, dividing them evenly between each jar.

6   Add the carrots, packing them tightly, leaving ½ inch of headspace. Gently jostle the jars or use the handle of a spoon to release any air bubbles. To prevent them from floating, seatbelt them in place (page 18). Wipe the rims of the jars, apply the lids, and process for 15 minutes (if you live higher than 1,000 feet above sea level, refer to the Adjust for Altitude chart on page 17 for additional processing time).

7   Remove the jars and allow them to cool.

VARIATIONS: Swap out the horseradish for the same amount of hot pepper flakes or omit the spice element altogether. Use white wine vinegar instead of distilled, or replace the sugar with 1 cup of honey.

CENTER OF THE PLATE: Eat as is, or add to salads, wraps, or sandwiches. I like these best when chilled—it makes them crunchier.

Croque Monsieur with Carrot Lime Pickle and Aged Cheddar

SERVINGS: 2

EFFORT: 15 MINUTES

ELAPSED: 25 MINUTES

1 cup homogenized milk

1 Tbsp unsalted butter, chilled

1½ Tbsp all-purpose flour

Salt

Black pepper

1 bay leaf

12 oz aged cheddar (preferably white), grated and divided

4 croissants

4 oz shaved ham

¼ Spanish onion, shaved as thinly as possible

¼ cup carrot lime pickle, finely chopped after measuring (page 156)

My nieces, Astrid and Leti, spent their formative years in France and introduced me to the Croque Monsieur when they were young. They were still toddlers when they swore to me that the secret to French bread was the amount of salt used by bakers. I don't know if that's true but using preserved limes adds salt and I'm sure they'll approve!

1 Measure the milk and set aside to allow it to warm slightly.

2 Preheat the oven to 425°F.

3 Melt the butter in a small pot over medium-high heat. Add the flour and cook, stirring, for 2–3 minutes.

4 Add the milk, a little at a time. If you add too much at once, you will end up with lumps that you can only remove with a lot of whisking.

5 Once all of the milk is incorporated, season with salt and pepper. Add the bay leaf and gently simmer, stirring frequently, until the sauce has thickened, about 4 minutes.

6 Remove from the heat, discard the bay leaf, and allow pot to cool for a few minutes. Add three-quarters of the cheese and stir to incorporate.

7 Cut the croissants in half like buns. Use three-quarters of the sauce to spread on the insides of the croissants.

8 Divide the ham between the sandwiches. Place a layer of onion and then pickle on top of the ham.

9 Close the sandwiches and place them on a baking sheet lined with parchment paper. Drizzle the remaining sauce evenly over top of the croissants and sprinkle with the remaining cheese.

10 Place in the oven until the cheese is golden brown and bubbly, about 10 minutes.

PANTRY RAID: Hot sauce (page 176), flavored salt, or fermented green chutney (page 228) would all be delicious with this sandwich.

Fridge Pickles with Mirin

These are addictive. We add them to everything! We also reuse the brine several times by boiling it and adding more carrots. Shred 4 cups of carrots and place them in a 1-quart Mason jar. Make a brine by boiling 2 cups of water, 1 cup of mirin (brown rice vinegar), 3 Tbsp of maple syrup, 24 peppercorns, and 1 tsp coarse salt for 3 minutes, uncovered. Remove the peppercorns, pour the liquid over the carrots, and leave on the counter, uncovered, for 6 hours before securing with the lid and storing in the fridge.

Fish Tacos with Pickled Carrots

SERVINGS: 2–3 (4 MEDIUM OR 8 SMALL)

EFFORT: 30 MINUTES

ELAPSED: 45 MINUTES

YOGURT SAUCE:

3 green onions, thinly sliced

1 Thai chili, thinly sliced, or fermented hot pepper slices (page 177)

¼ cup cilantro

1 cup plain Greek yogurt

3 Tbsp lime juice (about 1½ limes)

1 Tbsp olive oil (optional)

Salt

QUICK SLAW:

1 cup cider vinegar

⅓ cup honey

½ green cabbage, shredded

½ Spanish onion, sliced thin

1 apple, peeled and julienned

¾ cup pickled carrots (page 157), diced then measured

Salt

Pepper

TACOS:

½ cup all-purpose flour

Salt

Pepper

2 eggs, lightly beaten

¾ cup cornmeal or polenta

2 tsp ground cumin

1 tsp chili powder

¾ tsp salt

Black pepper

1 lb white fish, portioned into 8–12 pieces. I like thin fish, such as perch

Oil for frying (I like coconut oil)

4 medium or 8 small taco shells

Lime wedges and hot sauce

I hear a lot of people writing off tacos as trendy, but I grew up with them and will always have a special place in my heart for taco night. If you're less sentimental, you can always skip the shells and plate this same meal as a fish fry! Use your favorite pickled carrots for this one.

MAKE THE YOGURT SAUCE:

1   Stir the green onions, chili, cilantro, yogurt, lime juice, and olive oil together and season to taste with salt. Cover loosely and refrigerate for at least 30 minutes before eating.

MAKE THE SLAW:

2   To make the slaw, bring the vinegar and honey to a boil in a pot over medium heat. Add the cabbage and onion and boil for 1 minute, stirring to prevent anything from sticking. Remove from the heat, add the apple, pickled carrots, and salt and pepper to taste. Stir and set aside.

PREP THE TACOS:

3   Place the flour on a medium-sized plate and season liberally with salt and pepper.

4   Place the eggs in a bowl large enough to hold the fish.

5   Mix together the cornmeal, cumin, chili powder, salt, and pepper on a medium-sized plate.

6   Working with one piece at a time, pat the fish dry, dip it in the flour, then the egg, and then the cornmeal. Place in a single layer, on a plate or baking tray.

7   Heat a frying pan on medium-high heat. Add enough oil so that a wooden spoon leaves a trail when you run it across the pan (at least ⅛ inch).

8   Cook the fish for 3 minutes, flip and cook for an additional 2–3 minutes.

9   Line each taco shell with yogurt sauce, add fish, and top with drained slaw. Serve with lime wedges and hot sauce.

PANTRY RAID: Hot sauce (page 176), pickled ginger, pickled garlic, and powder from dehydrated pickles could all be served with these tacos.

Cherries

One of the most interesting cherry preserves I've made was a batch of sour cherries in sugar and 190-proof grain alcohol. I had no idea what I'd do with them, but they seemed like a good idea.

We opened a jar two years later for Sunday Service: a small event, which is essentially a potluck on steroids. Our friends Pat and Jessie compete on the BBQ circuit and return from weekend competitions with a plethora of leftovers. Some other friends, Kerry, Corey, Ayngelina, and Dave, all live in the same building and co-host the event.

I brought a few jars of these sour cherries. A sip of the liquid felt innocent—the first taste was fruity, semi-sweet and pleasant. The big surprise happened as I chewed the fruit; it exploded with the taste and burn of booze (I've since learned that fruit often absorbs much of the taste of alcohol in long infusions). The cherries were nearly addictive and the jars were emptied quickly. It was an afternoon full of laughter and one that's been long remembered.

Preserving food—and sharing it with friends and family—creates and nurtures community. Even when "nurturing" comes in the form of 95% alcohol and fuzzy memories.

PRESERVING NOSE-TO-TAIL

- **PITS** Similar to apricot and peach pits, cherry pits contain small amounts of cyanide. I recommend researching this so that you're comfortable using the pits (or not).
- **JUICE** Cherries can be juiced, and the juice is often frozen, canned, or fermented into country wine.
- **FLESH AND SKIN** The flesh and skin of a cherry are difficult to separate from one another, though leftover solids from infusions or fermentations can (and should) be dried whole or as leather. They freeze very well.

TIPS FOR STORING

Fresh cherries should be kept cold as long as possible. Store in an airtight container at the back of your fridge.

If you're in a pinch, you can juice cherries or macerate them with ⅛ their volume of sugar. Either technique will extend their life anywhere from five days to two weeks.

FILLING THE PANTRY

CANNED
Juiced or canned pitted in simple syrup. Also cooked as jam, jelly, or chutney.

CELLAR
They freeze very well after pitting.

DEHYDRATED
Cherries dry wonderfully.

FERMENTED
Cherry wine is easy to make, and cherries can be easily transformed into soda or liqueur.

INFUSED
Naturally juicy and great to infuse alcohol or vinegar.

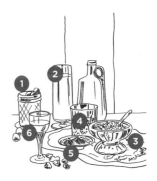

1 Pickled Cherries
2 Cherry Ginger Beer
3 Smoked Cherry Salt
4 Bourbon Cherries
5 Dehydrated Cherries and Cherry Espresso Powder
6 Cherry-Infused Brandy

CHERRIES

163

Batch-It

Cherry-Infused Brandy

INFUSE

LEVEL: ● ○ ○

YIELD: 1 QUART JAR

EFFORT: 10 MINUTES

ELAPSED: 1 MONTH

DRINK: WITHIN 2 YEARS

6 cups sweet or sour cherries, pitted
   (2–2½ lb)
2½ cups (1¼ lb) granulated sugar
26 oz brandy

YOU WILL NEED
Dehydrator

Dehydrated Cherries and Cherry Espresso Powder

DEHYDRATE

LEVEL: ● ● ○

YIELD: ¼–½ CUP

EFFORT: 20 MINUTES

ELAPSED: 1 DAY

EAT: WITHIN 2 YEARS

1 quart (4 cups) cherries, pitted
½ cup water
2 Tbsp espresso beans, ground
2 Tbsp brandy, bourbon, or dark rum

YOU WILL NEED
Cherry pitter
Parchment paper or Silpat mat
Spice grinder or high-speed blender
Dehydrator
Kitchen scale

The first steps in both of these recipes are the same, so these are a natural pair.

I love dehydrated cherries. The idea of infusing them with extra flavor came after I saw some incredibly expensive espresso powder. This recipe adds the natural sweetness of cherries and the butter-like quality of bourbon for even more decadence.

DAY 1: MACERATE THE CHERRIES FOR THE BRANDY:

1 Weigh the cherries. Add 50% of this weight in sugar. Place in a large bowl, cover tightly and refrigerate for 24 hours, stirring a few times.

DAY 2: DEHYDRATE THE CHERRIES FOR BOTH RECIPES:

2 Strain the cherries from Day 1, reserving the sugary juice in the fridge. Spread them on a dehydrator tray.

3 Spread the cherries for the powder on a separate tray.

4 Partly dry the cherries in a dehydrator at 135°F for 4 hours.

FINISH THE CHERRY BRANDY:

5 Place half of the brandy-destined cherries in a 1-quart Mason jar. Add the reserved cherry-sugar juice from the fridge and top with brandy. Cover tightly and store in a dark and cool place. Wait at least 1 month before tasting.

MAKE THE CHERRY ESPRESSO POWDER:

6 Place the water in a pan, add the espresso beans, and bring to a boil over high heat. Simmer for 3 minutes, add the bourbon, and reduce by half, about 5–10 minutes.

7 Add the espresso powder–destined cherries to this liquid, and continue to simmer, stirring, until most of the liquid has evaporated. This should only take a few minutes.

8 Line a dehydrating tray with parchment paper and return the cherries to the dehydrator. Dry at 135°F until dry and brittle, 4–8 hours. (Start checking them at the 4-hour point.)

9 Store in a jar with a lid. When you need powder, freeze the needed amount for 5 minutes to make them brittle, and pulverize in a spice grinder.

Pickled Cherries

LEVEL: ● ○ ○

YIELD: 4 PINT JARS

EFFORT: 40 MINUTES

ELAPSED: 1½ HOURS

EAT: WITHIN 1-2 YEARS

3 cups red wine vinegar

2 cups water

2 cups brown sugar, lightly packed

2 Tbsp coarse salt

4 Tbsp lime juice, about 2 limes

Zest of 2 limes, finely chopped

1½ Tbsp black peppercorns

3 dried chili peppers (page 174)

1 Tbsp coriander seeds

3 bay leaves

4 lb sweet cherries, pitted after
    weighing

Cheesecloth

Canning pot and rack

I'm a big fan of combining sweet and sour. Cherries are the closest thing to natural candy that I know, so pickling them makes a whole lot of sense. I sometimes freeze a few of these, making sure they don't touch while in the freezer, to snack on or to use as ice cubes.

1   Prepare your canning pot and rack, and sterilize your jars and lids (see page 17).

2   Combine the vinegar, water, sugar, salt, and lime juice and zest in a pot and place over high heat. While this liquid is heating, wrap the peppercorns, peppers, coriander seeds, and bay leaves in a cheesecloth bag and add to the pot. Add the cherries once the mixture begins to simmer and reduce the heat to medium. Continue to simmer, uncovered, for 10 minutes.

3   Remove the jars from the canner and turn the heat to high.

4   Use a slotted spoon to scoop out the cherries from their cooking liquid. Divide the cherries between the jars. Carefully pour in the hot cooking liquid until the jar is full, leaving ½ inch of headspace. Gently jostle the jars or use the handle of a spoon to release any air bubbles. Wipe the rims of the jars, apply the lids, and process for 15 minutes (if you live higher than 1,000 feet above sea level, refer to the Adjust for Altitude chart on page 17 for additional processing time).

5   Remove the jars and allow them to cool.

VARIATIONS: This works equally well with sour cherries or a mixture of the two.

CENTER OF THE PLATE: Try these in sandwiches, with cheese, or served on tacos or fish. They work especially well with lemon flavors.

Cherry Ginger Beer

FERMENT

LEVEL: ● ● ○

YIELD: 5 26 OZ (750 ML) BOTTLES

EFFORT: 60 MINUTES

ELAPSED: 10–20 DAYS

DRINK: WITHIN 1 MONTH

4 quarts filtered water

1½ cups granulated sugar, plus up to ¼ cup for the bug

10-inch piece of ginger (up to 2 inches for the bug and 8 inches for bottling), roughly chopped

1 pint cherries (sweet bing are my preference)

6 Tbsp fresh lemon juice, about 2 lemons

YOU WILL NEED

Cheesecloth

5 sterilized plastic home-brew bottles (26 oz/750 mL), screw-tops and bottle sanitizer

Ginger beer is easy to make. It's crisp and spicy, and it tastes far superior to anything you'll ever buy. It's fermented with the wild yeasts present in the air of your house, which I find fascinating!

There are three things to keep in mind with live ferments like this:

- Because it uses yeast naturally present in your house, each batch will be different because of changes in the environment.
- This is a live ferment. Do not bottle it in glass and do make sure to store it in the fridge to release pressure (see note on page 48).
- The process can create alcohol. Measure the percentage before pouring glasses for children or those who avoid alcohol.

MAKE A GINGER BUG (2–7 DAYS; IT WILL BE FASTEST IN WARM WEATHER):

1 Place 1 cup of the water, 2 tsp sugar, and 2 tsp of the finely chopped ginger in a clean jar. Stir well, cover loosely with a clean cloth. Place in a warm location out of direct sunlight.

2 Add the same amount of sugar and ginger each day until the liquid turns fizzy. It will bubble slightly, but sometimes only after you stir it. When this happens you are ready to make the ginger beer and bottle it (but if you don't have time you can feed it for another few days and bottle when convenient).

FERMENT AND BOTTLE THE SODA:

3 Pit the cherries, chop them roughly, and place them in a bowl. Add the 1½ cups of sugar, mix to coat the cherries, cover tightly, and refrigerate for 1–24 hours (you will get more vibrant cherry flavor by waiting longer).

4 Place the cherries in a pot. Cover with 4 cups of filtered water and boil over high heat for 10 minutes. Strain the liquid (reserving the cherries for eating or dehydrating).

5 Roughly chop 8 inches of ginger and place in a separate pot. Cover with 4 cups of water and boil for 10 minutes. Strain and add to the cherry water.

6 Strain the ginger bug and add it to the cherry-ginger water along with the lemon juice.

7 Clean and sanitize the bottles.

8 Divide the liquid evenly among the bottles, adding water to leave 1 inch of headspace. Put the screw-tops on the bottles.

9 Store in a warm, dark place in your kitchen, squeezing the bottles daily. When the bottles are firm, they should be transferred to the fridge to slow the fermentation and stop the pressure from continuing to build. This should take two to five days, depending on how warm your kitchen is.

10 Open slowly over a large bowl in case of volatility.

VARIATIONS: You can replace the cherries with other fruit. Solid fruit like blueberries or cranberries will make a clearer soda than fleshy fruit like peaches or plums.

CENTER OF THE PLATE: Mix 2 oz of dark rum, 3 oz of cherry-ginger beer, and a ½ oz of lime juice for a Dark and Stormy cocktail. Serve in a glass filled to the rim with ice.

Bourbon Cherries

Place pitted cherries in a jar and add enough bourbon to cover them by an inch or more. Cover with a lid and store in a dark and cool place for four to six weeks or longer. Eat the cherries and drink the bourbon!

10 Minutes or less

Smoked Cherry Salt

SMOKE

LEVEL: ● ● ○

YIELD: 1 CUP

EAT: WITHIN 1–2 YEARS

1 cup salt (use Maldon salt if you really want to spoil yourself)

1 cup cherries, measured then pitted and roughly chopped

Smoke maze

Wood chips or pellets (cherry is obvious but oak would also work)

BBQ

This was partially inspired by Japanese cherry salt, which contains no cherries at all. Smoke extra cherries to eat, cook with, or infuse while you make this. (See page 66 for more info on smoke mazes and smoking in general.)

Mix the cherries and salt in a bowl and leave covered tightly in the fridge for 24 hours. Leaving your BBQ unlit, line the top rack (or one half of BBQ) with aluminum foil and spread the salt mixture on it. If you'd rather avoid aluminum, use a cedar plank. Place the smoke maze on the opposite side, light it, and cold smoke for 5 hours. Store in a Mason jar for up to two years. It will not be completely dry, so don't worry if you feel moisture. Use the cherries and salt in the place of regular salt to season grilled meat, fish, or roasted vegetables.

Bourbon Cherry Hand Pies

SERVINGS: 4 (2 HAND PIES PER PERSON)

EFFORT: 45 MINUTES

ELAPSED: 6 HOURS

PASTRY:

1 cup frozen butter

2 cups all-purpose flour, plus extra
   as needed

1 tsp granulated sugar

1 tsp coarse salt

¼ cup ice water

2 eggs, lightly beaten

Icing sugar (optional)

FILLING:

⅓ cup pickled cherries (page 165),
   tightly packed

⅓ cup goat cheese

1 Tbsp honey

1 Tbsp bourbon

⅛ tsp dried thyme, finely chopped

1 tsp black pepper

Salt

YOU WILL NEED

Box cheese grater

2 baking trays

Parchment paper or 2 Silpat mats

Pastry brush

Fine sieve

I met Chris "Skip" Sweeney when I was five years old, and although we don't see each other as often any more, I'm proud to call him my oldest friend. When we were teenagers, Skip fell in love with pre-made pastries that we would warm up in a toaster. This recipe is a nod to those special friendships with shelf lives longer than frozen pastries'.

1   Grate the frozen butter and put it back in the freezer to chill.

MAKE THE FILLING:

2   In a bowl, mix together the cherries, goat cheese, honey, bourbon, thyme, pepper, and a pinch of salt. Set aside.

MAKE THE PASTRY:

3   In a separate bowl, mix together the flour, sugar, and salt. Add the butter and, using a spoon, mix until the mixture forms pebbles. Add the ice water, 1 Tbsp at a time, and continue to stir until the dough comes together. Divide in half, wrap each half in plastic, and refrigerate at least 1 hour.

4   On a floured surface, roll each sheet of dough into a 12- x 12-inch square (don't worry about being perfect). Cut each square into 8 pieces. Toss each piece lightly in flour.

5   Cover the baking trays with the parchment paper. Place four pieces of pastry on each tray. Place 1½ Tbsp filling on each piece and cover with another rectangle of pastry. Seal the sides with a fork and, pushing gently, spread the filling through the tarts with your fingers.

6   Cut 3 small slits in the top of the pastry and brush with egg.

7   Preheat the oven to 375°F. Divide your oven into thirds using the racks.

8   Place a tray on each rack and bake for 15 minutes. Swap the trays over and bake for 10–15 minutes further, until the tarts are golden brown.

9   Remove from oven and place pastries on racks to cool. Sift icing sugar over top before serving, if you like.

PANTRY RAID: Replace the bourbon with cherry-infused brandy or apricot-infused kirsch (pages 164 and 95), or add 2 tsp dehydrated cherry powder to the honey when mixing.

Hot Chocolate with Cherry Powder

SERVINGS: 2 LARGE MUGS

EFFORT: 10 MINUTES

ELAPSED: 15 MINUTES

1 quart (4 cups) milk

12 dried cherries (optional)

4 oz cherry-infused brandy
 (page 164) (optional)

3 Tbsp cocoa powder

2½ Tbsp maple syrup

½ tsp cayenne

2 Tbsp cherry espresso powder
 (page 164)

We eat many of our preserves in the winter, and the thought of cherries and coffee fills my head with memories of coming in from a cold walk with our dog, Shaeffer, and looking for a way to warm up. This recipe can be easily doubled on the coldest days.

1 Heat the milk and cherries, if using, in a pot over medium-high heat until nearly simmering.

2 While the milk heats, scatter the cherry espresso powder on a small plate. Dip the rim of each cup in water and then dredge through the powder.

3 When the milk reaches your ideal temperature, add the brandy, if using, the cocoa powder, maple syrup, and cayenne, and stir to incorporate. Divide the cherries between the four cups and serve.

PANTRY RAID: If you want to push this recipe even further, place 2 Tbsp of cherry espresso powder at the bottom of a French press and, after removing the cherries from the mixed beverage, allow the hot milk to steep for 5 minutes in the French press before straining and serving.

TIP: WASH YOUR BOWLS WITH CARBONATED WATER

When making jam or jelly, you may find yourself with a dirty bowl that has a small amount of leftover fruit droplets in it. There's not enough to scrape into your preserve and the only option appears to be a rinse in the sink. Pour a small amount of club soda into the bowl, swish it around, and pour the result into a glass for instant refreshment.

Chili Peppers

If you were to walk around our apartment, you'd find hot peppers in the oddest of spaces. You'd find them infusing vodka on the liquor shelf, hanging to dry from a lamp in the front room, dried and stored with our herbs, and fermenting in the dark recesses of our Great Wall of Preserves. And there's more than a gallon of different homemade chili sauces in the fridge. They're everywhere.

Although I've loved hot food for my entire life, I believe I misunderstood how to cook with it for a long time. I relied on phrases such as, "I love really flavorful hot sauce but not heat for the sake of heat," before re-examining my relationship with spices. A lot of commercial hot sauce is flavorful, but that flavor often comes from sugar and/or vinegar, which diminish the heat. To have any significant amount of heat in a dish, one has to add so much sauce that almost everything begins to taste like hot sauce.

Spreading a small amount of extreme heat across a dish allows you to enjoy spice while also allowing other flavors to come through.

PRESERVING NOSE-TO-TAIL

- **SKIN** The most bitter part of the pepper. It adds a base note to a preserve. The skin of thick-walled peppers can be removed by charring with intense heat. Thin-walled peppers dry the easiest and are most suited to air-drying.
- **FLESH** The sweetest part of the pepper. Many peppers become progressively hotter as you work your way from stem to tip. Commonly dried, fermented, and pickled.
- **PITH** Along with the seeds, this is the hottest part of the pepper. If you remove the pith, you can preserve it separately. Fermenting, curing, and dehydrating are typical techniques.
- **SEEDS** Hot and bitter. When fermenting hot sauce, you can blend the seeds and skins to make a thicker sauce or strain them through a colander. Dehydrate the solids to make a hot-and-sour powder that's a great substitute for dried chili flakes.

TIPS FOR STORING

Chili peppers should be stored the same way that other peppers are; see that section (page 279) for details on storing them.

FILLING THE PANTRY

CANNED

Hot sauce, pickled slices, and jelly.

DEHYDRATED

They dry easily with or without a dehydrator.

FERMENTED

Fermented hot sauce is the bomb.

INFUSED

Spicy vinegar or vodka is easy to make and a fantastic ingredient to cook with.

1 Wood-Fermented Hot Sauce
2 Chili Salt
3 Chili-Infused Vodka
4 Chili Oil
5 Fermented Slices

Batch-It

Air-Dried Hot Peppers

DEHYDRATE

LEVEL: ● ○ ○

YIELD: 1–1½ PINTS

EFFORT: 15 MINUTES

ELAPSED: 3–6 WEEKS

EAT: WITHIN 2 YEARS

Hot peppers (use at least a quart) with stems. I prefer thinner peppers (such as Thai) as opposed to thicker-walled varieties (such as jalapeño)

YOU WILL NEED

Butchers' twine

Chili Oil

INFUSE

LEVEL: ● ○ ○

YIELD: 1¼ CUPS

EFFORT: 10 MINUTES

ELAPSED: 1 HOUR

EAT: WITHIN 30 DAYS

1 cup peanut oil

1 Tbsp sesame oil

6 cloves garlic, finely chopped

2 inch piece ginger, finely chopped

1 cup whole dried chili peppers

Drying peppers can be as easy as tying them in a bunch and hanging them in a window. To use dried peppers, rehydrate them by covering them in boiling water. The spicy water is a great ingredient to add to rice, for example.

Chili oil, which can be made after you've dried some peppers, is a common ingredient in Asian and Mexican cuisine. Use it when oil is called for, or in place of hot sauce.

DEHYDRATE THE PEPPERS:

1 Wash and dry the peppers. Inspect them for bruises or soft spots. Remove any problematic parts.

2 Cut butchers' twine into different-sized pieces between 12–18 inches. Lay them on top of each other and tie one big knot in the middle to bind them together into a single package of string. Tie the free ends of the strings around the pepper stems.

3 Repeat until all the peppers are tied. Hang in a sunny, dry window and leave for two to four weeks. Inspect daily and run your fingers through them to allow the air to circulate. If you find a pepper is going moldy, remove it from the group and discard.

4 Store the dried peppers in a jar with an airtight lid for the best flavor retention (alternately, many people leave the peppers hanging in place). If you want to make chili powder, grind some dried peppers as you need them. This will help preserve their flavor better than if you grind them all at once.

MAKE THE CHILI OIL:

5 Mix the oils with the garlic and ginger in a pot over high heat for 4–5 minutes, before the garlic and ginger start to cook. Remove the pot from the heat and set aside.

6 Remove the stems from the dried peppers. Blitz in a food processor or blender to make flakes, then transfer to a dry container with a tight-fitting lid, such as a pint jar.

7 Pour the oil through a sieve to remove the garlic and ginger. I pour it into a bowl while it's still hot then pour it over the peppers immediately. Reserve the garlic and ginger for other cooking, such as a stir-fry.

8 Tightly cover the jar of oil and store in the fridge.

10 Minutes or less

Chili Salt

SALT

LEVEL: ●○○

YIELD: 2 CUPS

EAT: AFTER 10 DAYS AND
WITHIN 1–2 YEARS

2 oz (about ⅓ cup) hot chilies such
as ghost peppers

2 cups coarse/Maldon salt

This technique is the best way to add subtle heat to dishes, even though it uses hot, hot chilies. The salt draws water and capsaicin from the peppers and into its grains. This means that you are left with spicy salt that can be used in the place of normal salt in any dish. As the salt dissolves you will find that the heat will spread across the entire dish (unlike chunks of hot pepper) and allow you to raise the heat a little at a time.

Puree the peppers in a blender or food processor. Mix with the salt and place in a clean jar. Place a lid on top. Shake every few days for a month (you can use it at any time during and after this process). Store on a shelf away from sunlight.

Chili-Infused Vodka

It doesn't get any easier than this: Place whole chili peppers in a clean jar and cover them with vodka. However, I have a trick: I pack a 1-quart Mason jar with as many peppers as I can (I like to cut the tops off) and cover with vodka. This makes an EXTREMELY hot vodka base. You can dilute it with regular vodka to lessen the heat or add it to cooking. And, yes, the peppers are edible! I have kept peppers in vodka for years.

Wood-Fermented Hot Sauce

FERMENT

LEVEL: ● ● ○

YIELD: 2 QUARTS PURE HOT SAUCE, UP TO
 4 QUARTS IF YOU DILUTE WITH
 VINEGAR TO LESSEN HEAT

EFFORT: 45 MINUTES

ELAPSED: 4–6 WEEKS

EAT: WITHIN 1–2 YEARS

4 lb hot peppers (mix and match for
 more complex flavors!)

6 Tbsp coarse salt

3 whole bulbs garlic, cloves
 separated and peeled

1–2 quarts filtered water

YOU WILL NEED

Large container such as a crock or
 cookie jar

A plate to use as a weight to
 submerge the peppers

2 cups wood chips

Cheesecloth

Kitchen gloves

Making your own hot sauce is fantastically simple and a great gateway to preserving. If you're a chili head but haven't worked with hot peppers, these recipes are a perfect place to start!

1 Cut the tops off the peppers. I use gloves for the entire process but always manage to rub my eyes . . . or worse!

2 Place the garlic in your fermenting vessel.

3 Add the peppers then the salt and use your hands to mix.

4 Place your weight on top of the peppers and let sit overnight, covered loosely.

5 Toss the wood chips in a large colander and shake to remove any small bits.

6 Optional: toast the wood chips in a frying pan, stirring often. This can get smoky if you don't watch it closely.

7 Pour the wood chips (cooled, if you toasted them) onto a sheet of cheesecloth. Create a tea bag by tying the cheesecloth multiple times. You don't want it to open, as wood chips will be almost impossible to remove from the sauce and will ruin it.

8 Place the wood chip tea bag under the weight, and add water to submerge everything.

9 Ferment for five to thirty days, checking the brine daily after two or three days. Remove the wood when you are happy with the taste; if you leave it in for the entire time, it may become too "woody." As with any ferment, remove foam or mold as it appears. The peppers will soften in time; I move to the next step at the first sign that some have gone limp.

10 To make the hot sauce, puree the peppers in a blender. Add more brine to smooth the flavors (it is arguably the best part). You can also cut it with up to 50% vinegar.

11 Place in clean jars and store in the fridge.

VARIATIONS: Some like to strain hot sauce so that it's liquid. I prefer the body of this sauce. If you do strain it, use the solids for dehydrating or in chili salt (page 175).

CENTER OF THE PLATE: Leftover brine? Use it to marinate meat or tofu, or reduce to make a spicy concentrate.

10 Minutes or less

Fermented Slices

FERMENT

LEVEL: ● ○ ○

YIELD: 1 QUART JAR

EAT: WITHIN 1 YEAR

1-quart wide-mouth Mason jar

1½-cup Mason jar

1–1½ lb hot peppers, sliced into rings
(seeds included)

2 tsp coarse salt

1 Tbsp whey

2–3 cups filtered water

As a teenager I loved the pickled jalapeños that decorated nacho towers. These slices take those green pucks to an entirely new level. Taste the slices often to find that magical combination where they still have a semi-firm texture but have developed an amazing pickle flavor.

Fill the larger Mason jar up to the neck with hot pepper slices, then add salt and whey and secure lid. Shake well to distribute the salt, remove the lid, and cover loosely with a clean towel. Leave on the counter overnight. The next day, cover the peppers with filtered water, place the small Mason jar on top to submerge the peppers, and loosely cover with a clean towel. Leave in a cool spot. Check daily and skim off any foam that appears. Begin tasting after two to three days; it will become less salty and more sour with time. When you are happy with the taste and texture, transfer to the fridge where it will last most of the winter. I do this before they go soft, which will happen faster in warm kitchens than cool ones.

TIP: LORD OF THE FLIES

A common problem when fermenting, especially during summer months, is fruit flies. An airlock will keep them out, but otherwise you'll need to loosely cover the jar while fermenting. Instead of using a clean cloth, I have half a dozen reusable coffee filters (from the dollar store) that I place on top of jars to keep the bugs away.

Penne à la Chili-Infused Vodka

SERVINGS: 4

EFFORT: 20 MINUTES

ELAPSED: 2–2½ HOURS

2 Tbsp olive oil

1 medium onion, chopped

2 cloves garlic, minced

4 oz prosciutto or bacon, chopped
   into thin strips

Hot peppers from the chili-infused
   vodka (page 175) (as many as you
   like), chopped small

2 tsp dried oregano

1 cup chili-infused vodka (page 175)

1 quart (32 oz) canned plum
   tomatoes and juice

1 lb penne

1 cup heavy (35%) cream

Fresh lemon juice to taste

Coarse salt

Black pepper

3 Tbsp total of fresh oregano,
   parsley, basil, chives, or a
   combination

Parmesan cheese, grated, to garnish

YOU WILL NEED

Oven-safe pot with a tight-fitting
   lid, large enough to hold all
   ingredients. I use a 5½-quart
   Dutch oven.

This recipe calls for 1 cup of vodka and is a prime example of why I insist on over-spicing chili infusions. If your infusion is mild, you'll need to use an entire cup of it, whereas if you make a super-spiced infusion, you can top it up with fresh vodka and still achieve the same level of heat.

1 Preheat the oven to 375°F.

2 Heat the oil in the oven-safe pan over medium heat. Add the onion and cook until slightly browned.

3 Add the garlic and cook for 1 minute.

4 Add the prosciutto, hot peppers, and oregano, and cook for 3–4 minutes.

5 Drain off any excess fat from the pot and then add the vodka and juice from the tomatoes. Reduce by half, about 10–15 minutes.

6 Roughly chop the tomatoes, add them to the pan, cover the pan with its lid, and bake in the oven for 90 minutes.

7 If the sauce is too chunky for your taste, use a potato masher to crush the tomatoes further.

8 Cook the pasta in a large pot of salted, boiling water until al dente.

9 Remove the sauce from the oven, add the cream, and taste. Add lemon juice 2 tsp at a time; the sauce should taste slightly acidic but not lemony. Season to taste with salt and pepper.

10 Toss the pasta into the sauce and warm through. Add the fresh herbs and cheese right before serving.

PANTRY RAID: You can substitute every hot preserve you have on hand! This can also be a neat opportunity to create an automatic pairing by making a Bloody Mary while you have the infused vodka by your side. You can also substitute the salt with the same amount of herbes salées (page 229).

Charcoal Corn with Lime, Crema, and Dried Chili

SERVINGS: 6

EFFORT: 20 MINUTES

ELAPSED: 6–18 HOURS

1 cup heavy cream

1 cup sour cream

Salt

3 limes

6 cobs corn, husks on

4 air-dried chili peppers (page 174)

Aged white cheddar or Parmesan,
  finely grated (optional)

This is the simplest of recipes but it makes for fantastic eating. If you don't have a charcoal grill, or you have a large amount of corn to cook, you can easily cook the corn as described in a campfire or on top of a hot gas grill.

1 To make the crema, mix the cream and sour cream with a pinch of salt and the juice of one lime in a bowl. Cover tightly and leave in a warm spot in your kitchen for 6–18 hours. The longer you leave it, the thicker it will become.

2 Three hours before cooking dinner, soak the corn, still in the husks in water.

3 The key to this recipe is cooking the corn with the most amount of heat you can. Prepare a large bed of charcoal. If you are using a propane BBQ, preheat it on maximum. When I cook over charcoal, I don't use a grill.

4 Place the corn (still with husks on) on the BBQ. When the husks darken on the bottom, rotate by 90 degrees to expose fresh husk to the heat. Once that side has darkened on the bottom, do this once more and you're done!

5 While the corn cooks, blend the chilies into powder or rough chop them into flakes.

6 Allow the corn to rest for a few minutes then carefully remove the husks. Place the corn on a serving plate and squeeze the two remaining limes over top.

7 Apply the crema to the corn. I use a squeeze bottle and put as much crema as I would put butter, and scatter with chili powder.

8 Top the corn with cheese (if you're using any) before serving.

PANTRY RAID: Frozen herb butter (page 227) works really well on corn. Remove it from the freezer just before serving dinner and apply it like lipstick!

Citrus

While the majority of the food we bring into our house is local, we are not dogmatic about it. We frequently cook with citrus and enjoy that it's readily available in the winter when there are fewer local ingredients around to preserve.

The tipping point for including this chapter came from the realization that citrus has its own distinct category of preserves: marmalade. And it's a fascinating category—one that people generally have very strong feelings about. I have friends who hate the stuff and others who love it so much that they participate in and organize festivals and competitions dedicated to it.

Me? Despite it not being a local ingredient, I'm a fan of citrus and I love its versatility when used in cooking or preserving.

PRESERVING NOSE-TO-TAIL

- **ZEST** Although there are specialized tools to remove the zest of citrus fruit, I use a sharp bow-shaped vegetable peeler before chopping it with a knife. It can be dehydrated and candied or used for marmalade.
- **FLESH AND JUICE** Pulp is usually incidental (there's no advantage to removing it). Juice is frozen or canned.
- **PITH** It's the most bitter and isn't always avoided; for example, whole citrus slices (dried and fresh) are common ingredients in the Middle East and Asia, and lime pickles are a common ferment in India.
- **SEEDS** These are bitter and could be infused or dried and pulverized into a powder that could be mixed with sugar for a cocktail rimmer, or used to contrast with sweet fruit or candies. I generally discard them.

TIPS FOR STORING

Separate citrus from other fruit and veg by keeping it refrigerated in an airtight container of its own. A lot of fruit (including bananas, pears, plums, peaches, apricots, and tomatoes) produces ethylene, which reduces shelf life and promotes fungus in lemons, so store them separately from these things. They can be stored in the fridge in a plastic bag or container for several weeks. The best taste will come from storing on the counter.

If you're in a pinch, juice citrus and freeze it in ice cube trays. Use melted cubes for salad dressing, glazing protein (including tofu), or tossed, whole, into a cocktail.

FILLING THE PANTRY

CANNED

Marmalade (with and without zest), jelly, chutney, and concentrated juices.

DEHYDRATED

Whole fruit or slices can be dried.

CURED

Salt-preserved lemons are a common ingredient in Moroccan cuisine.

INFUSED

Slices of citrus are often used for quick infusions, such as lemon water, and sometimes used to make liqueur, such as limoncello.

1 Bourbon Marmalade
2 Limoncello
3 Lemon Squash with Hopped Strawberries
4 Shaved Citrus Slices
5 Candied Lemon Rind
6 Salt-Preserved Lemons and Limes

Batch-It

Lemon Squash with Hopped Strawberries

WATERBATH

LEVEL: ● ○ ○

YIELD: 4–5 HALF-PINT JARS

EFFORT: 25 MINUTES

ELAPSED: 1½ HOURS

EAT: WITHIN 2 YEARS

14 large lemons

1 oz hops of your choice

1½ cups honey

2 cups strawberries, pureed

Candied Lemon Rind

DEHYDRATE

LEVEL: ● ● ○

YIELD: 1–2 CUPS

EFFORT: 25 MINUTES

ELAPSED: 6–8 HOURS

EAT: WITHIN 6 MONTHS

Peels from the lemon squash

½ cup honey

2 tsp pure vanilla extract
   or ¼ cup bourbon

¼ tsp freshly ground nutmeg

¼ cup granulated sugar

¼ cup ground pistachio nuts

YOU WILL NEED

Dehydrator

I first read about lemon squash in The River Cottage Handbook No. 2, *Preserves*, by Pam Corbin. The term "squash" is a British one for a concentrated fruit drink. Just add water (or spike with rumtopf, page 323) when you're ready to serve.

Because squash uses so many lemons, it provides a great opportunity to make candied lemon rind. Instead of throwing the peels of the lemons into the compost you can candy part of the "waste."

PREP THE LEMON SQUASH:

1 Remove the zest of the lemons with a vegetable peeler, set them aside, and juice the lemons. You will need 3 cups of lemon juice.

2 Prepare your canning pot and rack, and sterilize your jars and lids (see page 17).

3 In a large pot, mix the hops with 3 cups of water and the honey and bring to a simmer over high heat. Let simmer for 1 minute, then turn off the heat and allow to steep for 10 minutes.

4 Remove the jars from the canner and turn the heat to high.

5 Using a sieve, remove the hops from the pot (they can be discarded), and add the pureed strawberries. Simmer for 3 minutes. Skim off any foam (you can put it in a glass and drink it later).

6 You may wish to strain the strawberry seeds from the liquid with a sieve. I don't mind the consistency and leave them (they can also be strained when opening each jar, if you'd rather).

7 Divide evenly between the five jars and add water until you have ¼ inch of headspace. Gently jostle the jars or use the handle of a spoon to release any air bubbles. Wipe the rims of the jars, apply the lids, and process for 5 minutes (if you live higher than 1,000 feet above sea level, refer to the Adjust for Altitude chart on page 17 for additional processing time).

8 Remove the jars and allow them to cool.

MAKE THE CANDIED LEMON RIND:

9 In a large pot, cover the peels with cold tap water. Bring to a boil, then reduce the heat and simmer over medium-high heat until soft, about 30 minutes.

10 Drain the peels in a colander and discard the liquid. Use a teaspoon to remove most of the pith from the peels, and slice them into narrow strips.

11 Place 1 cup of water into the same pot and add the honey, vanilla, nutmeg, and lemon peels. Simmer until you have a thick, translucent syrup, about 15 minutes.

12 Remove the peels from the syrup. Keep the syrup in the fridge as a sweetener for tea or use as a glaze when roasting root vegetables. It will store for weeks.

13 Place the peels on a dehydrator rack and dehydrate at 135°F for 1 hour.

14 Then, toss the peels in the sugar, making sure they are fully coated. Run your fingers through them to separate them. Spread the peels in a single layer on the dehydrator rack again and continue to dry at 135°F for about 4 hours, until they are dry but pliable. Store on a dark shelf in an airtight container.

> **TIP:**
> **A WREATH OF JAR BANDS**
> If you've been preserving for any length of time, you'll know how easy it is to end up with a giant pile of jar rings that can be a pain to store. We store them on a long piece of butchers' twine that has a loop tied at each end. The loops slip over a butchers' hook or can be put in a drawer. It's worth taking the time to hang wide-mouthed rings on one side and conventional on the other for quick and easy access when you need them.

Salt-Preserved Lemons and Limes

Preserved lemons are common in Moroccan cuisine. Place a few pieces on top of a roasting chicken or fish, or use the flavored salt directly from the jar like you would use any other salt. Cut three lemons into quarters and place them in a 1-quart jar. Add the juice of another lemon and add ¾ cup coarse salt. Place a lid on top, tighten, and shake the jar. Shake it daily for three to four days and store on a shelf out of direct sunlight. They will keep for five or six months and are best for eating after the first few weeks.

Bourbon Marmalade

LEVEL: ◉ ◉ ○

YIELD: 3-4 HALF-PINT JARS

EFFORT: 1 HOUR

ELAPSED: 1½ HOURS

EAT: WITHIN 1-2 YEARS

8 Seville oranges

1½ cups honey

1 stick cinnamon

2 oz bourbon

½–¾ tsp saffron (optional)

The arrival of Seville oranges and lemons marks the start of another season of jam and jelly in our kitchen. We don't make a lot of marmalade, but I enjoy it as a cooking ingredient and find it to be a versatile addition to our pantry.

1 Peel and juice the oranges, and reserve the solids.

2 In a large pot, cover the orange solids with 4 cups of cold water and simmer, uncovered, until soft, about 30 minutes. Strain and discard the water. Allow the peels to cool before removing the seeds and membrane with a spoon. Try to remove everything but the zest.

3 Chop the zest into small pieces.

4 In the same pot, combine the honey, 2 cups cold water, and cinnamon. Bring to a boil before reducing to a simmer, uncovered, removing any foam that appears, until the marmalade reaches 220°F or it sets (use the freezer test on page 13). This should take 10–15 minutes but will vary depending on the shape of your pan.

5 Prepare your canning pot and rack, and sterilize your jars and lids (see page 17).

6 Remove the jars from the canner and turn the heat to high.

7 Remove the cinnamon stick, add the bourbon and saffron, and fill the jars, leaving ¼ inch of headspace. Use the handle of a spoon to release any air bubbles.

8 Wipe the rims of the jars, apply the lids, and process for 5 minutes (if you live higher than 1,000 feet above sea level, refer to the Adjust for Altitude chart on page 17 for additional processing time).

9 Remove the jars and allow them to cool.

VARIATIONS: Use blood oranges or replace the bourbon with red wine.

CENTER OF THE PLATE: Mix 2 parts marmalade with 1 part butter and add 1 part fresh herbs. Place this spread under the skin of a chicken before roasting it.

10 Minutes or less

Shaved Citrus Slices

DEHYDRATE

LEVEL: ● ○ ○

YIELD: 1 QUART

EAT: WITHIN 1–2 YEARS

8–10 medium organic lemons or
    citrus of your choice

YOU WILL NEED
Dehydrator

You can dry any thickness of citrus effectively. If you leave limes or lemons whole on a rack, you can even dry them intact! I find that thin pieces are the most versatile for cooking and easier to work with. Add them to tea, toss them in stir-fries or rehydrate them in warm water for 10 minutes and place them on top of roasting vegetables, fish, or chicken.

Cut the lemons into rounds or shave them as thinly as possible, removing the seeds as you go. Place them in a single layer on a dehydrator sheet. Dry at 135°F until brittle. Thin slices should take 6–8 hours. I store these in an airtight container out of direct sunlight where they will last for years.

Limoncello

INFUSE

LEVEL: ● ○ ○

YIELD: 26 OZ (750 ML)

DRINK: AFTER 3 MONTHS, AND
    WITHIN 1–2 YEARS

1 26 oz (750 mL) bottle vodka
2 whole organic lemons

YOU WILL NEED
2 ft piece of cheesecloth
½- or 1-gallon jar (such as a cookie
    jar) with a lid, large enough to
    hold the vodka and suspend the
    lemons without touching it
The vodka bottle for long-term
    storage
Plastic wrap

So many of us have had our taste buds corrupted by commercial varieties of limoncello made with synthetic lemon. This technique uses a hammock to suspend the lemons over the vodka (the liquid never touches them) to infuse their flavor.

Pour the vodka into the jar. Tie a knot in the center of the cheesecloth. Tie a lemon on either side of the knot and suspend over the vodka, making sure the lemons don't touch the liquid. Do this by hanging the ends of the cheesecloth outside of the jar, securing them with the jar's lid, and tying the ends of the cheesecloth together. Seal the top from flies by wrapping it tightly with plastic wrap. Leave on a shelf out of direct sunlight and begin tasting after three weeks. Age for up to two months. Remove lemons when you like the taste; the early stages will taste bright and crisp while longer aging will produce more traditional, bitter flavors. Transfer clear liquid to its original bottle or a jar for longer storage and drink at any time.

Serve by mixing 2 parts Limoncello with 1 part simple syrup (a 50:50 mixture of water and granulated sugar).

Orange Beef

SERVINGS: 4

EFFORT: 40 MINUTES

ELAPSED: 1 DAY

BEEF AND MARINADE:

⅓–½ cup dehydrated orange slices
   (page 187), roughly chopped

2 cloves garlic, minced

1½ inch piece ginger, minced

¼ cup soy sauce

3 Tbsp fresh orange juice
   (about ½ an orange)

2 Tbsp oyster sauce

1 Tbsp honey

1 Tbsp chili flakes (page 174)
   or store-bought

Coarse salt

Black pepper

1 lb lean sirloin, cut into thin strips
   against the grain

FOR THE REST OF THE DISH:

1 Tbsp peanut or vegetable oil

⅓ cup beef stock

3 Tbsp fresh orange juice (about ½
   an orange)

1 bell pepper (or ½ red bell pepper
   plus ½ green bell pepper), diced

½ onion, diced

4 cups steamed long-rain white rice

3 orange segments

Dehydrated citrus and dried
   kumquats, for garnish (page 187)

I ate mostly vegetarian for almost eight years. A few years in, my friend Sherwin, who happens to be first-generation Canadian as well as a long-time vegetarian, said, "It's easier for you to be a vegetarian than me." I could tell he was referring to the differences in our ethnic backgrounds (his parents were from Hong Kong).

"Your family recipes use meat as a dish. Mine use it as an ingredient." He meant that I could skip a dish at a family meal and avoid meat, but his family ate less meat overall but cooked it into almost every dish.

I've found weekly inspiration in that statement for the last decade. Now, instead of serving a giant steak, we often portion meat as an ingredient in a dish rather than serving it on its own.

MARINATE THE BEEF:

1 Combine all of the marinade ingredients in a large container. Place the beef in the marinade, cover, and refrigerate for 12–24 hours.

COOK THE BEEF:

2 Remove the beef from the marinade, reserving the marinade.

3 Heat a frying pan on medium-high heat. Add oil and wait until it just begins to smoke. Toss the beef in the pan but don't overcrowd the pan; you may need to do this in two batches. The beef will appear to stick to the bottom but don't panic. When it's ready to be turned, it will release from the pan.

4 While the beef is cooking, place the reserved marinade in a small pot over medium heat. Bring to a simmer, and reduce by half, about 5–10 minutes. Add the stock and orange juice and reduce by half again, about 15–20 minutes.

5 Add the pepper and onion to the frying pan when you turn the beef for the final time and cook, stirring, for 2 minutes.

6 Remove the beef from pan, and let it rest on a plate for a few minutes. Add the reduced marinade to the frying pan, stirring to remove any sticky bits on the bottom.

7 Serve the beef and veggies with steamed rice. Garnish with the dried citrus.

PANTRY RAID: Serve with chili oil (page 174) or a cup of warm broth containing a few dried vegetables to drink as you eat it.

Chicken Stew with Salt-Preserved Lemons

SERVINGS: 6–8

EFFORT: 30 MINUTES

ELAPSED: 2 HOURS

1 cup all-purpose flour

1 tsp chili powder (page 174)
  or store-bought

1 tsp dried rosemary, roughly
  chopped then measured, divided

2 tsp powdered mustard

Preserved lemon salt, to taste
  (page 185)

3 lb chicken legs and thighs,
  skin on and bone in

¼ cup rendered pork fat, or
  coconut, peanut or vegetable oil

1½ lb butternut squash (weighed
  before peeling), peeled and cut
  into chunks

1 large onion, cut into chunks

3 garlic cloves, thinly sliced

½ cup carrot cut into chunks

½ cup celery, cut into chunks

2 cups wild, oyster, or Portobello
  mushrooms, roughly chopped

2–4 preserved lemon quarters
  (page 185) to taste, finely diced

Black pepper

2 cups chicken stock

1 cup flat-leaf parsley, divided

1 tsp ground cumin

YOU WILL NEED

Oven-safe pot with tight-fitting lid
  that will contain all ingredients
  with additional space

Immersion blender (optional)

This is loosely inspired by North African cuisine, though the ingredients are far more reflective of where we live. It can be eaten on its own or served on rice or couscous. Do not substitute fresh lemons for preserved lemons here; they are a key part of the recipe and add a unique flavor.

1 Preheat the oven to 325°F.

2 Preheat a large frying pan on medium-high.

3 Prepare a dredge by combining the flour, chili powder, rosemary, mustard, and ¾ tsp preserved lemon salt. Pat the chicken dry, dredge it in flour, and place on a clean plate.

4 Place the fat in the hot pan. When it just begins to smoke, add the chicken in one layer, making sure there is space between the pieces (you will have to do this in batches). Turn once so that the chicken is browned on both sides, about 5 minutes per side, and then place the chicken in the oven-proof pot.

5 Once the chicken is done, add a bit more fat, then add the squash in a single layer, and cook until it just starts to soften, stirring occasionally. You may have to work in batches here as well. Add the squash to the pot with the chicken.

6 Turn the heat to medium, add more fat if needed, and place the onion, garlic, carrot, and celery in the pan and cook for 2 minutes, stirring occasionally. Add the mushrooms and season with more of the lemon salt and pepper. Cook for another 2 minutes and add to the chicken pot.

7 Add the stock, half the parsley, cumin, and preserved lemon quarters. Stir to combine everything, place the lid on top, and bake for 1 hour.

8 Carefully remove 1½ cups of vegetables from the pot and puree until smooth. Add them back to the pot and mix.

9 Season with additional salt and pepper to taste and garnish with the remaining parsley before serving.

PANTRY RAID: Add canned tomatoes (page 333) at the end of cooking. Serve with slices of toast topped with herb-infused honey (such as the thyme-infused honey on page 229).

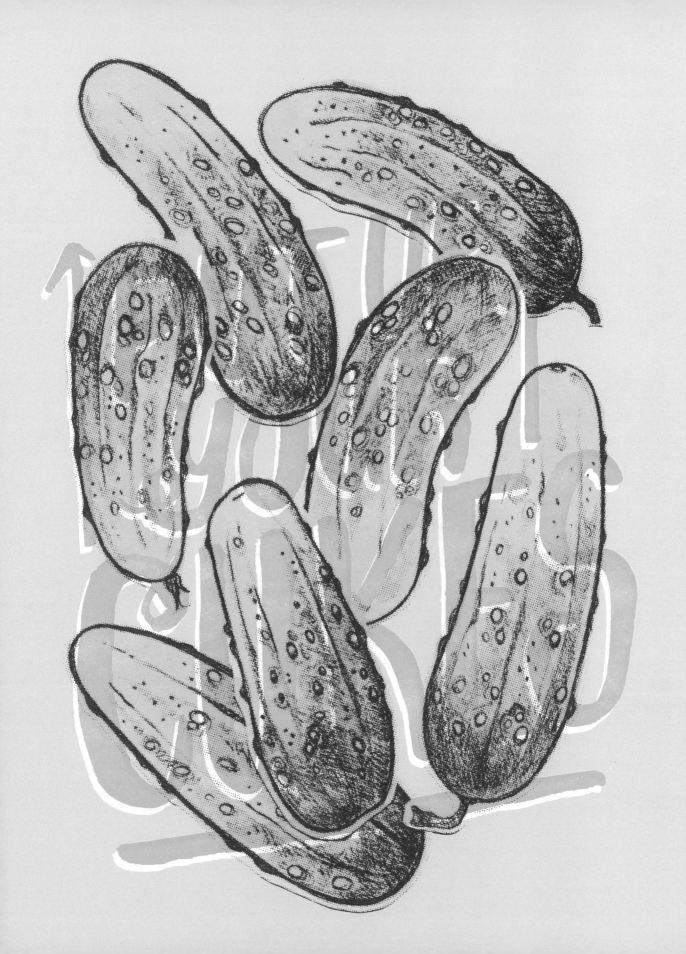

Cucumbers

I bought 10 lb of pickling cucumbers at the market and raced home. I was beyond excited at the prospect of my first attempt at fermenting.

I had started to read a recipe earlier in the week. "Started" being the key word.

It wasn't until the second or third day of fermenting that I decided to read the rest of the recipe. The final step described storing them in a cold cellar or fridge to stop them from fermenting. We owned a small apartment-sized fridge that was already stuffed to capacity.

I gave a lot of pickles away that year.

Fermented cucumbers aren't difficult to make, but they do require care. When I remember to check them daily and taste them often, they work out wonderfully. If I forget about them for a few days, they tend to rebel, leaving me with cucumber mush. Believe me, 12 hours and room in your fridge can make all the difference.

PRESERVING NOSE-TO-TAIL

Smaller cucumbers make crispier pickles.

- **SKINS AND SEEDS** The most bitter parts. If you like bitter flavors, leave cucumbers intact when infusing, or infuse a batch of liquid using only the seeds and skins. Removing the skins will make for less bitter preserves but will also produce much softer (and sometimes mushy) results.
- **ENDS** One end of a cucumber was connected to the stem. The other end, the blossom end (the smaller blemish) contains an enzyme that can soften pickles when fermenting and should be removed. Remove both ends if you're not sure which is which.

TIPS FOR STORING

Cucumbers are best stored at room temperature until cut. Keep them out of direct sunlight and store them away from onions, garlic, and bananas.

If you are worried about losing them, cucumbers can be stored in an airtight container in the fridge for three to five days. Or try the quick fridge pickles on page 194.

FILLING THE PANTRY

CANNED
Vinegar pickles and relish.

FERMENTED
Deli or kosher pickles.

INFUSED
Cucumbers are great for short infusions.

1 Fridge Pickles
2 Quick-Infused Vodka or Water
3 Vinegar Pickles
4 Awesome Relish
5 Fermented Dill Pickles
6 Curry Cucumber Pickle

Batch-It

Fridge Pickles

CELLAR

LEVEL: ● ○ ○

YIELD: 1½ CUPS

EFFORT: 5 MINUTES

ELAPSED: 45 MINUTES

EAT: WITHIN 24 HOURS

1 lb cucumbers (any type will do)

2 tsp sesame oil (optional)

½ cup white vinegar

1 Tbsp fresh lemon juice

2 tsp sesame seeds

Fermented Dill Pickles

FERMENT

LEVEL: ● ● ○

YIELD: ½ GALLON

EFFORT: 20 MINUTES

ELAPSED: 3–14 DAYS

EAT: WITHIN 6 MONTHS

2 lb small pickling cucumbers

8 cloves garlic, peeled

6 dried grape leaves (optional)

¼ cup fresh dill, chopped then measured, or 4–5 heads of dillweed, chopped

1 Tbsp coarse salt

1–1½ quarts filtered water

YOU WILL NEED

½-gallon wide-mouth Mason jar or fermenting crock

Fermented pickles, also called kosher or deli pickles, are as good as it gets when it comes to preserving. But because fermented pickles need several days before they are ready, I often make fridge pickles at the same time for a quick fix! Fridge pickles were a common staple at my Meme and Pepe's house. By making both recipes at the same time, we have pickles now and later.

PREP THE CUKES:

1 Cut the blossom end off all the cucumbers (for both recipes) to preserve texture. If you're not sure which end is the blossom, you can trim both ends.

PREP THE FRIDGE PICKLES:

2 Peel and slice the cucumbers into ½-inch-thick rounds.

3 Toss the cucumbers with sesame oil and allow them to rest for 10 minutes.

4 Add the vinegar and lemon juice, and rest for an additional 20 minutes.

5 When ready to serve, remove the pickles from the liquid and scatter with sesame seeds and salt to taste.

PREP THE FERMENTED PICKLES:

6 Lightly crush the garlic.

7 Place the grape leaves, if using, along the bottom of the ½-gallon Mason jar. Add the cucumber rounds, garlic, and dill. Wedge the last few cucumbers under the neck of the jar to prevent them from floating (see Seatbelting on page 18).

8 Add the salt, secure the lid on top, and carefully shake to distribute. Remove the lid and add water to cover the cucumbers, stopping just where the neck of the jar begins and making sure that the cucumbers are fully submerged.

9 Loosely cover with a towel and put the jar on a plate (in case the ferment bubbles over and makes a mess), out of direct sunlight. Taste after three days (they will get increasingly sour but lose texture with each additional day). In warm rooms, the cucumbers will ferment within as little as three days; in cooler spaces they will take as long as two weeks.

10 Store in fridge where they will last for months.

Vinegar Pickles

WATERBATH

LEVEL: ● ● ○

YIELD: 8 QUART JARS

EFFORT: 1 HOUR

ELAPSED: 2 HOURS

EAT: AFTER 6 WEEKS
    AND WITHIN 1–2 YEARS

6 lb Persian or pickling cucumbers

8 cups white vinegar (5% or more)

8 Tbsp pickling or kosher salt

16 tsp dill seed

16 bay leaves

8 Tbsp mustard seeds

8 tsp coriander seeds

8 inches ginger (16 tsp), peeled and
    minced fine

16 tsp chili flakes

16–32 cloves garlic, peeled and left
    whole, depending on your taste

This style of pickles is similar to the pickles you find in the condiment aisle of the grocery store and less like the ones you find in the deli. They will store on a shelf for up to two years and are at their crispest when chilled before serving.

You'll likely have to do these in a few batches (unless you have a pot big enough to hold eight jars). I promise it will go faster than you think! You can also cook the awesome relish (page 197) while you process the pickles.

1   Prepare your canning pot and rack, and sterilize your jars and lids (see page 17).

2   Wash and dry the cucumbers. Trim the ends.

3   Place 8 cups of water and vinegar in a large pot with the salt and bring to a boil over high heat. Because cucumbers come in drastically different sizes, you may find that you need significantly more or less brine. Large pickles use more brine.

4   Remove the jars from the canner and turn the heat to high.

5   Divide the spices and garlic evenly among the jars, fill them with cucumbers (vertically or horizontally), and secure them by placing several cucumbers across the top but under the level of the jar neck (see Seatbelting, page 18).

6   Completely cover with brine, leaving ½ inch of headspace. Gently jostle the jars or use the handle of a spoon to release any air bubbles. Wipe the rims of the jars, apply the lids, and process for 15 minutes (if you live higher than 1,000 feet above sea level, refer to the Adjust for Altitude chart on page 17 for additional processing time).

7   Remove the jars and allow them to cool.

VARIATIONS: Double the amount of mustard seeds or garlic.

CENTER OF THE PLATE: Chop these pickles into mayo, bread and fry them whole, or eat them straight from the jar.

TIP: PICKLING WITH SHOT GLASSES

When I pickle, I divide out my dry spices in shot glasses before I begin, which allows me to quickly pour them into the individual jars and ensure that the spices are distributed evenly.

Curry Cucumber Pickle

WATERBATH

LEVEL: ● ● ○

YIELD: 7 PINT JARS

EFFORT: 1 HOUR

ELAPSED: 1 DAY

EAT: AFTER 6 WEEKS
AND WITHIN 1–2 YEARS

6 lb pickling cucumbers, sliced
¼-inch thick

1 medium onion, diced

2 Tbsp pickling salt

2¾ cups white vinegar (5% or
greater)

¼ cup bottled lemon juice

¾ cup honey (or 1¾ cups
granulated sugar)

4 inches (8 tsp) minced ginger

¼ cup mustard seeds

2 Tbsp curry powder, spice level
to your taste

4 tsp dried dill weed

2 tsp ground turmeric

1 tsp celery seeds

This is a twist on a traditional bread-and-butter pickle. A slight sweetness is offset by the heat of the curry and ginger, and is balanced by the sourness of the vinegar and lemon. Dill is a surprisingly suitable ingredient in this mix.

1   Mix the cucumbers with the onion and salt. Place in a non-reactive bowl, cover tightly, and refrigerate for 24 hours.

2   Remove the cukes from their soaking water and rinse well (taste while rinsing to ensure the cukes aren't too salty). Discard the soaking water.

3   Prepare your canning pot and rack, and sterilize the jars and lids (see page 17).

4   Place the vinegar, lemon, and honey in a large pot and bring to a boil over high heat.

5   Add the cucumbers, ginger, curry powder, dill weed, turmeric, and celery seeds, and return to a boil, uncovered, over high heat before turning down the heat to a simmer for 3 minutes (moving to the next step as you wait).

6   Remove the jars from the canner and turn the heat to high.

7   Tightly pack the cucumber mixture into the jars using a slotted spoon. Then pour the brine overtop, leaving ½ inch of headspace. Gently jostle the jars or use the handle of a spoon to release any air bubbles. Wipe the rims of the jars, apply the lids, and process for 10 minutes (if you live higher than 1,000 feet above sea level, refer to the Adjust for Altitude chart on page 17 for additional processing time).

8   Remove the jars and allow them to cool.

VARIATIONS: Replace the ginger with an equal amount of dried pepper flakes (page 281).

CENTER OF THE PLATE: Add this to tuna or egg salad, eat it with anything salty, and use a touch of the brine when cooking rice or stir-fries.

Awesome Relish

WATERBATH

LEVEL: ● ● ○

YIELD: 3 HALF-PINT JARS

EFFORT: 30 MINUTES

ELAPSED: 2½ HOURS

EAT: AFTER 6 WEEKS

   AND WITHIN 1–2 YEARS

2 lb pickling cucumbers

¾ cup red onions, diced then measured

½ large red bell pepper, diced

1 Tbsp pickling salt

1 cup white vinegar (5% or higher)

2 Tbsp bottled lemon juice

½ cup granulated sugar

2 cloves garlic, minced

2 Tbsp cilantro, finely chopped then measured

2 Tbsp mustard seeds

½ tsp celery seeds

Quick Infused Vodka or Water

Peel and slice the cucumbers into rounds and add them to vodka or water for a refreshing drink (I use a 5:1 ratio of liquid to cuke for both). Water is infused for a few hours in the fridge; vodka can take two to six days on the counter. If the cucumber begins to disintegrate, you can remove it by straining. Water is best used quickly. The vodka will last indefinitely, but is best in its first few months.

In my opinion, relish is a dish best served cold. There is something magical about the contrast of cold, acidic relish clashing against hot, charred proteins (meat or otherwise). Add a layer of fat, such as aged cheddar, and I'll eat an entire meal without speaking a word . . .

1   Leaving their skins on, dice the cucumbers as small as possible, either by hand or in a food processor.

2   Toss the cucumbers with the onion, red pepper, and salt in a large bowl. Cover loosely with a cloth and leave for 2 hours on the counter.

3   Prepare your canning pot and rack, and sterilize your jars and lids (see page 17).

4   Remove the jars from the canner and turn the heat to high.

5   Rinse the vegetables several times, draining well and pressing out any remaining liquid. Taste to ensure they aren't overly salty (if they are, continue to rinse or soak in fresh water until palatable).

6   Place the vinegar, lemon juice, sugar, garlic, cilantro, and mustard and celery seeds in a large pot and bring to a boil over high heat. Add the cucumber mixture and reduce to a simmer. Simmer uncovered for 30 minutes, stirring occasionally.

7   Remove the jars from the canner and turn the heat to high.

8   Fill the jars, leaving ½ inch of headspace. Gently jostle the jars or use the handle of a spoon to release any air bubbles. Wipe the rims of the jars, apply the lids, and process for 10 minutes (if you live higher than 1,000 feet above sea level, refer to the Adjust for Altitude chart on page 17 for additional processing time).

9   Remove the jars and allow them to cool.

VARIATIONS: Add 2 red jalapeños, chopped fine, for a burst in flavor.

CENTER OF THE PLATE: Mix with olive oil, fresh lemon juice, and canned tuna for an amazing sandwich (or arancini) filler.

Pickled Baked Falafel Lettuce Wraps

SERVINGS: 2–4 (12–16 FALAFELS)

EFFORT: 45 MINUTES

ELAPSED: 1 DAY

FALAFELS:

1 cup dried chickpeas

1 cup fermented pickle brine (page 194) (see note)

½ onion

2 cloves garlic

¼ cup pickles (from the brine used above), diced small

1–2 dried chili peppers (page 174) or 2–3 tsp of chili flakes

¼ cup chopped flat-leaf parsley, cilantro, or a combination of the two

1 tsp ground cumin

Coarse salt

2–3 Tbsp all-purpose flour

Olive oil

¼ cup sesame seeds (optional)

PICKLED TAHINI SAUCE:

½ cup tahini

3 cloves garlic, finely minced

2 Tbsp olive oil

1 Tbsp pickle brine (or more to taste). Use the same brine as above

1 Tbsp chopped flat-leaf parsley or cilantro

Salt

TO SERVE:

Large leaf lettuce

Pickles of any type

Hot sauce

Dana adores pickles. She's also a fan of falafels. So, her typical falafel sandwich includes "a lot of pickled things." Instead of loading pickles onto wraps, though, this recipe packs the patties full of pickles and brine.

1 Pour the chickpeas into a 1-quart Mason jar and add the pickle brine and 1 cup of tap water. Loosely cover with a clean dish towel and leave for 24 hours on the counter, topping with additional water if the chickpeas become exposed.

2 Make the tahini sauce by placing the tahini, garlic, oil, brine, parsley, and ½ tsp salt in the blender. Pulse to combine. Transfer to a bowl, cover, and refrigerate. You don't need to rinse the blender.

3 To make the patties, place the onion, garlic, pickles, dried peppers, cilantro, cumin, and ½ tsp salt in the food processor. Process just until coarse.

4 Drain the chickpeas, discarding the liquid, and pour them into the food processor. Pulse until a coarse mixture (but not a uniform paste) forms.

5 Pour this mixture into a large bowl. Add the flour, 1 Tbsp at a time, mixing with a large spoon, until the mixture sticks together but doesn't cling to your fingers.

6 Cover tightly and refrigerate for 2–3 hours.

7 Preheat the oven to 400°F. Line a baking sheet with parchment paper.

8 Form the falafel mixture into golf balls and flatten. Lightly brush each with olive oil, roll in sesame seeds, and place on the prepared baking sheet. Bake until golden, turning once, 12–15 minutes in total.

9 To serve, line a leaf of lettuce with tahini sauce, add 2–3 falafels, and dress with as many pickles that will fit. Finish with hot sauce.

NOTE If you are using non-fermented pickles made with vinegar, such as the ones on page 195, use ½ cup of brine.

PANTRY RAID: Fermented turnips, pickles (pages 194 and 195), quick pickles (page 194), or fermented carrots (page 155) are great toppings.

Fish Fry with Homemade Tartar

SERVINGS: 4

EFFORT: 30 MINUTES

ELAPSED: 45 MINUTES

HOMEMADE DILL MAYO:

1 egg yolk

1½ tsp fresh lemon juice

1½ tsp pickle brine (any pickle will
do; I prefer dills, page 194)

½ tsp Dijon mustard

1 cup neutral-tasting oil, such as
grapeseed

2 Tbsp chopped fresh dill or 1 tsp
dry dill weed

TARTAR SAUCE:

1 cup mayonnaise

¼ cup pickles (dill if you have them
but any will do), diced small

¼ cup fresh dill, chopped fine

1 Tbsp fresh lemon juice

Cayenne pepper

Powdered mustard

Salt

FISH:

¾ cup all-purpose flour

Salt

Black pepper

2 eggs

Peanut or vegetable oil for frying

1 lb sustainable white fish fillets,
such as perch

My mom was born in Nova Scotia, but it's my dad who is
the King of the Fish Fry. I know that he asked a lot of questions of my Pepe and learned the two secrets to non-greasy
fish: use lots of oil and make sure it gets screaming hot!

This is traditionally served with boiled potatoes seasoned with salt, tartar sauce, and quick pickles. My dad
would preheat the oven to 200°F and keep the fish warm
as he cooked the rest of the meal.

YOU WILL NEED

You can make the mayo with a whisk, but it's easier with a
high-speed blender.

MAKE THE MAYO:

1 Place the egg yolk with the lemon juice, brine, and Dijon in
a blender and mix until incorporated, about 10 seconds.
With the machine still running, slowly drizzle in the oil. It
should take almost 5 minutes to add all the oil, so be patient.
Add the dill right at the end and blend for 5 more seconds.

MAKE THE TARTAR SAUCE:

2 In a bowl, mix the mayonnaise with the pickles, dill, and
lemon juice. Add cayenne pepper, powdered mustard, and
salt to taste. Mix to combine, cover, and refrigerate for at
least 30 minutes.

PREP THE FISH:

3 Scatter the flour on a large plate. Season liberally with salt
and pepper. Place the eggs in a bowl and lightly beat.

4 Preheat a frying pan on medium-high until it's very hot.
Add at least ⅛-inch layer of oil and heat until it just begins to
smoke. Prepare the fish while it heats.

5 Take a piece of fish, pat it dry with paper towel, then dip it
in egg, dredge in flour, and transfer to the pan.

6 Fry until just opaque, 2–3 minutes, flipping once. Repeat
with the remaining fish.

PANTRY RAID: Use infused salt (such as the peach salt on
page 263), herbes salées (page 229), a touch of vinegar, or
dried herbs (page 227) to season the flour.

Rainbow Trout
Kelsere Springs
ON
$14/lb. whole
$16/lb. 6/74
$14/lb. +

ARCTIC
CHARR

WASHINGTON
STATE

Fish

My Meme and Pepe lived in a small fishing village in Cape Breton, Nova Scotia. When they came to visit us in Toronto one year, we indulged my grandmother's deep-seated love for Chinese food by going to a fancy Chinese restaurant for dinner. Shortly after we ordered, the waiter arrived at our table with a covered plate and yanked the cover off to reveal our meal. It was looking right at me.

My grandfather wasted no time. He skillfully portioned and served the fish. He then severed the skull and plopped it onto his plate. He harvested the tongue, cheeks, and eyeballs—his favorite parts. He let me try a cheek, and I was hooked (excuse the pun). He emphasized the importance of using every part of the fish.

In the years that followed, I joined my grandfather on fishing trips for mackerel, and on each trip I saw the fish stock decrease.

Just as the mackerel began to disappear, so did the cod. And then the tuna. And then the fish plant. People started moving west to find work, and communities began to disappear. Sustainable fishing isn't just about sustaining the ocean, it's also about sustaining the communities that depend on it.

There are many apps and websites that can help you identify species and sources of sustainable fish. If you're going to preserve fish, please consider the source. You'll be looking after our oceans and the people who depend on them.

PRESERVING NOSE-TO-TAIL

When I preserve fish, I usually do so one method at a time, although it's quite easy to make several types of jerky, different forms of pressure canned fish, or a combination of the two.

TIPS FOR STORING

Alton Brown has long argued that most frozen fish is fresher than allegedly fresh fish! If you're going to freeze fish, clean and gut it (if necessary), wrap individual pieces in butchers' paper, label them, and store in an airtight bag. To freeze shellfish, remove all the meat from the shells and freeze in a light saltwater brine, which you can rinse off before eating. Lean fish will last up to six months in a freezer while other fish and seafood is typically best if used within two to four months. As with meat, fish should be thawed slowly in the fridge.

FILLING THE PANTRY

CHILLED
Although you can purchase pickled fish, like herring, it is best as a quick pickle and stored in the fridge.

PRESSURE CANNED
Much better than canned fish from the grocery store.

DEHYDRATED
Jerky is delicious.

FERMENTED
Fish sauce is common, and is often unknowingly consumed as Worcestershire sauce.

CURED
Smoked (hot and cold) and salt-cured fish are fantastic.

1 **Smoked Mussels in Olive Oil**
2 **Salmon or Trout Jerky**
3 **Salt-Cured Gravlax in Olive Oil**
4 **Canned Tuna Escabèche**
5 **Cured Sardines**

Smoked Mussels in Olive Oil

SMOKE

LEVEL: ● ● ●

YIELD: 2-3 CUPS

EFFORT: 20 MINUTES

ELAPSED: 2-3 HOURS

EAT: WITHIN 2 DAYS

2 Tbsp unsalted butter, chilled

¼ cup finely chopped onion
  or shallots

3 cloves garlic, thinly sliced

Salt

Black pepper

1 cup chicken or vegetable broth

½ cup dry white wine

3 lb mussels in their shells

1 cup olive oil

YOU WILL NEED

Cold smoker or BBQ with a smoke
  maze (see page 66 to learn how
  to make and use one)

Block of ice and aluminum foil. If it's
  a hot day, cover the ice with foil
  and place the mussels overtop
  before putting them in the smoker.

One night Dana and I were having dinner with our friends
Dan and Kristin Donovan, owners of Hooked and the source
of much of my knowledge about sustainable fish and seafood. We were surprised and delighted when a tray of
crackers, cheese, and smoked mussels marinated in olive
oil appeared on the table. It was the best part of the meal.

COOK THE MUSSELS:

1 In a large pot, melt the butter over medium-high heat. Add
   the onion and garlic, and season with a pinch of salt and
   pepper to taste. Cook until semi-translucent, 4–5 minutes.

2 Add the broth and wine. Turn the heat to high, cover the
   pot, and bring to a boil.

3 Inspect the mussels to make sure they close after being
   lightly tapped on the counter. Discard any that remain
   open—they could be spoiled.

4 Once the broth is boiling, add the mussels to the pot, and
   cover and steam for 5 minutes, or until most of the mussels
   have opened. Discard any that remain closed. Allow the
   mussels to cool enough to handle.

COLD SMOKE THE MUSSELS:

5 Prepare and light your smoker.

6 Open the shells and remove the mussel meat, making sure to
   reserve all the liquid (you can use it to brine scallops or add
   a bit to a stir-fry, chowder, or Bloody Mary).

7 Place the mussels in the smoker and smoke for 90 minutes
   before tasting. If you like the taste, remove them; otherwise,
   continue to smoke for an additional 30–60 minutes.

8 Pack the mussels in a clean jar and cover with olive oil and
   place lid on top. Allow them to rest in the fridge for at least 1
   hour and up to two days. Eat within a week. You can extend
   unused oil or mussels by freezing up to two months. Store it
   in the fridge at all times.

VARIATIONS: If you have a hot smoker, smoke them at 145°F
  for 90–120 minutes in Step 7.

CENTER OF THE PLATE: Eat these with cheese, stir them into
  an omelet, or serve them with pasta and tomato sauce.

Salmon or Trout Jerky

DEHYDRATE

LEVEL: ● ● ○

YIELD: ¼–½ LB

EFFORT: 20 MINUTES

ELAPSED: 1 DAY

EAT: WITHIN 3–6 MONTHS

½ cup cedar wood chips (optional)

¾ cup soy sauce

2 Tbsp rice vinegar

1 Tbsp wasabi (use less if you
    prefer mild)

2 Tbsp honey

2 lb salmon or trout, skin removed

Vegetable oil

YOU WILL NEED

Dehydrator

This jerky isn't subtle. Some of the flavors of the salmon will be engulfed by the stronger flavors of the wood-infused soy sauce and wasabi. The heavier flavors are inspired by the way I eat sushi (with too much wasabi and soy sauce) and they taste great with an ice-cold lager in the hottest days of summer.

1 In a well-ventilated kitchen, place the wood chips, if using, in a large pot and heat on medium-high until they just begin to smoke (this will only take a few minutes). Cover them with the soy sauce, rice vinegar, and honey, and boil on high for 3 minutes. Remove from the heat and allow the mixture to cool for 30 minutes. Pour the liquid through a fine sieve to separate out the wood chips. Set the wood chips aside and use them to smoke other things on another day.

2 Add the wasabi to the marinade as it cools.

3 Cut fish into 4-inch-long by ¼-inch-thick strips, taking care to cut in the direction of the grain.

4 Place the fish and marinade in a container. Cover and refrigerate for 30 minutes and up to 3 hours, but no longer.

5 Strain the fish and pat it dry to remove any excess marinade. Brush your dehydrator trays with vegetable or cooking oil, and place the fish in a single layer with space between pieces for the air to flow. Dehydrate at 155°F for 8–10 hours.

6 When the jerky is dry, preheat the oven to 275°F. Spread the jerky in a single layer on rimmed baking trays and bake for 10 minutes. Allow the pieces to cool, blot the surfaces (some final moisture may have released from the fish in the oven), and seal in airtight containers. Store in the fridge.

VARIATIONS: Adding 2 Tbsp chopped garlic and/or ginger and ¼ cup orange juice while the marinade cooks (and before straining) is another neat combination.

CENTER OF THE PLATE: I eat this as is, but you could make a sandwich out of it (it is an awesome replacement for bacon in a BLT), add it to a hearty salad, spoon it on top of cooked rice, or warm it in evaporated milk like my Pepe would do!

Salt-Cured Gravlax in Olive Oil

SALT

LEVEL: ● ○ ○

YIELD: 1 LB

EFFORT: 15 MINUTES

ELAPSED: 2 DAYS

EAT: WITHIN 10 DAYS

1 lb salmon fillet, skin on

1 Tbsp maple syrup

1 Tbsp powdered mustard

3 Tbsp kosher salt

3 Tbsp fresh lemon juice

2 tsp lemon zest

3 shallots, shaved with a mandolin

3–4 bay leaves

2–3 large sprigs of dill
    (or 2 tsp dried dill weed)

Olive oil

YOU WILL NEED

Terrine pan, bread pan, or small
    bowl that will hold the salmon

Gravlax is one of the easiest preserves in the world to make. Season the fish, cover it in salt and something sweet, and wait for a few days before rinsing well. This recipe elevates it further with a soak in a bath of oil.

1 Coat the salmon in maple syrup before scattering the mustard and salt on all sides. Press the dried ingredients into the fish to coat. Mix together the lemon juice and zest, shallots, bay leaves, and dill to make a cure. Place the salmon in a snug container, pour over the cure, seal tightly, and refrigerate for 24 hours.

2 Thoroughly rinse the fish under running water, discard any liquid, and clean the container and return the fish to it.

3 Cover the fish with olive oil, cover tightly, and refrigerate for another 24 hours.

4 To serve, cut into thin slices. As your knife nears the skin (which will be thick from curing), turn it away from you to remove the skin.

VARIATIONS: Replace the maple syrup with honey, add black peppercorns to the cure, or cold smoke for 2 hours after curing and before resting in olive oil.

CENTER OF THE PLATE: Serve with bagels and cream cheese, or create a wonderful sandwich with aioli. You can also make a salad by chopping some and mixing it with diced fresh English cucumbers (with the seeds removed), dill, salt, Spanish onions, and a touch of crème fraîche.

TIP: TRANSPORTING FROZEN FISH

My parents frequently brought fish home from Nova Scotia on summer road trips. When packing, Pepe would tell us that "cold eats cold." He meant that once frozen fish started to thaw, it would pull the cold out of the other fish and start to thaw them. If you want to keep fish frozen in a cooler, each piece should be individually wrapped in newsprint to insulate it from the other fish and prevent any thawing. We used this technique for years and would often arrive home after two days of driving with a cooler filled with completely frozen fish.

Canned Tuna Escabèche

PRESSURE CAN

LEVEL: ● ● ○

YIELD: 3-4 HALF-PINT JARS

EFFORT: 30 MINUTES

ELAPSED: 2½ HOURS

EAT: WITHIN 6-9 MONTHS

1½ lb fresh tuna (avoid the
   darkest cuts), skin removed

½ cup olive oil

¼ cup white wine vinegar

¼ cup dry white wine

6 garlic cloves, shaved

2 tsp sweet paprika

2 tsp coarse salt

1 tsp black pepper

When we turned 40 we decided to celebrate by joining two friends, Paul and Paul, on a once-in-a-lifetime trip to Spain. We chose Spain in large part because of their reverence for preserved food.

Canned tuna is often considered better than fresh fish in Spain. The homemade version is more expensive than store-bought, but it's better in every other way.

Small magnesium-phosphate crystals sometimes form in canned tuna. According to the National Center for Home Food Preservation, these usually disappear when heated and are safe to eat.

1   Prepare the pressure canner, jars, and canning supplies (see pages 21–23).

2   Cut the fish into 1-inch cubes (approximately).

3   Prepare the brine by placing the oil, vinegar, and wine in a large pot and adding the garlic, paprika, salt, and pepper. Bring to a boil on high before lowering to a simmer for 3 minutes. Reduce the heat to just below a simmer until you're ready to process.

4   When your canner is near boiling, assemble the jars. Pour some brine into each jar, pack with a layer of fish, add more brine, and repeat until the jars have only 1 inch of headspace. Use the back of a spoon or a chopstick to release any air bubbles and ensure the fish is covered.

5   Wipe the rims, place lids on top, and secure rings in place. Pressure can at 10 lb of pressure for 100 minutes following the instructions of your canner (if you live higher than 1,000 feet above sea level, refer to the Adjust for Altitude chart on page 25 for additional processing time).

6   Turn the heat off and allow the canner to cool naturally for at least 1 hour. Store the jars on a shelf out of direct sunlight.

VARIATIONS: Add a hot pepper or 1 tsp of mustard seeds to the bottom of each jar before filling.

CENTER OF THE PLATE: A sandwich or casserole are obvious uses; you can also eat it straight from the jar.

Freezing Shellfish

To preserve shellfish, cook it, remove the shells, allow it to cool, and submerge the meat in salt water in freezer bags. If you don't have access to seawater, you can make your own version at home. The best way to make salt water is with a scale, as the different sizes of salt grains alter the volume dramatically. The salt should weigh about 2½%–3½% of the weight of the water.

Cured Sardines

SALT

LEVEL: ● ○ ○

YIELD: 4 APPETIZERS (12 SARDINE
FILLETS)

EFFORT: 20 MINUTES

ELAPSED: 1–2 DAYS

EAT: WITHIN 1–2 DAYS

3 preserved or canned plum
tomatoes (page 333) plus 3 Tbsp
of the liquid

¼ cup olive oil

2 cloves garlic, shaved

¼ cup flat-leaf parsley, chopped fine
then measured

Coarse salt

Black pepper

6 fresh sardines, filleted with skin on

1 lemon

2 tsp white wine vinegar

2 Tbsp chives, finely chopped
then measured

Filleting a sardine is easier than it may sound: assuming it has been gutted and cleaned, you remove the tail and dorsal fin. You then cut around the head, touching the spine but not severing it, and then use your fingers to "unzip" the spine and separate the bones from the head to the tail. A friendly fishmonger may be willing to do this for you but I think you're up for the challenge!

This recipe is inspired by the venerable Alice Waters, who consistently inspires us in and out of the kitchen. If you're hosting a dinner party, you can assemble this one or two days in advance, as it will improve over time.

1 Place the liquid from the tomatoes in a bowl. Cut the tomatoes in half, and squeeze as much of their liquid as you can into the bowl. Finely chop the tomatoes and add any excess liquid to the bowl. Set the tomato pieces aside.

2 In a large pot, place the olive oil, garlic, parsley, and tomato pieces and add ½ tsp salt and pepper. Heat on medium-high until the oil shimmers, about 3–4 minutes. Remove the pot from the heat and transfer the contents to a bowl. Cover and chill in the freezer for 10 minutes.

3 Season the fish with salt and pepper.

4 Cut the lemon in half. Squeeze the juice of one half into the oil mixture. Add the tomato liquid and vinegar to the oil for your brine. Cut the remaining lemon half into extra-thin slices, add them to the brine, and then add the fish. Make sure the fish is well coated, then cover tightly and refrigerate. It is ready to eat after 1 hour but will improve in the next 24–48 hours.

5 To serve, remove the fish from the brine and lightly drain it or pat it dry. Garnish with chives before serving.

VARIATIONS: Replace 2 Tbsp of the olive oil with sesame oil or replace the white wine vinegar with sherry vinegar.

CENTER OF THE PLATE: Serve the fish as is on a cheese tray with crackers, or overtop a plate of arugula dressed with lemon juice and olive oil. They can also be lightly fried or grilled.

Fishcakes

SERVINGS: 4

EFFORT: 30 MINUTES

ELAPSED: 45 MINUTES

½–1 cup gravlax (page 206), according to taste, roughly chopped then measured

3 cups mashed potatoes, with or without skins (5–6 medium potatoes if boiling from scratch)

1 egg, lightly beaten

1 large onion, diced

2 tsp powdered mustard

½ tsp sweet paprika

Coarse salt

Black pepper

⅓ cup all-purpose flour

Vegetable oil for frying

Although crab cakes take center stage at most restaurants, fishcakes are the star of the show in my family. They were often made from leftover boiled or mashed potatoes with other leftover veggies tossed in. We ate these with a salad for dinner and with fried eggs for breakfast. And I liked to add ketchup or mustard pickles. You can keep the cooked fishcakes warm in a 200°F oven while cooking the others. These also freeze well. To do so, lay them on a cookie sheet and wrap in plastic. Once they are frozen solid (overnight will do), transfer to a container with as much air removed as possible.

1 If the gravlax is very salty, you can soak it in cold water for an hour or more before cooking. Taste as it soaks (cooking will not remove the salt). My family preferred very salty fishcakes and often made them from salt cod when the fish still thrived in the Atlantic.

2 Mix the potatoes with the gravlax, egg, onion, mustard, and paprika in a large bowl. Season liberally with salt and pepper.

3 Spread the flour on a plate and season liberally with salt and pepper.

4 Form the mixture into 8–10 large patties, about ⅔ cup of the mixture in each.

5 Preheat the oven to 200°F.

6 Dredge the cakes in the flour and place them in a single layer on a plate or baking tray.

7 Heat a large frying pan on medium-high then add enough oil to shallow-fry the cakes. The oil should be at least ⅛-inch deep. Cook the fishcakes in batches, adding oil as needed, making sure to leave room between each one. Keep the cooked cakes warm in the oven while you cook the rest.

PANTRY RAID: Serve with pickled beets (page 124), hot sauce (page 176), tartar sauce (page 200), quick pickled onions, or cucumbers.

Maritime Chowder with Smoked Mussels

SERVINGS: 6–8

EFFORT: 25 MINUTES

ELAPSED: 45 MINUTES

1 Tbsp unsalted butter, chilled

1 Tbsp olive oil

1 large onion, chopped into
    ½-inch pieces

2 cloves garlic, minced

3 medium carrots, shredded

2 stalks celery, chopped into
    ½-inch pieces

¼ tsp dried thyme

¼ tsp sweet paprika

6 medium red potatoes, skin on,
    chopped to ½-inch cubes

Salt (the salt and/or liquid from
    preserved lemons on page 185
    is ideal)

Black pepper

3 medium red potatoes, skin on,
    grated

6 cups (1–1½ quarts) fish or chicken
    stock

2 bay leaves

1 lb skinless white fish, cut into
    bite-sized cubes

1 lb or more smoked mussels
    (page 204), weight with the shell
    on

1 cup evaporated milk or heavy
    (35%) cream

2 Tbsp fresh lemon juice
    (about ½ lemon)

¼ cup flat-leaf parsley, measured
    then chopped

Once you've made chowder a few times you'll find it's a pretty easy dish to put together. This recipe was my grandmother's, and it always seemed to taste better on Day 2. Serve this as a main or a side with some tea biscuits (see page 222).

1 Heat a large frying pan over medium-high heat. Add the butter and olive oil.

2 When the oil and butter just begin to smoke, add the onion and garlic and cook for 90 seconds, stirring occasionally. Add the carrots, celery, thyme, and paprika and cook for 3 more minutes, stirring occasionally.

3 Add the potato cubes, season with salt and pepper, and cook for 3 minutes, stirring occasionally.

4 Transfer the cooked veggies to a large pot and add the grated potatoes, stock, and bay leaves. Place over high heat and cook until it begins to simmer. Turn down the heat and maintain at a low simmer for 10 minutes.

5 Add the fish and continue to simmer for 5 minutes.

6 Remove the mussels from oil and allow them to drain for a few minutes (there's no need to pat them dry). Add the mussels to the pot.

7 Once the mussels are warm, about 3 minutes, finish with evaporated milk, lemon juice, and parsley. Add salt and pepper to taste.

PANTRY RAID: Try serving with a touch of hot pepper or pickle brine (page 195), or celeriac powder. A side of fermented carrots (page 155) works with this, too.

Grapes

Grapes are an amazing fruit. Their tough skin protects the delicate flesh from the extremities of the outside world. I had dehydrated several things before I decided to make raisins. With blissful ignorance I placed small bunches (the stems still attached) onto drying racks and put them in the dehydrator. I was sure that they'd be done overnight.

When I woke up the next morning, the grapes looked identical to the night before. They were slightly smaller after 24 hours. By "slightly," I mean they hadn't really changed at all.

A tiny bit of progress was showing after the second day. And a bit more after the fourth. By the sixth day it was clear that something was happening but it was going to take a lifetime to make raisins. I gave up.

A few years later I went back to the drawing board. This time I used a large needle to poke holes into them (this allows the moisture to escape) and the results were staggering!

There are few homemade foods that are so much better than their commercial counterpart than the humble raisin. They are candy-like in their initial sweetness but the tartness of their skin balances the flavors in a way that demands your attention!

PRESERVING NOSE-TO-TAIL

- **SEED** Bitter and inedible.
- **FLESH** The sweetest part. It is remarkably easy to peel grapes: blanch them in boiling water and put in an ice bath to cool.
- **JUICE** Extracted by a food mill, juicer, or steam juicer. Fermented, frozen, or waterbathed.
- **SKIN** More bitter than the sweet flesh behind it. It can be a pleasant contrast when the flavors are concentrated (as happens when you make raisins or jelly). Can be dehydrated into powder.
- **STEMS** Not a great preserving ingredient but useful as a handle when blanching large amounts or for processing with a steam juicer.

TIPS FOR STORING

Store, unwashed, in an airtight container pushed against the back wall of your fridge (where it is coldest).

FILLING THE PANTRY

CHILLED
Quick pickle or freeze the fruit and juice.

CANNED
Jelly, juice, and jam.

DEHYDRATED
Raisins!

FERMENTED
Wine is a specialized skill, and many people spend a lifetime perfecting it. Homemade (alcoholic) cordial can be a surprising alternative.

1 Grape Cordial (non-alcoholic)
2 Grape Hooch (alcoholic)
3 Roasted Grape Onion Chutney
4 Raisins
5 Quick Pickled Grapes

Batch-It

Roasted Grape Onion Chutney

CELLAR

LEVEL: ● ● ○

YIELD: 1½–2½ CUPS

EFFORT: 15 MINUTES

ELAPSED: 45 MINUTES

EAT: WITHIN 3 MONTHS

2 Tbsp fat (lard or any
    vegetable oil), divided

6 medium white onions

2 cloves garlic, minced

Coarse salt

Black pepper

Ground cinnamon

Cayenne or chili powder

2–3 lb seedless grapes, stems
    removed (I use a combination
    of red and white)

3 Tbsp maple syrup

1½ Tbsp balsamic vinegar

2 Tbsp fresh lemon juice
    (about ½ a lemon)

A steam juicer makes preserving fruit juices a breeze. We put 5–6 lb of grapes (stems included) into our juicer and are rewarded with pure fruit juice within 30–40 minutes.

Although chutneys are most commonly associated with waterbath preserving, I like to make them for the fridge/freezer because I tend to eat small amounts of them. Because the chutney involves roasting the grapes, you'll find that you have ample free time to make the cordial. I often make combinations like this during the week as a way to relax and unwind from my day.

ROAST THE GRAPES AND CARAMELIZE THE ONIONS FOR THE CHUTNEY:

1   Preheat the oven to 500°F. Grease a rimmed baking tray with 1 Tbsp of the fat and place it in the oven.

2   Cut the onions in half between the root and stem. Then cut rounds, and halve them so you get strips (not rings).

3   When the oven reaches temperature, carefully scatter grapes on baking tray (it may splatter) and cook for 4–5 minutes. Carefully shake the grapes at least once in this process. When done, remove from the oven and set aside.

4   Place a large frying pan over medium-high heat. Add the remaining 1 Tbsp of fat and heat until it just begins to smoke. Add the onion strips, garlic, ½ tsp salt, and pepper to taste. Finish with a ¼ tsp of cinnamon and the same amount of cayenne. Cook for 5 minutes, stirring frequently to prevent burning.

5   Add the maple syrup, vinegar, and lemon juice, and cook, stirring occasionally to prevent burning, until the onions are caramelized. This should take 20–25 minutes. Remove from the heat.

Grape Cordial (Non-Alcoholic)

WATERBATH

LEVEL: ● ● ○

YIELD: 4 HALF-PINT JARS

EFFORT: 10 MINUTES

ELAPSED: 1½ HOURS

DRINK: WITHIN 1–2 YEARS

4 lb grapes
Sugar or honey to taste (optional)

YOU WILL NEED

Juicer (steam or conventional).
If you don't have a juicer, you can cook the grapes with ½ cup of water, crushing them as they cook and then straining. Because the yield will be less with this method you should double the amount of grapes.

JUICE, REDUCE, AND BOTTLE THE CORDIAL:

6 Prepare your canning pot and rack, and sterilize your jars and lids (see page 17).

7 Juice the grapes and bring them to a simmer over medium-high heat. Add sweetener to taste.

8 Remove the jars from the canner and turn the heat to high.

9 Fill the jars with grape juice, leaving ¼ inch of headspace. Gently jostle the jars or use the handle of a spoon to release any air bubbles.

10 Wipe the rims of the jars, apply the lids, and process for 5 minutes (if you live higher than 1,000 feet above sea level, refer to the Adjust for Altitude chart on page 17 for additional processing time).

11 Turn the burner off, leaving the pot in place, and allow the jars to sit in the canner for 20–30 minutes (this will help prevent syphoning which is common in thin liquids such as cordials). Remove the jars and allow them to cool.

COMPLETE THE CHUTNEY:

12 Allow the grapes to cool. Roughly chop them and add to the onions. Add the lemon juice. Reduce the mixture by simmering on medium-high until a thin layer of liquid remains on the bottom of the pot. Taste and season to taste with additional salt, pepper, or maple syrup. Transfer to a clean Mason jar or other airtight container and store in the fridge. If you plan to use this for cooking, such as adding to roast chicken or vegetables, this will also freeze well in a yogurt tub where it will keep for three to six months.

10 Minutes or less

Grape Hooch (Alcoholic)

FERMENT

LEVEL: ● ● ○

YIELD: 32 OZ/1 QUART

DRINK: AFTER 3 MONTHS AND WITHIN 2–3
   YEARS (WILL IMPROVE WITH AGE)

1½ –2½ lb Concord grapes
   (other varieties will work)
Granulated sugar
½ tsp champagne or ale yeast
Filtered water

YOU WILL NEED

1 quart standard mouth Mason jar
Airlock with a size 12 or 13 stopper

Most people I speak with are surprised by how easy it is to make booze. I often make a quart at a time using this technique (it works equally well with cherries and other fruit). We kiddingly refer to this as "hooch" and it shouldn't be confused with wine. It's a simple alcohol that can be made with 5 minutes of free time and a bit of patience.

DAY 1:

1 Cut enough grapes in half to fill the Mason jar. Add sugar to fill the spaces between the fruit. Place the airlock on top. Allow to ferment out of direct sunlight.

DAY 10:

2 Strain the solids from the liquid. You can dehydrate these solids though they will taste very boozy. Return the juice to the Mason jar (no need to clean it as it will likely have some yeast inside), add ¼ cup sugar, and stir until dissolved. Add the yeast and top with filtered water, leaving 1 inch of headspace. Place the airlock on the jar and leave for three weeks (ensuring the water in the airlock stays topped up), or until the fermenting subsides. Rack into a new jar or bottle, taking care not to transfer any sediment. Drink fresh, age in the fridge, or bottle as you would for fruit wines for longer storage. You can also age in the Mason jar you made it in as long as you are vigilant about keeping the water in the airlock topped up.

TIP: A SECRET STASH

I keep two large Tupperware containers hidden in our basement. One is filled with sugar, vinegar, salt, various pickling spices, a large bottle of filtered water, and a bottle of vodka. The other contains lids and jars of all sizes. These are my emergency supplies, and they have bailed me out many times when I'm in the middle of a preserving session and realize I am missing something. I rotate the inventory to keep things fresh and I have never been caught short!

10 Minutes or less

Quick Pickled Grapes

CELLAR

LEVEL: ● ○ ○

YIELD: 1 QUART

EAT: AFTER 1 WEEK AND WITHIN 3
MONTHS

1 organic lemon
1½–2½ lb grapes
1 cup white wine vinegar
¼ cup honey

I love combining sweet and sour, and pickled grapes are an easy way to do that. They can be eaten as a snack or added to salads or mild-tasting food like white fish and chicken. Try roasting them to intensify the flavor blend.

Cut the lemon into thin rounds, discarding the pith-filled tops and bottoms. Place the lemon in a 1-quart Mason jar (or other container). Clean and halve the grapes, removing any seeds, and filling the Mason jar as you go. Leave 1 inch of headspace. Place the vinegar, 1 cup tap water, and honey in a pot and bring to a boil over high heat. Immediately pour the liquid into the jar to cover the grapes leaving 1 inch headspace (it's OK if you have more than this; just shake the jar a few times a day for the first few days to distribute the grapes). Place an airtight lid on top and transfer to the fridge to sit for a week before eating.

Raisins

DEHYDRATE

LEVEL: ● ○ ○

YIELD: 1 CUP

EAT: WITHIN 1–2 YEARS

1 bunch (2–3 lb) seedless grapes

YOU WILL NEED
Dehydrator
A large sewing needle
or old meat thermometer

I will never tire of watching people's reactions to their first taste of homemade raisins. I place a bowl of them in front of unsuspecting guests as often as possible. It doesn't take long before they absent-mindedly reach into the bowl and pop a few homemade raisins into their mouth. The look on their face when the explosion of flavor hits them makes me smile every time.

Boil the needle to sterilize it. Gently rinse the grapes and remove them from their stems. Working carefully, stick the needle cleanly through each grape. The holes will be hidden by the wrinkles in the raisins. Any grapes you miss will take far longer to dry. Spread the grapes on dehydrator trays, leaving space between them. Dry at 135°F until completely dry, about 16–20 hours. Store in a container with a lid.

Roasted Chicken with Pickled Grapes

SERVINGS: 3-4

EFFORT: 20 MINUTES

ELAPSED: 45 MINUTES

1½ tsp onion powder

1½ tsp celery or mushroom powder
(page 251)

½ tsp cayenne pepper

½ tsp sweet paprika

Salt

Black pepper

Chicken thighs and legs (3 pieces of
each), bone in and skin on

½ cup chicken stock

½ tsp grape pickle brine (page 219),
or more to taste

1 cup quick pickled grapes
(page 219)

YOU WILL NEED

Roasting pan with rack

Chicken thighs and legs are often not only the cheapest parts of the chicken but also the most flavorful.

1 Preheat the oven to 350°F.

2 Mix the onion powder, celery powder, cayenne, and paprika with ¾ tsp of salt and pepper to taste. Pat the chicken dry and rub the spice mixture into each piece.

3 Place the chicken on the roasting pan, leaving space between each piece. Bake, uncovered, for 30–40 minutes, or until the chicken reaches an internal temperature of 165°F.

4 Once the chicken is done, remove the baking tray and rack from the oven. Place the rack on a cutting board. Tent with aluminum foil and let the chicken rest for 10–15 minutes.

5 Carefully add the stock and brine to the roasting pan. Stir to deglaze the pan and then transfer the contents to a small pot. Skim off any fat, bring to a simmer over medium heat, and add the pickled grapes.

6 Transfer this sauce to a serving dish and lay the chicken on top (this will keep the skin crunchy).

PANTRY RAID: Instead of using pickled grapes, rehydrate raisins in grape juice. You can also add herbes salées (page 229) or fermented hot sauce (page 176) to season.

Frozen Grapes

Frozen grapes are lousy when they're thawed but they're amazing to eat frozen—or to use as ice cubes. Remove and discard the stems. Wash the grapes and toss them in sugar while still damp (optional). Place them on a towel to air-dry for 15 minutes (you could also put them in the dehydrator on its highest setting for 5 minutes to dry), transfer to a rimmed baking tray, and spread in a single layer. Freeze until solid and then transfer to a freezer bag or airtight container.

Tea Biscuits with Raisins and Pistachios

MAKES: 10–12 BISCUITS

EFFORT: 20 MINUTES

ELAPSED: 40 MINUTES

¼ cup raisins (page 219)

3 Tbsp roughly chopped pistachios (measured after chopping)

2 cups all-purpose flour

4 tsp baking powder

1 tsp sea salt

2 Tbsp frozen butter, grated with a cheese grater and returned to freezer until needed

2 Tbsp lard (or butter)

1 cup cold buttermilk

2 tsp maple syrup or honey

2 eggs, lightly beaten

I'm a big fan of tea biscuits. We slather them with jam, dip them in soup, and eat them with BBQ food. It's also a highly adaptable recipe; replace the raisins and pistachios with other preserves and you'll have success every time.

Work the dough as little as possible to keep the butter from melting before it's added to the stove. You may even wish to chill your spoon and bowl before using them, but don't be overly concerned.

1 Boil a pot of water. Place the raisins in a mug or heat-proof pan, cover them in boiling water, and allow them to rest at least 10 minutes before draining and patting dry.

2 Preheat the oven to 425°F.

3 Mix the raisins, pistachios, flour, baking powder, and salt in a large bowl. Add the frozen butter and the lard with a spoon. Use a spoon to mix it to prevent the butter from melting.

4 Create a well in the center of the dry ingredients. Add the buttermilk and maple syrup. Stir with the handle of the spoon to incorporate.

5 Rinse your hands under the coldest water you can stand for at least 30 seconds. Wipe them dry and lightly flour your hands before proceeding.

6 Scatter flour on a cutting board and place your dough on top. Stretch and fold the dough onto itself five or six times and lightly press down on it until it is 1 inch thick.

7 Use a 2-inch cookie cutter or a glass to cut out the biscuits. You can assemble any trimmings into another sheet and cut again. These "seconds" won't be as flaky as the original cuttings and are often my testers.

8 Brush the egg wash on the biscuits.

9 Bake for 12–15 minutes, until brown and cooked throughout.

10 Serve immediately with butter and jelly!

PANTRY RAID: It's easy to make and you can add up to ⅓ cup of additional ingredients to make it sweet or savory. Replace the raisins and pistachios with 2 Tbsp of chopped fermented hot peppers (page 177) and a ¼ cup of cheddar, or ¼ cup of dried cherries and ¼ cup of brie.

Herbs

My mom has always grown herbs, sometimes in pots, sometimes scattered through a flower garden, but they were always something to proud of.

I was in my late teens or early twenties when I read that sage could be dried and burned like incense. When Mom told me she was done gardening for the year, I started drying bunches of sage. Once the leaves had curled into cylinders, they were easy to pluck, and I'd light them on fire before quickly blowing them out and letting them smolder for a few seconds. The smoke has no intoxicating properties and turning my sage into incense became a lovely tradition, and one I took with great seriousness.

It took me almost two decades to realize that I could have cooked with that sage and other herbs.

As a side note, there is no Batch-It recipe in this chapter since herbs are so quick and easy to work with. The recipes are easy to combine, so experiment and try a few!

PRESERVING NOSE-TO-TAIL

Herbs come in all shapes and sizes. They generally have two parts, but I see them as three:

- **LEAVES.** Commonly used and fragile. Often dried or salt-cured.
- **EDIBLE STEMS.** These are flavorful and can be eaten. Long, flexible stems, such as parsley or basil stems, can remain whole and be eaten, dried, fermented, and more.
- **WOODY ENDS.** Found in thyme, for example, these are not edible but are useful when drying. They keep the leaves from falling off until you want to remove them. Remove dried herbs from woody stems by placing the dried product in a large jar or a bowl with a lid and shaking it like mad. The stems aren't overly useful, but could be turned into a gentle smoke.

TIPS FOR STORING

Herbs are easy to store, though they can be a little picky. If you wrap them too tightly, they will mold. I have found the best way to store them is to wrap them loosely in a paper towel and store them in a container.

FILLING THE PANTRY

CANNED
Mint and other jellies.

DEHYDRATED
Herbs dry remarkably well.

CURED
Herbes salées, or herbs preserved in salt, are an absolute must-have in our fridge. We use them throughout the winter in almost all of our cooking.

INFUSED
Herb vinegars are easy to make and store well.

1 Fermented Green Chutney
2 Lemon-Mint Fridge Jelly
3 Air-Dried Herbs
4 Herbes Salées
5 Thyme-Infused Honey
6 Frozen Herb Butter

Lemon-Mint Fridge Jelly

CELLAR

LEVEL: ◉ ◉ ○

YIELD: 1 PINT JAR

EFFORT: 15 MINUTES

ELAPSED: 45 MINUTES

EAT: WITHIN 10 DAYS,
   BUT WILL LAST LONGER

6 lemons (about 1 cup after cooking
   and juicing per below)

½ cup honey, divided, plus more to
   brush the lemons

2 tsp calcium water

2 tsp Pomona's Pectin

2 loose cups fresh mint, divided

When making jelly, one often needs to use pectin as a thickener. Most commercial pectin is incredibly bitter and requires a lot of sugar to make the jelly edible; a notable exception is Pomona's Pectin. I used it to make this very tart jelly. I prefer not to waterbath my herb jelly as it allows me to add a touch of fresh herbs at the end, which bring out the flavors.

1 Heat the BBQ to medium-high. Wash the lemons and cut them in half horizontally. Spread a light coat of honey on the lemon flesh and place on the grill, flesh side down. BBQ until the lemons are golden brown, about 5–10 minutes. Remove from the BBQ, allow to cool, then juice them. If you don't have a BBQ, char them in a dry frying pan.

2 Combine the lemon juice with ¼ cup honey and calcium water.

3 In a separate bowl, combine the pectin and ¼ cup honey and stir well. Set aside.

4 Place ⅔ of the mint in a pot with 1⅔ cup tap water, bring to a boil over high heat, and boil for 1 minute. Remove from the heat and allow mixture to steep for 10–15 minutes.

5 Strain the solids from the mint-infused water, discard them, and combine the liquid with the lemon-honey calcium water.

6 Bring the ingredients to a full boil on high heat. Add the honey-pectin water, and boil for 1 minute.

7 Remove from the heat and test the jelly for set (see the freezer method on page 13). If it doesn't set, bring it back to a boil for another minute and test again.

8 Chop the remaining mint, add it to a clean jar, and pour the jelly into it. Place the lid on, and shake to distribute the herbs. Store in the fridge for two to three months.

VARIATIONS: You can also add two mint tea bags to step 4 to make this even mintier!

CENTER OF THE PLATE: I use this for glazing meat and fish or serving as a condiment to anything that's been roasted.

10 Minutes or less

Frozen Herb Butter

CELLAR

LEVEL: ● ○ ○

YIELD: 2 CUPS (1 LB)

EAT: WITHIN 3 MONTHS

2 cups room-temperature butter

1 cup chopped fresh herbs (I like a
    mixture of thyme, rosemary, sage,
    and chives)

2 cloves garlic, finely chopped

Air-Dried Herbs

DEHYDRATE

LEVEL: ● ○ ○

YIELD: 1 BUNCH

EAT: WITHIN 1–2 YEARS

1 bunch herbs such as thyme,
    parsley, or chives. Avoid basil.

My garden generally produces lots of herbs in the late fall, and I always look for quick ways to preserve them through the winter. This butter is fantastically easy and very versatile.

Mix the butter with the herbs and garlic in a large bowl. Scoop onto plastic wrap and form into a "sausage." Freeze solid. When you want to use a piece, heat a knife under hot running water and cut what you need. You can add it to a frying pan (or other hot cooking) from frozen or let it thaw first.

Thick-skinned herbs, such as sage, thyme, rosemary, and summer savory, preserve really well; thinner-skinned herbs, such as parsley and basil, don't. I have several small S-hooks in my kitchen that allow me to hang herbs almost anywhere. If you live in a dusty environment, you may wish to wrap the herbs in a paper bag that has holes poked in it for the drying process.

Clean and dry the herbs. Grab them in a bunch, tie their stems together, and fan the ends to give them room to breathe. Hang on a shelf or in a closet until they are bone dry and brittle (this should take a few days depending on how humid your house is). After drying, store herbs whole in a clean, dry container.

> **TIP: BIG OVER SMALL**
>
> Many grocery store herbs and spices have sat in shipping containers, warehouses, and stores for weeks, months, or even years before you bring them home. In some cases, they are stored in open oxygen or environments that will degrade their flavors. Nothing can compare to the flavor of home-dried herbs and spices. And you know exactly how fresh they are. When storing homemade herbs, keep in mind one golden rule: larger pieces will retain their flavors longer than smaller pieces (including powders).

Fermented Green Chutney

FERMENT

This is loosely based on a South Indian green chutney I once tried. When done right, green chutney is the most flavor-balanced food I've ever eaten. I like to cook the herbs and ingredients because it helps stimulate their natural oils and produce more flavor.

LEVEL: ● ○ ○
YIELD: 1 QUART
EFFORT: 15 MINUTES
ELAPSED: 3–7 DAYS
EAT: WITHIN 1 MONTH

2 cups fresh mint, chopped then measured

1 cup cilantro, chopped then measured

1 small onion, chopped then measured

6 cloves garlic, chopped then measured

4 Thai chilies, chopped fine

2 Tbsp ginger, chopped then measured

1 Tbsp olive oil

⅔ cup almonds, roughly chopped after measuring

1 Tbsp cumin seeds, roughly chopped after measuring

1 Tbsp honey

1 Tbsp salt

1 cup filtered water

¼ cup whey

YOU WILL NEED
1-quart Mason jar with airlock

1 Add the oil to a heavy frying pan on medium-high heat. Wilt the mint and cilantro, for 30–90 seconds, remove from the pan, and set aside.

2 Place the onion, garlic, chilies, ginger, and carrot in the frying pan and cook until they just begin to soften, about 5 minutes.

3 Toast the almonds and cumin seeds in a separate, dry pan until the almonds just begin to darken (this should only take a few minutes).

4 Add all ingredients to a blender or food processor and puree to desired thickness (I like to see some chunks; others like a uniform consistency).

5 Place the chutney in a clean Mason jar. If the jar is not completely full, add filtered water until the level reaches the neck of the jar.

6 Secure with an airlock and place out of direct sunlight. Check daily. If scum appears, skim it off, but otherwise leave the jar undisturbed. Taste after three or four days. It will become increasingly sour with time, but you can refrigerate it when you're happy with the taste (it is generally ready within a week of starting).

VARIATIONS: Add extra hot pepper, use 2 Tbsp sugar instead of the honey, or add ¼ cup chopped chives.

CENTER OF THE PLATE: Use this anywhere you would use salsa or relish.

10 Minutes or less

Herbes Salées

SALT

LEVEL: ● ○ ○

YIELD: 1 QUART

EAT: WITHIN 6–12 MONTHS

2 cups fresh parsley, chopped
   then measured

½ cup fresh chives, chopped
   then measured

2 Tbsp fresh thyme, chopped
   then measured

1 Tbsp fresh rosemary, chopped
   then measured

1 cup carrots, diced then measured

1 cup leeks, diced then measured

¾ cup coarse salt

1 tsp celery seeds

YOU WILL NEED

You can use a food processor to
   speed up this recipe and chop the
   herbs. I generally spend a bit
   more time and chop everything
   by hand.

This is a staple in our kitchen. There's no measuring or ingredient list; we simply combine all the herbs we can get (other than basil) with salt, and add them to a half-gallon jar. Not everyone is so freewheeling. My mother is French Canadian, and her family recipes contain carrots, onions, and summer savory. This recipe is inspired by those traditions.

Toss all ingredients in a large bowl. Transfer ingredients to a clean 1-quart Mason jar. Cover with the lid and place in the fridge. It will take four to five days for the flavors to develop and will get better with time. Store on a cool, dark shelf and use wherever salt is called for.

Thyme-Infused Honey

It's important to use dried thyme for this (the water content in fresh thyme can pose a risk as honey removes oxygen). Lightly toast ten sprigs of thyme to help release the oils, place them on a large cutting board, and lightly pound for a few seconds to bruise slightly. Tie the thyme in a cheesecloth sack and place in a clean pint jar and secure with lid. Top with 1–2 cups of honey.

Taste after three days. You can leave the thyme in place for up to thirty days. Remove it when you like the taste of the honey. Store, covered with the lid, on a dark, cool shelf (it will keep indefinitely).

Roast Leg of Lamb with Goat Cheese

SERVINGS: 6–8

EFFORT: 20 MINUTES

ELAPSED: 1½ HOURS

STUFFING:

¼ cup olive oil

2 large onions, diced

2 cloves garlic, minced

6 Tbsp fermented green chutney
(page 228)

1 tsp Dijon mustard

⅓ cup soft goat cheese

LAMB:

3–4 lb boneless leg of lamb
(weighed without bone); remove
from fridge an hour before
cooking

Coarse salt

Black pepper

⅓ cup Dijon mustard

2 Tbsp spicy green chutney

3 Tbsp vegetable oil

¼ small onion, diced

½ small carrot, diced

1 stalk celery, diced

YOU WILL NEED

Butchers' twine

Meat thermometer

Removing the bone from the leg of lamb creates a natural place for stuffing and speeds up the cooking time. Don't fret too much about doing it perfectly; tie the roast into a cylinder with butchers' twine. Ask your butcher to debone the lamb for you if you don't know how.

PREP THE STUFFING:

1 Heat the oil in a large pan set over medium heat, add the onions, and cook until browned.

2 Add the garlic and cook for 1 minute.

3 Add the chutney and mustard, cook for 30 seconds just to warm them through, and transfer them with the onion and garlic to a bowl. Mix in the goat cheese and set aside to cool.

PREP THE LAMB:

4 Season the lamb liberally with salt and pepper.

5 Mix the mustard and chutney together in a bowl and then rub evenly all over the lamb.

6 Stuff the cavern of the lamb (where the bone was) with the cooled goat cheese stuffing. Tie up with twine.

COOK THE LAMB:

7 Preheat the oven to 325°F.

8 Place a large frying pan (big enough to hold the lamb) on the stovetop over medium heat. Add the oil and heat until it nears its smoking point.

9 Add the onion, carrot, and celery and cook, stirring, until brown.

10 Remove the veggies and place them in a roasting pan. Place the frying pan over high heat, add additional oil, and wait until it just begins to smoke. Sear the meat until brown on all sides, about 2 minutes per side.

11 Rest the lamb on top of the veggies and insert meat thermometer into the thickest part. Roast for 1 hour and check. It is medium-rare when the internal temperature reaches 130°F, which should take about 80 minutes.

12 Remove from the heat, loosely tent with foil, and allow to rest in the pan for 10 minutes.

PANTRY RAID: The lemon-mint fridge jelly (page 226) is an obvious addition when serving.

Roast Potatoes with Herbes Salées

SERVINGS: 4–6

EFFORT: 10 MINUTES

ELAPSED: 45 MINUTES

2½ lb potatoes (Yukon Gold are my
favorite for roasting)

4 Tbsp duck fat, lard, or vegetable
oil, divided

1 Tbsp all-purpose flour

Herbes salées to taste (page 229)

Fresh lemon juice for serving
(optional)

My Aunt Audrey made the best roasted potatoes when I was a child, and I've spent most of my life trying to recreate them. I don't know that I've met her level of potato awesomeness but I know I'm getting close! If there is one Golden Rule about roasted potatoes, it's this: make sure that they are not crowded in the roasting pan. If they are too close they will steam and never brown.

1 Place a large pot of salted water on high heat and bring to a boil.

2 Peel and cut the potatoes into 1-inch cubes. Make sure the cubes are uniformly sized so that they cook evenly. Soak them in cold water until you're ready to cook them.

3 Preheat the oven to 400°F.

4 Put 3 Tbsp of the fat in a roasting pan and melt in the oven while it comes to temperature.

5 When the water is at a full boil, add the potatoes and cook until the edges just begin to soften, about 5 minutes.

6 Drain the potatoes well. Pour them into a large bowl, add the remaining 1 Tbsp of fat, and vigorously toss to coat them in oil and roughen their exteriors. Scatter the flour over the potatoes and toss again.

7 Remove the roasting pan from the oven. Carefully add the potatoes to it (the fat should sizzle!), leaving space between the potatoes so they don't steam up. Roast for 15 minutes, then flip them. Cook for an additional 10–15 minutes, or until all sides are golden brown.

8 Remove from the oven, toss with herbes salées, drizzle with lemon juice if you like, and serve at once.

PANTRY RAID: Add a dusting of any dehydrated food before serving. Mushroom, kimchi, or celeriac powder will all work.

Meat

I have a complicated relationship with meat.

I learned to skin rabbits at five years old, sent pigs to slaughter at twelve, and watched deer get shot at fourteen. I stopped eating red meat, game, and fish for eight years in my twenties, and by my mid-thirties I was the leader of my hunting camp.

I'm proud of the hunting traditions that run deep in my family, and it excites me to share them with Dana and our friends. We use every part of the animal that we can. Hides are donated to the Aboriginal communities, bones are for broth, fat is used for cooking, and inedible trim becomes snacks for my dog.

Hunting has made me far more conscious of my decision to eat meat and how it made it onto my plate. Being closely connected to the death of an animal makes it far more difficult to avoid the questions connected with eating meat and the economic systems that produce it.

Meat plays a central role in our winter diet because it is one of the few local ingredients available in abundance during the shortest days of the year. Chicken carcasses are pressure canned as stock, meat is cured for sandwiches, and jerky is loaded into the car in case we get stranded in a snowstorm. Preserving meat doesn't need to be a complicated task; most of the techniques predate almost all of the technology that we take for granted in our kitchens today.

PRESERVING NOSE-TO-TAIL

When I preserve meat it tends to be a solo act—I don't preserve other things at the same time—with two exceptions:

- When smoking, frying, or curing meat, I often make other recipes using the same technique, such as smoking peppers (page 281) while I smoke bacon.
- Some of the flavors I add to the meat, such as fresh herbs, become secondary preserves once I'm done with my meat recipe and left with extras.

TIPS FOR STORING

Meat has a relatively short shelf life in your fridge. Remove any plastic encasing it, place it in an airtight container, and store toward the back of your fridge on the bottom shelf.

continued . . .

FILLING THE PANTRY

CHILLED

Frozen is most common. It is best to wrap it tightly with butchers' paper (which is moisture and vapor resistant). Historically, meat was stored in a cellar, in large crocks surrounded by salt.

CANNED

Not recommended and not considered safe, though many still do.

PRESSURE CANNED

Meat can be pressure canned, though there is some debate around the safety of including the bones.

DEHYDRATED

Jerky.

CURED

Brine brisket and corned beef, cure bacon and charcuterie.

1 Pressure Canned Beef Stock
2 Bacon
3 Brined Slow-Cooker Brisket
4 Home-Cured Curry Pastrima
5 Bulgogi Beef Jerky

Not all meat freezes equally well. In *The River Cottage Meat Book*, author Hugh Fearnley-Whittingstall explains that much of the meat available in supermarkets is not aged long enough; to cut costs, the meat is often denied the hanging stage that allows some of the water to evaporate and makes it tender. Meat that hasn't been hung, or hasn't been hung long enough, freezes poorly because excess moisture affects the structure and results in dry, tough meat.

When my father freezes meat, he wraps the package from the store in a layer of butchers' paper, shiny side in, and writes the date and contents on each package. If you have a small freezer, place the new meat on the bottom and rotate older cuts to the top to be used first.

You should never thaw meat outside of the fridge. Although it takes longer, the fridge is the safer option.

 # Pressure Canned Beef Stock

PRESSURE CAN

LEVEL: ◉ ◉ ○
YIELD: 3–5 QUART JARS
EFFORT: 45 MINUTES
ELAPSED: 24 HOURS
EAT: WITHIN 1 YEAR

5 lb beef bones (you can use them straight from the freezer if you've been storing them)
2–4 Tbsp tomato powder or paste (page 332)
2 large onions, halved with skin on for color
2 medium carrots, cut into 2–3 large pieces
2 stalks celery, cut into 2–3 large pieces
3 cloves garlic
3 Tbsp olive oil
Black pepper
3–4 bay leaves

On a cold winter day you are likely to smell gently simmering stock wafting through our house. I often start my stock on a cozy Saturday morning before chilling it overnight and canning it the next morning.

Pressure canning stock lets me keep it on the shelf, giving me easy access to it whenever I need it. This recipe uses beef bones, but I make it from vegetable scraps, beef, chicken, or deer bones. Stock is one of my main uses for pressure canning.

MAKE THE STOCK:

1 Preheat the oven to 400°F.

2 Baste the bones with tomato paste and scatter them on a roasting pan.

3 Add the onions, carrots, and celery, garlic, and olive oil. Season liberally with pepper and place in the oven.

4 Bake for 60–90 minutes, flipping once. Remove when the bones have completely browned.

5 Place the roasted ingredients in a large pot with the bay leaves. Cover with cold tap water. Bring to a low simmer, uncovered, over medium-high heat. You should barely see any bubbles. Skim off any froth that appears (this will happen for the first hour or so).

6 Keeping the stock at a low simmer, add water as needed to keep the bones submerged. Cook for 10 hours or more (I generally cook it until I'm just about ready for bed).

7 Strain the stock. I strain it multiple times starting with a pasta colander and finishing with a fine sieve (this makes the job faster as the sieve doesn't clog). The solids will contain meat and fat that has lost most of its flavor from the long simmer. I dehydrate them and sprinkle them onto our dog's dinner (he's a lucky dude!).

8 Chill overnight. In the winter I chill it outside in my pressure canner (the design of the pot prevents critters from getting into it).

PRESSURE CAN THE STOCK

9 Skim off any fat from the stock with a spoon and reserve it for other cooking. Measure the liquid. You want 4–5 quarts. Reduce the liquid by simmering or increase the volume by adding water as required.

10 There will be some harmless sediment in most homemade broths. You can remove this by carefully syphoning with a tube (the same way you rack fermented alcohol, page 46) or straining multiple times through a clean dishcloth and a sieve. I don't bother.

11 Pour the hot stock into quart jars, leaving 1 inch of headspace. Gently jostle the jars or use the handle of a spoon to release any air bubbles. Process with 10 lb of pressure for 25 minutes at sea level (if you live higher than 1,000 feet above sea level, refer to the Adjust for Altitude chart on page 25 for additional processing time).

VARIATIONS: Deer stock is made identically to beef stock. To make chicken stock, follow the same instructions but omit the tomato paste, roast the chicken carcasses for 45–60 minutes (until brown) and simmer the stock for 4–5 hours.

CENTER OF THE PLATE: It's stock! Make soup, braise with it, or cook rice in it. The possibilities are endless.

 # Bacon

LEVEL: ● ○ ○

YIELD: 3-5 LB

EFFORT: 20 MINUTES

ELAPSED: 8 DAYS

EAT: WITHIN 1 YEAR

2 lb pork belly, rind on

5 cloves garlic, minced

1 oz coarse salt

1 Tbsp coarsely ground coffee
    (optional)

1-2 tsp black pepper

¼ cup maple syrup

2 Tbsp bourbon

YOU WILL NEED

Optional: cold smoker or BBQ and
    smoke maze (page 66) with apple
    or maple wood chips

Homemade bacon is surprisingly easy to make and is far superior to store-bought. Most pork bellies come with the rind (skin) intact. Some people like to peel it off, as it can be dense and chewy, but I think it makes for better bacon.

Many bacon recipes call for pink salt (page 65). I'm not opposed to using it, but I prefer to cure bacon with coarse salt. If possible, use local-pastured pork for a fattier and more flavorful product. I used to measure the salt by volume but found the results to be drastically different from each other. The salt should be between 2½% and 3½% of the weight of the belly. This bacon will freeze well if wrapped in butchers' paper.

1 If you don't have a big enough container for the belly, chop it into pieces (I often make 4- x 4-inch squares of bacon). If you've never bought pork belly before, don't be surprised if you find nipples on it; you can leave them on or cut them off.

2 Mix together the garlic, salt, coffee (if using), pepper, maple syrup, and bourbon to make a cure. Massage it into the pork belly and place in the container. Refrigerate for eight days, shaking the container or flipping the belly daily to distribute the cure. You will feel the texture of the meat become firmer.

3 Discard the cure and rinse the pork under cold running water.

4 Preheat the oven to 200°F. Bake the pork until its internal temperature reaches 150°F, about 1½ hours. Allow it to cool.

5 If smoking, smoke for 4–5 hours until it is dark yellow.

6 Let the pork cool before wrapping it tightly in butchers' paper.

VARIATIONS: Add any spice/sweet combination that you like. Skip the coffee, maple, and bourbon and substitute 2 Tbsp brown sugar and 1 Tbsp dried chipotle flakes; or 2 Tbsp brown sugar, 1 Tbsp smoked paprika, and 10 slices dehydrated apple.

CENTER OF THE PLATE: Although you can slice and fry this like you would breakfast bacon, I cut the bacon into lardons (a.k.a. matchsticks) to use in other cooking.

Brined Slow-Cooker Brisket

SALT

LEVEL: ● ○ ○

YIELD: 4–5 LB BRISKET

EFFORT: 45 MINUTES

ELAPSED: 3½–5½ DAYS

EAT: WITHIN 6 MONTHS (IF FROZEN)

4–5 lb brisket with a nice fat cap
   (i.e., not trimmed of all fat)
Salt and pepper

FOR THE BRINE:

2 onions, cut in quarters, skin on
8 cloves garlic, slightly crushed,
   skin on
⅓ cup plus 2 Tbsp coarse salt
¼ cup brown sugar, loosely packed
4 bay leaves
2 Tbsp whole black peppercorns
2 Tbsp powdered mustard
1 Tbsp sweet paprika

FOR THE SLOW COOKER:

4 cups beef broth
2 garlic cloves, minced
1 onion, cut into ¼-inch wide strips
½ cup red wine or beer

FOR THE DRY RUB:

¼ cup brown sugar, lightly packed
1½ Tbsp powdered mustard
2 tsp sweet paprika
1 tsp cayenne pepper
1 tsp ground cumin
1 tsp black pepper

YOU WILL NEED

Slow cooker

This calls for some planning: the brisket should brine for three to five days and will take up considerable room in your fridge. If you're short on space, consider removing your crisper for a few days and storing the brining container there.

1   Season the brisket with salt and pepper.

2   In a large bowl, mix the onions, garlic, salt, sugar, bay leaves, peppercorns, mustard, and paprika with 3 quarts of tap water. Add the brisket and submerge in the brine (if it's not fully submerged, flip the brisket a few times a day during brining). Cover tightly with a lid or plastic wrap and refrigerate for a minimum of three, maximum of five days, flipping once daily.

3   In a large pot, bring the beef broth and garlic to a boil over high heat, then lower the heat to control splatter. Reduce the broth by half, about 20–30 minutes.

4   Make the dry rub by mixing together the sugar, mustard, paprika, cayenne, cumin, and pepper.

5   Remove the brisket from the cure, rinse well, and pat dry. Massage the dry rub into the brisket.

6   Scatter half the onions into your slow cooker, place the brisket on top, and add the rest of the onions, reduced broth, and wine.

7   Cook on high for 6–8 hours, until fork-tender.

8   Remove from the slow cooker and tent loosely with foil for 12–15 minutes.

9   Cut across the grain, shaving thinly to serve. Extra portions will freeze well surrounded in cooking liquid, and they can be reheated or kept warm in it as well.

VARIATIONS: You can add any spices you like to the dry rub or cure. Capers, juniper berries, and ¼ cup of pickle juice are all interesting additions!

CENTER OF THE PLATE: Serve on a bun, in soup, or with baked beans. Or eat it cold. Reheat slices in broth or some reserved cooking liquid on the stovetop.

Home-Cured Curry Pastrima

SALT & SMOKE

LEVEL: ◉ ◉ ○

YIELD: ¾–1 LB CURED MEAT

EFFORT: 30 MINUTES

ELAPSED: 6 WEEKS

EAT: WITHIN 6 MONTHS

FIRST CURE:

2 lb steak (flank or hanger are ideal)

½ cup kosher salt

SPICE PASTE:

3 cloves garlic, minced

1-inch cube of ginger, minced

3 Tbsp smoked paprika

2 Tbsp fenugreek seeds, measured
then pulverized

2 Tbsp curry powder

1 Tbsp cracked black peppercorns

1½ tsp salt

1 tsp celery seeds

1 tsp ground cumin

1 tsp chili powder or cayenne
pepper

1 Tbsp maple syrup

YOU WILL NEED

Cheesecloth

Butchers' twine

A rock or weight that's at least the
same weight as the piece of meat
you are using (a 6-pack of beer
will work just fine!)

Cold smoker with wood chips
(optional)

Pastrima is similar to Italian bresaola. From what I've read, its roots are Turkish (though other countries in the Middle East also make it or a variant of it). It uses household ingredients and doesn't require a curing chamber. After an initial cure, the meat is coated in a spice paste (fenugreek is a common ingredient) and dried again. This is a longer-term endeavor.

PREP THE FIRST CURE:

1 Trim off as much of the fat and silver skin as you can.

2 Rub the salt thoroughly into the meat. Place the meat in a snug, airtight container, adding any remaining salt. Refrigerate for fourteen days. Drain any residual liquid daily.

3 Remove the meat from salt and rinse thoroughly. Cover with fresh, cool water, and refrigerate overnight.

4 The next step is to press the meat to help remove more liquid. Wrap the meat in a few layers of cheesecloth and place it in a bowl. Place a small plate on top of the meat and place the rock or weight on top. Refrigerate for two days.

5 Remove the cheesecloth, tie the meat with a butchers' knot (if you don't know how to tie one, just make sure the meat is securely tied). Hang in the fridge or a cool space that is below 50°F for two weeks.

PREP THE SPICE PASTE:

6 Place the garlic, ginger, paprika, fenugreek, curry powder, peppercorns, salt, celery seeds, cumin, chili powder, and maple syrup in a bowl. Slowly add about ¼ cup water, stirring to make a thick paste. Don't add too much water. You want it thick!

7 Spread the paste on the meat and hang it in a relatively cool (around 60 degrees is perfect), semi-humid part of your house for two weeks. The most common problems are mold or rotting, which are generally caused by skimping on salt at the start or hanging in an environment with extreme humidity or lack thereof.

8 Cold smoke for 2–4 hours (optional); I use apple or maple wood chips. If you're not smoking, move to the next step.

9 Wrap tightly with butchers' paper and store in fridge. Depending on the humidity in your fridge, it will last up to six months. If it dries out, it will become tough to slice but could be braised to soften, then chopped into soups, stews, curries, and pasta sauces.

VARIATIONS: Replace maple syrup with 2 Tbsp brown sugar or add 1 Tbsp chipotle powder instead of the cayenne.

CENTER OF THE PLATE: Shave it thinly across the grain. Eat it as is or with grainy mustard or strong hard cheese on a crunchy cracker. Thin pieces can also be great on a toasted sandwich with brie, arugula, and a small amount of olive oil.

TIP: MEAT HOOKS AREN'T JUST FOR MEAT

Four-inch meat hooks are affordable and can easily be attached to a metal rack. If you don't have a metal rack, you can hang a heavy duty towel rack out of reach of pets or curious fingers. Place metal hooks on it to dehydrate peppers or beans, or to hang other preserves in your kitchen.

Bulgogi Beef Jerky

DEHYDRATE

LEVEL: ● ● ○

YIELD: ⅓–½ LB JERKY

EFFORT: 15 MINUTES

ELAPSED: 1½ DAYS

EAT: WITHIN 2–3 MONTHS

2 lb flank steak

1–2 Tbsp sesame seeds

1 pear (Bartlett or Bosc are my
   faves), peeled and cored

6 green onions or 1 medium onion

4 cloves garlic

1-inch piece ginger, minced

1–2 dried chili peppers (page 174)

1 Tbsp brown sugar

2 tsp coarse salt

Black pepper

⅓ cup soy sauce

2 Tbsp sesame oil

1 Tbsp mirin, white wine,
   or cider vinegar

YOU WILL NEED
Dehydrator

Jerky should be made from lean cuts of meat; game, pork, and beef are the most common. This recipe uses a liberal interpretation of the marinade used for Korean bulgogi.

When making jerky, be conscious of the danger zone. Bad bacteria thrive between 70°F and 140°F. In order to avoid this, your dehydrator needs to maintain a temperature of at least 145°F. If you have a dehydrator with a single setting, you may want to consult the manufacturer to ensure that it is hot enough.

1 Cut off any excess fat from the meat and slice it into ¼-inch strips, cutting with the grain (not against it). This will add to the texture of the final product.

2 Toss the sesame seeds in a bowl with the beef.

3 Make a marinade by placing the pear, green onions, garlic, ginger, chili peppers, sugar, salt, and pepper to taste in a food processor with the soy sauce, oil, and vinegar. Blend into a paste.

4 Mix the marinade with the beef, stir well, and cover tightly with lid or plastic wrap. Refrigerate for 24 hours.

5 Remove the beef from marinade, draining off any excess. Transfer to a dehydrator tray, leaving ½ inch between each piece. Dry at 155°F for 6–12 hours, testing after 6 hours. The jerky is done once it is dry throughout yet still slightly flexible.

6 Preheat the oven to 275°F.

7 Scatter jerky in a single layer on rimmed baking trays. Bake for 10 minutes and allow then allow the jerky to cool on the tray. Blot any excess moisture from the surface and store in airtight containers in the fridge for maximum shelf life.

VARIATIONS: If you'd like to use wild game instead of beef, freeze it for thirty days before beginning the recipe to kill any parasites.

CENTER OF THE PLATE: This can be eaten as is, or rehydrated in heated water or stock to add to cooking. You can also pulverize it into a powder to use as a seasoning in other cooking.

Homemade Pizza

SERVINGS: 4

EFFORT: 25 MINUTES

ELAPSED: 1½ HOURS–2 DAYS

DOUGH:

Generous ¼ tsp instant active yeast

¾ cup warm water

2 tsp maple syrup

2¼ cups all-purpose flour

1 tsp salt

1 Tbsp extra-virgin olive oil

1½ tsp cider or malt vinegar

SAUCE:

1 cup tomato sauce or canned
   tomatoes and juice, pureed
   (pages 332–333)

2 Tbsp extra-virgin olive oil

Salt

Black pepper

½ tsp dried oregano, plus more
   to garnish

TOPPINGS:

6 oz of your choice of cured meat
   (pages 238–241)

6–8 oz cheese, cut into
   ½-inch cubes

½ Spanish onion, cut in rounds

5–6 jalapeño peppers, cut in rounds

½ tsp fresh rosemary

YOU WILL NEED

Food processor with a plastic blade
   or a stand mixer with dough hook

Rectangular baking sheet that's 12 x
   15 inches or larger

Pizza dough was one of the first doughs I learned how to make, after reading Jim Lahey's recipe for No-Knead Bread. The dough can rest for as little as 30 minutes, but it's even better after one or two days of resting in the fridge.

MAKE THE DOUGH AND SAUCE:

1   Place the yeast in a cup, add 2 Tbsp of the warm water and the maple syrup, and stir well. Place in a warm spot of your kitchen for 15 minutes, stirring once.

2   Place the flour and salt in a food processor fitted with the plastic blade or a stand mixer. Add the remaining warm water, oil, and vinegar and mix. Add the yeast-water mixture and process into a loose ball (this will take about 1 minute using the food processor, and 2–3 minutes if using a stand mixer). If it doesn't form a ball, add additional water 1–2 tsp at a time.

3   Dust your hands with flour. Form the dough into a ball and coat the outsides with a bit of flour. Place in a bowl, cover with a damp dishcloth, and leave in a warm, draft-free spot in your kitchen for 30–60 minutes. You can then use the dough or transfer it to the fridge. It will noticeably improve over the next two days.

4   To make the sauce, combine the canned tomatoes and juice, oil, salt, pepper, and oregano in a food processor and puree to desired thickness.

ASSEMBLE AND COOK THE PIZZA:

5   Place an oven rack in the middle of the oven. Preheat the oven to 500°F.

6   Pour some olive oil onto a rimmed baking tray and spread it over the entire surface, including the sides.

7   Spread the dough over the pan to make a rough oval. Spread it as thinly as you can without making it transparent, about ½ inch. If you tear the dough, cover the holes firmly with a fold of dough—make sure it is well-covered, as the sauce could leak through these holes and make the dough stick to the pan. If the dough is dry, add a little more olive oil as you go—it will add to the flavor.

continued . . .

8   Scatter the tomato sauce across the dough. Spread it evenly over the dough but avoid the edges.

9   Scatter the toppings overtop. The center should have the fewest toppings or it will get soggy and limp.

10 Bake the pizza for 12–15 minutes, or until brown.

11 Scatter the surface with more oregano to taste and serve.

PANTRY RAID: The possibilities are endless. Add herbes salées (page 229) as a garnish or mix it into the dough. Add pickled mushrooms (page 252), mix mushroom powder (page 251) into the sauce, season with chili salt (page 175), or serve with chili oil (page 174)!

Cherried Duck Prosciutto

I was introduced to duck prosciutto in Michael Ruhlman's *Charcuterie*. Weigh and record the weight of your duck breast. Score the fat and place it in a tight-fitting container surrounded by 2–3 cups kosher salt. Remove after three days, rinse well, and pat dry. Dust the duck with black pepper and 1 Tbsp of pulverized dried cherries (page 164). Wrap in cheesecloth and hang in your fridge (I tie it to a shelf at the back of the fridge) for one to two weeks. It will be done when the duck has lost 30% of its original weight. Remove the cheesecloth and store in fridge, wrapped tightly in butchers' paper or a snug container.

Potato, Leek, and Bacon Soup

SERVINGS: 6–8

EFFORT: 30 MINUTES

ELAPSED: 1½ HOURS

1½ quarts chicken or
vegetable stock

4 large leeks, cut into rings, roots
and dark green parts set aside

1½ lb Yukon Gold potatoes,
quartered with their skin on

½ lb bacon (page 238)

3 cloves garlic, minced

¼ tsp dried thyme

1 cup heavy (35%) cream

2 tsp cider vinegar

Cheddar cheese or sour cream to
serve (optional)

Chives to garnish

This is a simple winter soup that takes a relatively small amount of bacon and creates a flavor for an entire meal. The leftover fat from frying the bacon flavors the entire soup and is the secret star of the dish. You can cook this without cream, but I enjoy the texture and additional flavor that it brings.

1 Pour the stock into a large stock pot with the burner set to high. Add the reserved leek greens and wait for the stock to boil. Immediately reduce heat to a low simmer and cook for 10 minutes. Remove and discard the leek greens, add the potatoes, and simmer until soft, about 20 minutes.

2 Meanwhile, cut the bacon into lardons (thin strips). Fry in a separate pan over medium-high heat until crisp. Remove the bacon from the pan with a slotted spoon and set aside. Add the leek rings and garlic to the bacon fat in the pan and fry until translucent. Transfer the leeks and garlic to the stock pot, using a ladle to pick up the fat.

3 Puree the soup smooth with an immersion blender. Add the bacon, the thyme, and then the cream. Mix to combine.

4 Add 1 tsp of the cider vinegar, mix to combine, and taste the soup. You should taste a difference, though it shouldn't taste like vinegar. Add the second teaspoon if you like. You can thicken the soup by simmering it for longer or thin it by adding additional stock.

5 Garnish with cheddar cheese or sour cream and chives, and serve immediately.

PANTRY RAID: Finish with dried vegetable powder or a touch of homemade cider vinegar (page 82). Make it with mushroom stock (page 253) instead of chicken or vegetable.

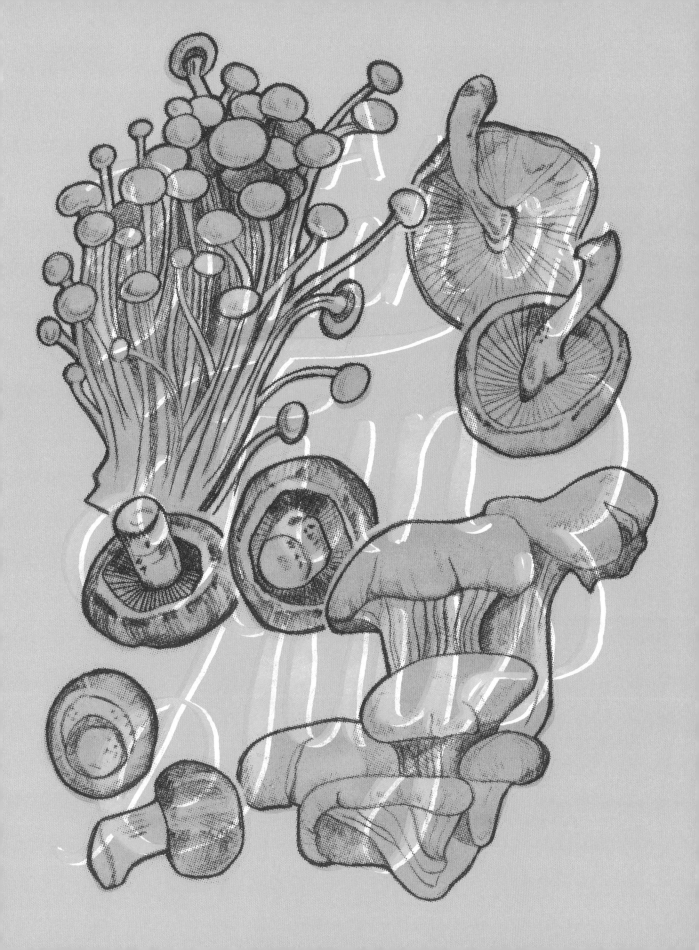

mushrooms

Dana bought me a dehydrator for Christmas a few years ago. I rifled through the fridge looking for things I could pop into it and found 3 or 4 lb of mushrooms.

Once the mushrooms had finished drying, I didn't know what to do with them. I threw them into our spice grinder, made them into a powder, placed it in a vintage Mason jar, and put it on the shelf beside a jar of onion powder.

I was cooking dinner for New Year's Eve a few days later when I reached for the onion powder. On a whim, I grabbed some mushroom powder as well and tossed a liberal amount of both into the gravy. A quick taste revealed a happy accident and I found myself reaching for the jar and adding more powder to the sauce—it was awesome!

Dehydrated foods are thickeners and, moreover, concentrated flavor bombs. Within weeks, I was adding mushroom powder to nearly everything. It started with soups, stews, stir-fries, and sauces. Then it made its way into pasta and pizza dough, rubs, and dressings.

Mushroom powder is magic. It changed my entire understanding of preserving and cooking. I realized that preserving could go beyond making condiments and be a tool to create ingredients.

PRESERVING NOSE-TO-TAIL

Mushrooms have stems and caps and, despite what you may have seen in many recipes, they can generally be used interchangeably.

If you'd rather preserve mushroom caps by themselves—they are arguably prettier than the stem—or want to avoid the thicker ends of larger mushrooms such as portobellos, dehydrate the stems and then tear them to make duxelles (see page 250).

TIPS FOR STORING

Mushrooms should be stored in an airtight container surrounded by a slightly damp cloth or layer of paper towel. You want a dark and slightly moist environment. If storing them in a paper bag, they are best left out of the crisper and kept on a shelf of the fridge. You can easily clean them with a soft brush or damp paper towel.

FILLING THE PANTRY

CANNED

Pickled is the only way to go if you're using a waterbath.

PRESSURE CANNED

Canned whole or in pieces, as ingredient in soup or stew, or made into stock.

DEHYDRATED

Drying mushrooms takes seconds with some basic equipment. Although you'll need to dry them fully for long-term storage, I love to cook with them after semi-drying slices for a few hours to concentrate their flavor.

1 **Mushroom Stock**
2 **Pickled Enoki Mushrooms**
3 **Canned Mushrooms**
4 **Air-Dried Mushrooms**
5 **Mushroom Powder**
6 **Mushroom Duxelles**

Batch-It

Canned Mushrooms

PRESSURE CAN

LEVEL: ● ● ○

YIELD: 5 PINT JARS

EFFORT: 45 MINUTES

ELAPSED: 1½ HOURS

EAT: WITHIN 1 YEAR

8 lb button mushrooms

2½ tsp coarse salt

Mushroom Duxelles

CELLAR

LEVEL: ● ○ ○

YIELD: ½–1 PINT

EFFORT: 20 MINUTES

ELAPSED: 8 HOURS

EAT: WITHIN 1 YEAR

1 lb cremini mushrooms

2 Tbsp unsalted butter, chilled

2 Tbsp olive oil

2 large shallots, diced thin

1 clove garlic, minced

¼ tsp dried thyme (or 2 sprigs fresh thyme)

Salt

Canned mushrooms are the perfect "in case of emergency" food for any pantry. They last a long time and can be used in almost any recipe if you find yourself short of a few ingredients. And don't throw out the water from the jar; it can be used as a simple stock or reduced into 1 Tbsp of intense flavor booster.

The duxelles (most commonly used in beef Wellington) is a luxurious combination of mushrooms, butter, and aromatics that freezes very well.

When canning mushrooms, I sometimes remove the stems for esthetic reasons. The stems can be chopped and added to the duxelles, and both recipes are better for it.

PREP THE CANNED MUSHROOMS:

1 Clean off any visible dirt from the mushrooms, trim the ends, and soak in hot tap water for 10 minutes before inspecting for additional dirt.

2 Prepare your pressure canner and rack, and sterilize your jars and lids. (See pages 21–23.) Boil a kettle of water in case you need additional water to fill the jars.

3 Small mushrooms can be left whole, but larger mushrooms should be cut so that all the pieces are approximately the same size.

4 Place the mushrooms in a pot, cover with water, and simmer, uncovered, for 5 minutes.

5 Divide the mushrooms between the jars and cover with hot water from the pot and/or kettle. Add ½ tsp of salt to each jar.

6 Process in the pressure canner for 45 minutes with 10 lb of pressure at sea level (if you live higher than 1,000 feet above sea level, refer to the Adjust for Altitude chart on page 25 for additional processing time).

MAKE THE DUXELLES:

7 While the pressure canner is busy doing its thing, scrub the 4 cups mushrooms clean with your hands to remove any visible dirt.

8 Break the mushrooms up with your hands or slice them, whichever method you prefer.

9 In a large frying pan, heat the butter and oil over medium-high heat.

10 Add the shallots and garlic and sauté for 3 minutes.

11 Add the mushrooms and thyme and fry until soft, 5–10 minutes, stirring and seasoning to taste with salt and pepper as you go.

12 Remove the frying pan from the heat and allow the mixture to cool.

13 Scoop the mushrooms onto a piece of plastic wrap and roll into a sausage shape. If you are avoiding plastic, pack the mushrooms tightly into ice cube trays or muffin trays. Freeze until solid and then transfer to airtight containers.

10 Minutes or less

Mushroom Powder

DEHYDRATE

LEVEL: ● ○ ○

YIELD: 1 PINT JAR DRIED MUSHROOMS OR ¼–½ CUP MUSHROOM POWDER

EAT: WITHIN 1 YEAR

1 lb mushrooms

YOU WILL NEED
Dehydrator

Although you can air-dry mushrooms to make powder, I believe that many people will eventually want to dry larger quantities and use a dehydrator to do so. I store them in Mason jars and make ½–1 cup of powder at a time.

Clean the mushrooms and spread them on a dehydrating tray. Dry at 125°F until completely dry and brittle, about 6–8 hours. To make them into powder, pulverize the mushrooms in a high-speed blender or coffee grinder. Store the powder or mushrooms in an airtight jar on a dark shelf.

 # Pickled Enoki Mushrooms

WATERBATH

LEVEL: ● ● ○

YIELD: 4–5 HALF-PINT JARS

EFFORT: 45 MINUTES

ELAPSED: 1½ HOURS

EAT: AFTER 6 WEEKS AND WITHIN
    2 YEARS

4 lb enoki mushrooms

¼ cup bottled lemon juice

1¼ cups white vinegar (5% or
  higher)

1 cup olive oil

1 tsp canning or pickling salt

10 tsp chili flakes

1½ tsp fresh oregano leaves (or ½
  tsp dried oregano powder)

You can pickle any kind of mushroom that you want (the National Center for Home Food Preservation recommends using mushrooms that are less than 1.25 inches in diameter). Despite looking like an unmanageable clump, enoki have individual stems and can be easily loaded into a jar in small chunks. Every time I look at them I think of the Sentinels from *The Matrix* and that makes me smile!

1 Prepare your canning pot and rack, and sterilize your jars and lids (see page 17).

2 Place the mushrooms in a large pot, and add the lemon juice and enough tap water to cover. Bring to a boil before lowering to a simmer for 5 minutes. Carefully strain out the mushrooms (reserving the liquid for other cooking) and allow to cool.

3 Rinse the pot and add vinegar, olive oil, and salt to it. Bring to a boil before lowering to a simmer over medium heat.

4 Remove the jars from the canner and turn the heat to high.

5 Divide the chili flakes and oregano evenly between the jars.

6 If the enoki stems are in thick bunches, hold them in one hand and trim from the bottom to ensure the majority of mushrooms are separated into smaller clumps and are short enough to fit in the jars. The stems can be used in other cooking, especially stir-fries.

7 Carefully place the mushrooms in the jars, packing as tightly as they allow. Cover in hot brine.

8 Wipe the rims of the jars, apply the lids, and process for 20 minutes (if you live higher than 1,000 feet above sea level, refer to the Adjust for Altitude chart on page 17 for additional processing time).

9 Remove the jars and allow them to cool.

VARIATIONS: Use other types of fresh mushrooms, replace the oregano with thyme, or replace the white vinegar with white wine or champagne vinegar.

CENTER OF THE PLATE: Wrap a small clump of mushrooms with a stalk of asparagus in prosciutto, chop them on top of bruschetta, or use as a pizza topping.

 ## Air-Dried Mushrooms

Place clean mushrooms on a metal rack in a warm spot. Make sure they don't touch. Walk away. Leave them be until they're dry and brittle, two to five days, and store in a clean, airtight Mason jar on a shelf. It's that easy.

# Mushroom Stock

PRESSURE CAN

LEVEL: ● ● ○

YIELD: 5 QUART JARS

EFFORT: 1½ HOURS

ELAPSED: 2½ HOURS

EAT: WITHIN 1 YEAR

4 stalks celery

2 medium carrots

2 large Spanish onions

2 lb mixed mushrooms

1 head of garlic

1 Tbsp olive oil

Coarse salt

Black pepper

¼ cup mushroom powder (optional)

½ tsp cayenne pepper

2 bay leaves

½ tsp dried marjoram

½ tsp dried parsley

½ tsp dried thyme

2 tsp balsamic vinegar

If you've never had mushroom stock before, you're missing out. Mushrooms are full of umami and this savory stock can be slurped from a bowl or transformed into a soup.

1 Preheat the oven to 450°F.

2 Roughly chop the celery, carrots, onions, and mushrooms into 1-inch chunks. Cut the top off the garlic, exposing the flesh in each clove but keeping the head together. Toss the garlic and veg with the olive oil, salt, and pepper and place on a rimmed baking tray. Roast for 25 minutes, flipping halfway, until the veggies are soft but not cooked through.

3 Place the roasted veg in a large stockpot with the mushroom powder, cayenne, bay leaves, marjoram, parsley, and thyme. Add 6 quarts of tap water and vinegar. Bring to a boil, then lower to a gentle simmer for 1 hour. Prepare your pressure canner and jars while it simmers. (See pages 21–23.)

4 Remove the soup from the heat and strain it to remove any solids. If you pick out the herbs, the other veggies can be reserved to use in stocks and soups as a thickener.

5 Process at 10 lb of pressure for 45 minutes a sea level (if you live higher than 1,000 feet above sea level, refer to the Adjust for Altitude chart on page 25 for additional processing time).

VARIATIONS: Cooking scraps can be frozen over a period of weeks and then transformed into this stock. You can roast them from frozen as long as you stir them a few times.

CENTER OF THE PLATE: You can use this as a replacement for beef broth; add cream, lemongrass, or more mushrooms (fresh or dry) for an instant soup; or combine it with roast drippings to make the best gravy ever!

TIP: MEASURING LARGE QUANTITIES

When making recipes that call for large amounts of liquids, I find it frustrating to measure 1 cup at a time. Mason jars are a great shortcut for approximate measuring (each 1-quart jar = 4 cups). For more accurate measuring, measure 4 cups of water into a Mason jar and mark the jar with a piece of tape or grease pencil.

Tofu Wellington

SERVINGS: 2-4

EFFORT: 45 MINUTES

ELAPSED: 2-24 HOURS

1 lb firm or extra-firm tofu

Salt

1 cup of brine from fermented carrot
   pickles (page 155), sauerkraut
   (page 144), or kimchi (page 147);
   or 1 cup water + 1 Tbsp honey +
   1 Tbsp cider vinegar (page 82)

Black pepper

1 sheet of puff pastry (about 9 oz;
   this is generally half a box)

½–¾ cup mushroom duxelles
   (page 250)

¾–1 lb fresh spinach

½ cup feta cheese, crumbled
   then measured

1 egg, lightly beaten

This is a liberal reinterpretation of beef Wellington. Because it cooks in a hot oven, its ideal accompaniment is roasted vegetables. Cut an assortment of root vegetables into sticks, toss them in honey and olive oil, throw them onto a rimmed baking sheet, and add them to the oven 15 minutes before the Wellington goes in, checking regularly.

1 Drain the tofu and pat it dry. Season with salt, sit it on a plate, and cover loosely for 1 hour on your counter. Pat dry, gently squeezing to remove additional moisture.

2 Place the tofu in a tight-fitting airtight container and add the brine and pepper to taste. Refrigerate for 1 hour, or up to 24 hours.

3 Thaw out the puff pastry and mushroom duxelles, if need be.

4 Preheat the oven to 425°F.

5 Bring 1 cup of water to a boil over high heat. Add the spinach and cook for 1 minute. Drain the spinach (reserving the liquid for other cooking), let cool, and squeeze to remove as much moisture as possible.

6 In a large bowl, mix the mushroom duxelles with the spinach and feta.

7 Roll the pastry into a sheet large enough to completely wrap the tofu. Line the pastry with three-quarters of the mushroom-spinach mixture. Place the tofu on top, add the remaining mushroom-spinach mixture, cover with the pastry, and seal on all sides. Brush the surface with beaten egg, carefully flip onto a baking tray lined with parchment paper, and brush the top and sides with egg. Use a fork or a toothpick to poke a few small holes in the surface to allow steam to escape.

8 Bake until browned, 20–30 minutes.

PANTRY RAID: Hot sauce (page 176), smoked peach or pepper powder (pages 260 and 281), preserved lemons (chopped into the duxelles), or shredded fermented Brussels sprouts (page 145) can all add interesting twists to this dish.

Mushroom Polenta

SERVINGS: 4 SIDES

EFFORT: 5 MINUTES

ELAPSED: 30-40 MINUTES

1 cup cornmeal or polenta (coarse if possible)

½–1 cup mushroom powder (page 251)

1–2 air-dried hot peppers (page 281)

4–6 cups water or stock. Mushroom (page 253), vegetable, or chicken will all do

1–2 pints canned tomatoes (page 333) or 16–32 oz canned whole tomatoes, coarsely chopped, liquid included

Coarse salt

Black pepper

2 bay leaves

2 Tbsp unsalted butter, chilled

¼ cup Parmesan cheese, grated then measured

Chives, for garnish

Mark Trealout is a local organic farmer who introduced me to coarse cornmeal. It was unlike anything I had ever cooked with before and I fell madly in love with it. In fact, I bought 10 lb of it when I heard that his supply was drying up a few years back.

This is a no-fuss meal that takes moments to make and is as much about the hidden mushrooms as it is about the cornmeal. It will warm you on the coldest of days. If you happen to have truffle oil, add a few drops to each bowl as you serve it.

1   Preheat the oven to 425°F.

2   Combine the cornmeal, mushroom powder, and hot peppers with 4 cups of stock and the tomatoes and their liquid in a roasting pan. Season liberally with salt and pepper and add the bay leaves.

3   Place in the oven, stirring and checking after 20 minutes. If the mixture is threatening to stick to the bottom of the pan, add additional stock or water.

4   Cook until the polenta is soft, about 30–35 minutes total.

5   Remove the bay leaves and add the butter. If the texture is dry, add 2–3 Tbsp milk or heavy cream. If it's too wet (it should be close to the texture of porridge), stir it and return to the oven for a few more minutes. Spoon into bowls, top with shavings of Parmesan cheese and chives, and serve at once!

PANTRY RAID: Leftover liquid from any pressure canned veggies, a small amount of brine from kimchi (page 147), dried slices of mushroom, and dehydrated green onions all work well.

Peaches

For years, I peeled peaches without really knowing how to do it. I hacked away at them with a paring knife, almost destroying their shape, and I would give myself peach acid burns in the process. When I shared my troubles with a friend who also happens to be a chef, she asked me why I wasn't blanching them.

I've never peeled a peach with a blade since.

Peaches, like tomatoes, should be peeled with a quick blanch in boiling water or by charring with high heat (see page 261).

If you blanch the skins, be sure to dehydrate them and then add them to tea, ferments, infusions, or the coals of your BBQ for smoke!

PRESERVING NOSE-TO-TAIL

Like apricots, peaches have a pit that conceals a kernel. Read the Nose-to-Tail section on page 91 regarding the amount of cyanide in each and why I recommend further research before preserving or consuming these.

Keep your eyes out for any varieties marked "freestone," as these have the easiest pits to remove. This is true of all stone fruit.

The flesh of a peach is a versatile preserving ingredient that may be preserved with or without the skin. Firm peaches are much easier to peel than softer ones, and certain varieties are easier than others, too.

You can use unpeeled peaches in any recipe that calls for peeled fruit. Some claim a minor loss of texture but it's largely a matter of preference.

TIPS FOR STORING

Do not store peaches in the fridge until they ripen. They will always taste better at room temperature and will ripen well on the counter as long as there is enough air to circulate around them. Once they're ripe, store them in the crisper or in an airtight container on a shelf in the fridge.

CHILLED
Freeze slices, halves, or juice.

CANNED
Slices, chutney, jam, butter, BBQ or other sauces.

DEHYDRATED
Dried slices or halves, or make fruit leather.

1 Instant Hot Sauce
2 Charred Peach Slices
3 Smoke-Dried Peaches
4 Peach Salt
5 Peach Crème Fraîche
6 Peach-Bourbon BBQ Sauce

Batch-It

Smoke-Dried Peaches

SMOKE

LEVEL: ● ● ●

YIELD: 3 HALF-PINT JARS

EFFORT: 10 MINUTES

ELAPSED: 10–12 HOURS

EAT: WITHIN 1 YEAR

2 lb peaches (7–8)

1½ tsp fresh lemon juice

YOU WILL NEED

Smoke maze and BBQ (or smoker)

Smoke chips (I use apple or hickory)

Dehydrator

Canned Peach Slices

WATERBATH

LEVEL: ● ● ○

YIELD: 3–4 PINT JARS

EFFORT: 1 HOUR

ELAPSED: 1½ HOURS

EAT: WITHIN 1–2 YEARS

6 lb peaches (20–24 peaches)

¾ cup honey

1 tsp salt

These recipes work well together because the first steps are identical. I started peeling peaches on the BBQ because they are ripe when summer is at its hottest and I'd rather not have a boiling pot of water heating up my kitchen. This is also a good recipe for newbies, as many will find the idea of BBQing peaches familiar and fun.

Canned peaches are easy to make and versatile to use. Eat them from the jar or use for other cooking. Any leftover syrup is great for tea, as a glaze for meat, or for making popsicles!

Peaches can be smoked with any type of cold smoker. Using a smoker with a built-in thermostat is easiest, but I've had equally good results placing peaches on one side of a cool BBQ and lighting a smoke maze (page 66) on the other. We dry them on a dehydrator and add them to any dish that you would add BBQ sauce to (they add a touch of sweetness and smoke).

PEEL ALL THE PEACHES:

1. Heat your BBQ to high. Once it's hot, scorch all 8 lb of the peaches until they char. Flip until they're scorched on all sides.
2. Turn off the BBQ, place peaches into a bowl, and allow them to cool.
3. Peel the peaches before cutting them in half by slicing along the crease of the peach (this will make it easiest to remove the pit). Place three-quarters of them in one bowl for canning and set aside.

PREP THE PEACHES FOR SMOKING:

4. Toss the other peaches in the lemon juice.
5. Once the BBQ is cool, light the smoke maze, and place it on one side of the BBQ. Place the peaches on the other side. Cold smoke for 5 hours, checking the smoke maze occasionally.

WATERBATH THE PEACHES:

6 Prepare your canning pot and rack, and sterilize jars
and lids (see page 17).

7 Place the peaches, 4 cups of water, honey, and salt into a
large pot and bring to a boil over high heat. As soon as it
boils, lower the heat to a bare simmer and move to the
next steps.

8 Remove the jars from the canner and turn the heat to high.

9 Using a slotted spoon, fill the jars with the peaches.

10 Distribute the cooking syrup between the jars, leaving 1
inch of headspace. Gently jostle the jars or use the handle
of a spoon to release any air bubbles. If you have any leftover syrup, use it to sweeten tea or add lemon juice to taste
(I use 1–2 parts lemon to 1 part syrup) to make a peach
lemonade. Wipe the rims of the jars, apply the lids, and
process for 25 minutes (if you live higher than 1,000 feet
above sea level, refer to the Adjust for Altitude chart on
page 17 for additional processing time). Remove the jars
and allow them to cool.

DEHYDRATE THE PEACHES:

11 Spread the cold-smoked peaches on dehydrator racks and
dry at 125°F for 6–8 hours. They should be hard and firm
throughout when done. Store in Mason jars or other airtight
containers and store in a dark, cool place in your kitchen.

TIP: HOW TO PEEL A PEACH

To peel a peach or a tomato, lightly score an X into the
skin of the fruit with a paring knife, submerge it in boiling water for 30–60 seconds, and transfer to an ice
bath to cool before pulling the skin off.

Peach-Bourbon BBQ Sauce

WATERBATH

5 lb peaches, about 17–21 peaches

¼ cup brown sugar, lightly packed

1 cup minced onion

5 cloves garlic, minced

1-inch piece ginger, minced

1¾ cups cider vinegar

½ cup honey

¼ cup bourbon

1½ Tbsp smoked paprika

2½ tsp salt

2½ tsp chipotle powder (grind whole chipotles if you don't have any)

The smoky flavors in this BBQ sauce come from a combination of lightly roasting the peaches and adding chipotle powder. We discovered the magic of ground chipotles while on vacation with our dear friends "the Pauls" a few years ago. This recipe is a tribute to them.

1 Preheat the oven to 375°F.

2 Cut the peaches in half and place on a rimmed baking sheet cut side up. Scatter the brown sugar over top. Roast until the peaches just begin to brown, 35–40 minutes.

3 Place the peaches, including any peach juice created during roasting, in a large pot. Add the onion, garlic, ginger, vinegar, honey, bourbon, paprika, salt, and chipotle powder and bring to a simmer over medium-high heat. Mash the peaches as they cook and keep at a simmer until the sauce reduces and thickens by half, about 15 minutes. Leave the sauce chunky or blend it smooth with an immersion blender.

4 Prepare your canning pot and rack, and sterilize your jars and lids (see page 17).

5 Continue to reduce the sauce until it's as thick as you want it.

6 Remove the jars from the canner and turn the heat to high.

7 Fill the jars with the sauce, leaving ½ inch of headspace. Gently jostle the jars or use the handle of a spoon to release any air bubbles.

8 Wipe the rims of the jars, apply the lids, and process for 20 minutes (if you live higher than 1,000 feet above sea level, refer to the Adjust for Altitude chart on page 17 for additional processing time). Remove the jars and allow them to cool. Store in a dark, cool place in your kitchen.

VARIATIONS: You can roast the peaches on the BBQ to increase the smoke flavor, but you will lose some of the precious juices. Replace the honey with 2½ cups brown sugar for a more traditional BBQ sauce.

CENTER OF THE PLATE: Add this to any BBQ dish; it can also be added to tomato sauce (page 332) for an interesting pizza sauce.

10 Minutes or less

Peach Crème Fraîche

FERMENT

LEVEL: ● ○ ○

YIELD: 1¼–1½ CUPS

EAT: WITHIN 1 WEEK

1 cup heavy (35%) cream
2 Tbsp buttermilk
1 peeled peach, pulverized

YOU WILL NEED
1 pint jar or airtight container

Crème fraîche is similar to sour cream, though it's more luxurious and heavier in fat content. By fermenting it with peaches you'll be creating a more interesting ingredient, one that combines the thickness of sour cream with the sweetness of the peaches and the acidity of fermentation.

Mix the cream and buttermilk in a clean jar with the peach. Cover with a clean, dry cloth and place in a warm, draft-free space in your kitchen. Stir a few times as it thickens; most like it to be the consistency of sour cream. It is generally complete in 12–24 hours. Cover and store in the fridge.

Peach Salt

SALT

LEVEL: ● ○ ○

YIELD: 1 CUP

EAT: AFTER 6 WEEKS

½ cup finely chopped peach
  (1 small peach)
1 cup salt

Any coarse salt will do for this, though I'm a big fan of spending the extra money for Maldon salt here. Use this as a finishing salt on salads, pork, and barbecued foods or toss on toasted nuts, desserts, or even with toast and butter!

Mix the peach and salt in a clean half-pint Mason jar, secure the lid, and store in a cool location. Lightly shake the jar every few days for the first two weeks. It's best after six weeks and will keep for one to two years on your counter.

Instant Hot Sauce

The quickest hot sauce ever! This is an easy way to save peaches when they are starting to soften. Puree three or peaches with ½ cup white vinegar, ½ cup honey, and ¼ cup fresh hot peppers (or more to taste). Store in an airtight container in the fridge for six to twelve months.

Finger-Lickin' Ribs with Peach BBQ Sauce

SERVINGS: 4

EFFORT: 30 MINUTES

ELAPSED: 7-30 HOURS

2 racks of ribs, about 4–5 lb total

⅓ cup brown sugar

3 Tbsp powdered mustard

1 Tbsp ground cumin

1 Tbsp sweet paprika

1½ tsp coarse salt

1 Tbsp black pepper

2 tsp chili powder

1½ cups peach bourbon BBQ sauce
(page 262)

Ribs were a semi-frequent meal at our house and are a frequent meal at our hunting camp. We usually eat them with rice, but for a special treat we serve them with cheese biscuits—a modification of the biscuit recipe on page 222. We omit the raisins and pistachios, and add 1 Tbsp of the rub and ½ cup of cubed cheddar cheese and bake them while we grill and rest the ribs!

1   Remove the membrane from the bottom of the ribs if necessary: use a paring knife to separate this layer of skin from the bone, then peel it back with your hands. This will help the rub penetrate, improve the texture of your ribs, and allow them to fall off the bone more easily.

2   Mix together the sugar, mustard, cumin, paprika, salt, pepper, and chili powder to make a rub.

3   Rub the ribs thoroughly and evenly, cover with aluminum foil, and refrigerate for 2–24 hours.

4   Preheat the oven to 225°F.

5   Place the ribs side by side on a large rimmed baking tray. Bake uncovered for 3½ hours.

6   Brush the ribs liberally with the BBQ sauce and bake for an additional 1–1½ hours. Cut into them to check that they're done. If you fear that they are becoming too dark, tent them loosely with aluminum foil.

7   Once the ribs have finished baking, loosely tent a piece of aluminum foil overtop (if you haven't already done so), and allow them to rest for at least 20 minutes before cutting and serving. Some people like to finish the ribs on the BBQ by adding more sauce and grilling them on high for a few minutes before resting.

PANTRY RAID: Add up to 1 Tbsp of any of the following to the rub: hot sauce (page 263), smoked peach powder (page 260), peach salt (page 263), tomato powder (page 332), or mushroom powder (page 251).

Dr. Stanwick's Apple Galette with Peach Crème Fraîche

SERVINGS: 6–8

EFFORT: 30–40 MINUTES

ELAPSED: 2–3 HOURS

GALETTE CRUST:

4 oz frozen butter

8 oz all-purpose flour

½ tsp salt

3 oz ice water

1 egg, lightly beaten

FILLING:

4–5 apples (I use a mix of green
   Crispin apples and red Spartan)

Juice of half a lemon

½ tsp ground cinnamon

⅓ cup peach crème fraîche
   (page 263)

1 oz (2 Tbsp) honey

1 oz (2 Tbsp) bourbon

Salt

YOU WILL NEED

Large baking sheet

Parchment paper or a Silpat mat

My most influential mentor was Dr. Michael Stanwick, who taught me how to teach. He was very proud of his sour cream apple pie. This is my tribute to his trademark dish.

MAKE THE CRUST:

1 Grate the butter into a large chilled bowl. Return it to the freezer for a few minutes then place it in a large bowl.

2 Mix the flour with the salt. Add the flour mixture, a few Tbsp at a time, to the butter, gently tossing the bowl after each addition to coat the butter with flour. When the butter stops absorbing the flour, scatter it with ice water, 1 tsp at a time, and continue to toss until there is no visible loose flour. Rinse your hands under very cold water, then, handling the dough as little as possible, form it into a ball. Cover with a damp cloth and refrigerate for 30 minutes.

MAKE THE FILLING:

3 Peel and slice the apples into a large bowl, about ¼ inch thick. Scatter the lemon juice over the apples as you slice them to help control browning.

4 Sprinkle with the cinnamon, add the crème fraîche, honey, bourbon, and a pinch of salt. Let rest for 15 minutes, stirring a few times as you wait.

MAKE THE GALETTE:

5 Preheat the oven to 375°F.

6 Roll the dough into a flat disk on a lightly floured surface. Don't worry about making a perfect shape—this is rustic! Carefully transfer it to a baking sheet lined with parchment paper or Silpat mat.

7 Remove the apple slices from their liquid and arrange them on the center of the crust.

8 Fold one side of the crust toward, but not right into, the center. Work your way around the outside of the crust, folding it as you go, leaving the center of the filling exposed.

9 Brush the pastry with the egg and pour the reserved liquids into the middle of the pie just before placing it in the oven. The galette is done when golden brown, 25–35 minutes.

PANTRY RAID: Stir jam (page 301) or grind dehydrated berries (page 320) into a powder and add them with the apples!

Pears

I have ruined more pears than any other fruit. They were one of the first things I ever dehydrated. I shaved them razor thin and put them in the dehydrator for a day. I was beyond excited to try them. I hadn't seen dried pears for sale very often, and I was pretty sure that I was on the verge of a culinary breakthrough.

I rifled through the dehydrator looking for the results and found nothing! I eventually realized that the thin slices had almost evaporated and were too thin and fragile to remove from the tray.

Undaunted, I tried to make pear leather next but encountered the same problem—I poured it too thin and couldn't separate it from the tray.

I then abandoned my efforts at dehydrating and turned my attention to placing a bunch of pear slices in a Mason jar of vodka. I was surprised to learn that you could leave the fruit in too long and render the liquid undrinkable. It was full of minuscule pieces of pear flesh that rendered the drink close to sludge.

However, onward and upward, as they say. This chapter contains the results of some of my more positive experiments!

PRESERVING NOSE-TO-TAIL

A pear, for the purpose of preserving, contains all of the same parts that an apple does. Check out page 81 for ideas on how to preserve pears.

TIPS FOR STORING

If a pear feels hard, it is unripe. Ideally, it should be slightly harder than a grape and should only be refrigerated at that point.

Pears will ripen relatively quickly in a bowl on the counter (they won't properly ripen in the fridge, though they will soften). As they ripen they will darken naturally. If this concerns you, dip them in a 50:50 mixture of lemon juice (fresh or bottled) and water. Remove them, let them rest for a few minutes and dry them with a towel before storing them.

If you're desperate, you can blend soft pears into a puree (remove the cores; you can leave the skin on or take it off) and store for three to five additional days in the fridge or for one month in the freezer.

FILLING THE PANTRY

CHILLED
They will keep in the fridge for about 1 week after ripening.

CANNED
Pear sauce, butter, and chutney.

DEHYDRATED
Slices or leather. Some pears, such as Asian pears, will separate when you try to dry them into leather.

FERMENTED
"Perry" is a hard cider.

INFUSED
Infuse dried pears.

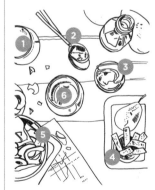

1 Pear Ginger Beer
2 Honeyed Pear Butter
3 Pear-Infused Brandy
4 Caramelized Pear Leather
5 Dehydrated Pears
6 Pear Skin Cider (Perry)

Batch-It

Honeyed Pear Butter

WATERBATH

LEVEL: ● ● ○

YIELD: 3–4 PINT JARS

EFFORT: 30 MINUTES

ELAPSED: 1 DAY

EAT: WITHIN 1–2 YEARS

8 lb Bosc pears (Williams
   or D'Anjou pears will also work)

1 lemon, zest and juice

2 cups apple cider

¼ cup honey

1 Tbsp ginger, grated then
   measured

1 tsp pure vanilla extract

YOU WILL NEED

Slow cooker

Pear Skin Cider (Perry)

FERMENT

LEVEL: ● ● ○

YIELD: 1 QUART

EFFORT: 5 MINUTES

ELAPSED: 1 MONTH

EAT: WITHIN 2 YEARS
   (IMPROVES WITH AGE)

1 cup honey

Filtered water

Approx 4 cups loosely packed pear
   skins (any skins left over from
   making the pear butter)

Ale or champagne yeast

Fruit butter is to jam what tomato paste is to sauce. These have a deep, intense flavor that goes a long way. Use this in the place of applesauce (page 82) or as a cooking ingredient.

You can either toss or use the peels you remove from the pears to make the butter. My preference is to make a quick and simple Perry. It's ready in a few weeks, but will improve over time in your fridge or in a sanitized wine bottle with a cork.

PREP THE PEAR BUTTER:

1   Peel the pears, reserving the skins, and chop into 1-inch cubes, discarding the seeds and hard parts of the cores. Place them in the slow cooker as you work. Juice and zest the lemon; grate the zest and add it to the pears with the juice.

2   Add the apple cider to the pears and turn the slow cooker to high, with the lid on, until the pot begins to simmer. Turn down the heat to low (you can leave it on low from the start though it will take longer to cook). If you can't fit all the pears in your slow cooker, begin this on the stove until it reduces enough to fit into the slow cooker.

3   Stir the pears from time to time. Once they have softened completely, mash them with a wooden spoon, still in the slow cooker.

4   Continue to reduce the mixture (with the lid on and heat on low) until it's twice the thickness of applesauce, stirring occasionally. Depending on your slow cooker, this could take 12–24 hours. Once done, add honey, ginger, and vanilla, and stir to finish.

MAKE THE CIDER:

5   Pour ½ cup of the honey and 1 cup of filtered water into a clean pint jar. Shake to mix. Fill the jar to the neck with pear peels (you can push to pack them tightly), and add additional water to cover if needed. Place an airlock on the jar and allow it to ferment for 1 week.

WATERBATH THE PEAR BUTTER:

6   Prepare your canning pot and rack, and sterilize your jars and lids (see page 17).

7   Remove the jars from the canner and turn the heat to high.

8   Fill the jars, leaving ½ inch of headspace. Gently jostle the jars or use the handle of a spoon to release any air bubbles.

9   Wipe the rims of the jars, apply the lids, and process for 10 minutes (if you live higher than 1,000 feet above sea level, refer to the Adjust for Altitude chart on page 17 for additional processing time). Remove the jars and allow them to cool before storing.

CONTINUE TO FERMENT AND AGE THE CIDER:

10 After 1 week, strain the concoction and discard any solids. Return the filtered "juice" to the Mason jar and add ½ cup more honey and 1 tsp of ale yeast, and fill the jar with filtered water to where the neck begins. Place the airlock on the jar, place the jar on a plate (in case it bubbles over), and ferment for three more weeks or until bubbling slows/stops.

11 Strain a final time and cover with a lid. This can age in the fridge for up to a year or you can bottle it in wine bottles (a walkthrough of the bottling process can be found on page 48).

Pear-Infused Brandy

Place 1 cup of dried pear slices in a clean Mason jar with 26 oz of brandy. Secure the lid and place in a warm, dark place in your kitchen. Age for up to three months, tasting occasionally. Strain out the pears and store them in the fridge in an airtight container. Use the pears in baking or added to ice cream. The brandy is fine in a bottle kept in a cabinet.

10 Minutes or less

Dehydrated Pears

DEHYDRATE

LEVEL: ● ○ ○

YIELD: 1 QUART

EAT: WITHIN 1 YEAR

2 lb pears (10–15 pears, depending on the varietal)

1 Tbsp fresh lemon juice

YOU WILL NEED

Apple corer

Dehydrator

I recommend a mandolin for this recipe, in order to keep your slices as uniform as possible.

Core the pears and slice with a mandolin to at least ¼ inch thick, tossing them in the lemon juice as you work. Spread the pears on dehydrating trays, ensuring that the slices don't touch. Dehydrate at 125°F until dried throughout, anywhere from 6–10 hours. Once cooled, they should be near brittle and dry when torn in half. Store them in a Mason jar on a shelf.

 # Caramelized Pear Leather

DEHYDRATE

6 Bartlett pears
¼ cup brown sugar, lightly packed
1 Tbsp balsamic vinegar
Salt

Pear leather roll-ups are fun treats. I think of them as candy, and caramelizing them was a natural next step to make them even yummier.

1 Peel the pears, cut them into quarters, and discard the seeds and core.

2 Place the sugar in a bowl, add the pear quarters, and coat all sides of each quarter with sugar.

3 Place a large frying pan on high heat.

4 Gently place the pears in a single layer (work in batches if necessary) in the pan. Once a side is golden brown, carefully turn it to cook the other side. The pan will begin to fill with the liquid from the pears. This can be a bit messy to clean but avoids oil, which can create an odd texture when dehydrating.

5 Puree the pears and their liquid with the balsamic vinegar and a pinch of salt.

6 Line a dehydrator tray with parchment paper, pour the leather in a ¼-inch-thick layer, and dry at 135°F for 6–10 hours. It should be slightly tacky but pliable. Don't spread it too thin, or you won't be able to get it off the tray!

7 Once done, keep the leather on the parchment paper (it helps keep the leather from sticking to itself) and roll it into a tight cylinder. Cut strips for individual portions. Store this in an airtight container in the fridge.

VARIATIONS: Use maple sugar instead of brown sugar or replace the pears with apples. You could also caramelize the pears on the BBQ to add a smoky flavor.

CENTER OF THE PLATE: Serve with nuts or granola, blend into a smoothie, or eat as is.

TIP: FUNNELS. BETCHA CAN'T HAVE JUST ONE!

Canning funnels range from cheap plastic ones to $15 metal ones (my preference). I've built up a small collection of funnels over the years and it makes filling jars a snap. I often work with five or six at a time.

Pear Ginger Beer

FERMENT

LEVEL: ● ● ○

YIELD: 4 26 OZ (750 ML) BOTTLES

EFFORT: 45 MINUTES

ELAPSED: 10–20 DAYS

DRINK: WITHIN 1 MONTH

4 quarts filtered water

1½ cups granulated sugar, plus more
for the bug

8-inch piece ginger, or more to
taste (some is used in the bug,
the rest during bottling)

1 cup dried pears

2 lemons

YOU WILL NEED

5 plastic bottles (like you would
bottle beer in), caps, bottle
sanitizer and a funnel

**I love homemade ginger beer, but remember that this is a
live ferment. Do not bottle it in glass and make sure to
store it in the fridge to release pressure.**

**The process can create alcohol. Measure the percentage before serving to children or those who avoid alcohol
(see page 48 for instructions).**

MAKE A GINGER BUG (2–7 DAYS; IT WILL BE FASTEST IN WARM WEATHER):

1 Place 1 cup of the water, 2 tsp sugar, and 2 tsp of the finely
chopped ginger in a clean jar. Stir well and cover loosely with
a clean cloth. Place in a warm location out of direct sunlight.

2 Add the same amount of sugar and ginger each day until the
liquid turns fizzy when stirred. When this happens you are
ready to make the ginger beer and bottle.

FERMENT AND BOTTLE THE SODA:

3 Roughly chop 6–7 inches of ginger, and place it in a large
pot. Add the pears, cover with 1 quart of the water and boil
over high heat for 10 minutes. Strain, and add more water to
make 16 cups and allow the liquid to cool.

4 Strain the ginger bug and add it to the pear-ginger water
with the juice of two lemons.

5 Bottle in clean, sanitized bottles, leaving 1 inch headspace.
If you don't have enough soda, divide what you have evenly
between bottles and top each bottle up with filtered water.
Store in a warm, dark place in your kitchen, squeezing the
bottles daily. When the bottles are solid, they should be
transferred to the fridge. This should take few days to a
few weeks.

6 Open the bottles slowly over a bowl to release excess
pressure.

VARIATIONS: This will work with any dried fruit; see dried
apple slices (page 85).

CENTER OF THE PLATE: Drink this cold or reduce it to a pear-
caramel syrup to intensify cocktails, glaze pork or fish, or add
to salad dressings or fruit salad.

French Onion Soup with Pear Brandy

SERVINGS: 6–8

EFFORT: 30 MINUTES

ELAPSED: 1½ HOURS

¼ cup unsalted butter, chilled

3 Tbsp olive oil

4 cloves garlic, finely chopped

4 lb onions, divided

4 sprigs fresh thyme
 or ¼ tsp dried thyme

3 bay leaves

Coarse salt

Black pepper

½–¾ cup pear-infused brandy
 (page 271)

10 cups beef stock (page 236)

1½ tsp cider vinegar

2 Tbsp soft butter

2 Tbsp all-purpose flour

6–8 pieces baguette, preferably
 thick-cut and a day old

3 cups Gruyère cheese, shredded
 then measured

YOU WILL NEED

Oven-safe bowls

This soup has a LOT of onions. I learned from Chef Jeff Dueck that cutting onions into rings will ensure they fall apart when cooking, adding texture to the dish, while cutting them in strips will preserve their shape and original texture.

1 Melt the ¼ cup chilled butter and oil in a large stockpot over medium-high heat.

2 Add the garlic, stir, and cook for 30 seconds.

3 Shave one-quarter of the onions into rings, add to the pot, and cook until they brown, stirring as you go.

4 Cut the remaining onions into ¼-inch slices. Add to the pan and cook, stirring to prevent them from burning, until they just begin to change color, about 5–7 minutes.

5 Add the thyme and bay leaves and season to taste with salt and pepper. Add the brandy and cook, stirring, for 3 minutes.

6 Add the stock, bring to a boil, and then lower to a simmer, partially covered, for 1 hour.

7 Discard the bay leaves. Add the vinegar ½ tsp at a time, stirring and tasting after each addition. You should be able to detect the increased acidity but not taste the vinegar.

8 Finish the soup by increasing the heat and bringing it to a noticeable boil. Make a beurre manié by mixing the 2 Tbsp soft butter with the flour to make a uniform paste. Add this to the soup and continue to simmer, stirring a few times, for 3 minutes. Remove from heat and proceed to serving instructions (or chill to serve next day).

TO SERVE:

9 Turn the broiler to maximum.

10 Pour warm soup into oven-safe bowls. Add a piece of bread and cheese to each bowl and place under the broiler until golden brown, about 4 minutes, but watch to make sure the cheese doesn't burn.

11 Serve carefully on top of a saucer or small plate.

PANTRY RAID: Replace butter with 1 cup mushroom duxelles (page 250), replace the salt with herbes salées (page 229) or finish with 2 Tbsp herb butter (page 227).

Roasted Duck with Pear Butter

SERVINGS: 4-6

EFFORT: 25 MINUTES

ELAPSED: 35 MINUTES

2 large duck breasts (8–12 oz each)

Coarse salt

Black pepper

⅓ cup walnuts, chopped
    before measuring

½ cup pear butter (page 270)

2 Tbsp white wine vinegar

YOU WILL NEED

Oven-safe pot (cast iron
    is my preference)

Duck should be served rare-medium. It's remarkably moist and a little goes a long way. You can easily double the sauce (no need to double the walnuts) to add additional flavor to the rice when you serve it.

1   Preheat the oven to 350°F.

2   Score the fatty side of the duck by cutting lines into the fat until you just reach the meat. Cut in diagonal grid lines (each line should be about ½ inch away from the next).

3   Season the duck liberally with salt and pepper.

4   Place the duck, fat side down, in the cold pan, then turn the heat to medium-high.

5   When the fat is crispy, 6–8 minutes, flip the duck and carefully transfer it to the oven for an additional 7 minutes, (loosely tenting it with aluminum foil will prevent a mess). It will be fairly rare when done.

6   Place the duck on a rack or plate, fat side up. Tent it loosely with aluminum foil and allow to rest for at least 10 minutes.

7   While the duck rests, toast the walnuts over medium-high heat in a separate pot for 2–3 minutes. Stir frequently; the nuts will darken slightly. Remove from the heat, and add the pear butter and vinegar to the pan. Mix to combine and set aside.

8   Cut the duck widthwise, on the bias, transfer to a serving dish, and pour the walnut mixture on top.

PANTRY RAID: Add a touch of pear brandy or apple-raspberry shrub (page 306) to the nuts while they toast.

Peppers

My parents spend a lot of time at our cabin in the late summer and fall. Despite being off-grid, it offers many creature comforts. Propane powers a stove, fridge, and BBQ; wood stoves bring heat; and a gas generator exists in case the isolation becomes too much. It rarely does for them.

In 2003, 50 million people lost power for several days on the east coast of North America. Frozen food defrosted, cash machines stopped working, and lineups clogged the few gas stations that managed to open. Life, as most of us knew it, stopped. My parents, on the other hand, had no idea. They had brought a bushel of Sheppard peppers into the forest and were blissfully transforming them into roasted pepper puree (a recipe inspired by them follows in this chapter).

Their experience during that week has long inspired me. Preserving can be easy. It doesn't require a lot of equipment. Learning to become self-sufficient (and protecting yourself from any potential zombie threat) is a great feeling—one that I'm reminded of every time I preserve peppers and think of my parents doing the same at the cabin!

PRESERVING NOSE-TO-TAIL

Sweet peppers contain the same components as chili peppers with two exceptions: Their flesh is sweeter (obviously), and their skin is more bitter.

I have several friends who believe they don't like sweet peppers. I believe that they don't like the bitterness of the skin; most have happily eaten pepper-based recipes I've made as long as I've peeled the peppers first.

The easiest way to peel the skins from a pepper is to char them over a fire. I use a BBQ set to the hottest temperature or place them under the broiler. Burn the outside of the peppers, cover them in a heat-safe bowl, allow them to cool, and peel by hand.

TIPS FOR STORING

Most peppers begin as green (the most bitter stage) and change colors as they ripen on the vine. This is why green peppers tend to store the longest. Whole peppers store best. Refrigerate them in an airtight container and they will keep for one to two weeks. If you don't have a large enough container, store them in the crisper away from watery veggies, such as exposed lettuce.

FILLING THE PANTRY

CHILLED

Frozen after peeling in slices or as puree. Giardiniera is a great fridge pickle, too!

CANNED

Pickled in vinegar or an oil and vinegar combination. Use great care when using oil, as peppers are not highly acidic. The recipe in this chapter adheres closely to the standards and guidelines from the National Center for Home Food Preservation.

DEHYDRATED

Peppers dry well, though the process tends to accentuate the bitterness of the skin.

1 Pickled Peppers
2 Pickled Sweet Cherry Peppers
3 Marinated Roasted Red Pepper
4 Giardiniera
5 Frozen Roasted Red Pepper Puree
6 Smoke-Dried Peppers

Batch-It

Marinated Roasted Red Pepper

WATERBATH

LEVEL: ● ● ○

YIELD: 4 PINT JARS

EFFORT: 1½ HOURS

ELAPSED: 2 HOURS

EAT: AFTER 1 MONTH
AND WITHIN 1–2 YEARS

5 lb red peppers (about 15 peppers)

½ cup Spanish onion cut into long,
thin strips then measured

2 cups sherry vinegar (5% or higher)

1 cup bottled lemon juice

1 cup olive oil

1 Tbsp dried oregano

8 cloves garlic cut as thinly
as possible

4 sprigs thyme

3 Tbsp smoked paprika

9 Tbsp red wine vinegar (5%)

A bushel of red peppers (around 30 lb) usually costs less than $1 per pound in the fall. Both of these recipes begin by charring peppers to remove the skins, which makes them a natural pair to batch.

Marinated roasted peppers are delicate and so are best added at the end of cooking or used as a topping on omelets, sandwiches, or pizza. Red pepper puree has been a staple in our pantry for more than ten years.

REMOVE THE SKINS FROM ALL 17 LB OF PEPPERS:

1 Preheat your BBQ on maximum, close the lid and allow it to heat for at least 10 minutes. If you don't have a BBQ, you can set your broiler to high and char the peppers on a baking sheet placed on a high rack in the oven.

2 Place the whole peppers on the grill. Wait for them to blacken on one side, and then rotate. Continue until most of the outside of the pepper is charred.

3 Place the peppers in a pot with a lid and cover (this will make them easier to peel). Pace on a heatproof surface, as the pot will get hot. Allow the peppers to cool enough to handle with a gloved hand.

MAKE THE MARINATED PEPPERS:

4 Prepare your canning pot and rack, and sterilize your jars and lids (see page 17) while the charred peppers cool.

5 Peel 5 lb of the peppers, removing the stems and seeds. Transfer peeled peppers to another pot as you work.

6 Place the onion, sherry vinegar, lemon juice, oil, and oregano in a pot and bring to a simmer over high heat.

PROCESS THE PEPPERS:

7 Remove the jars from the canner and turn the heat to high.

8 Divide the garlic, thyme, paprika, red wine vinegar, and peppers equally among the jars. Cover with the hot pickling solution, leaving ½ inch of headspace. Gently jostle the jars or use the handle of a spoon to release any air bubbles.

9 Wipe the rims of the jars, apply the lids, and process for 15 minutes (if you live higher than 1,000 feet above sea level,

Frozen Roasted Red Pepper Puree

CELLAR

LEVEL: ● ○ ○

YIELD: 1½ QUARTS/6 CUPS

EFFORT: 1–1½ HOURS

ELAPSED: 2½ HOURS

EAT: WITHIN 1 YEAR

12 lb red peppers (about 36 peppers)

1 tsp salt

1 tsp pepper

¼ cup olive oil

YOU WILL NEED

Containers to store the puree (I put
⅓-cup portions in 18 freezer bags
or oversized ice cube trays)

refer to the Adjust for Altitude chart on page 17 for additional processing time). Remove the jars and let cool.

MAKE THE PEPPER PUREE:

10 While the other peppers are waterbathing, place the remaining whole peppers in a food processor. Set aside the smoky liquid in the bottom of the bowl. Puree the peppers until smooth, season with salt and pepper, and taste. Add the olive oil and a small amount of the smoky liquid, puree, and taste again. Continue adding smoky liquid until you are happy with the taste of the puree. Season if needed.

11 Place the puree in freezer bags, remove all the air, and freeze flat. You can also freeze this in ice cube trays.

NOTE: Allowing the peppers to cool on a rack placed over a baking sheet will let the natural juices to gather on the sheet without steeping in the charred skins. This will make far more usable juice and will increase your yield (and flavor) dramatically in step 11.

10 Minutes or less

Smoke-Dried Peppers

SMOKE

LEVEL: ● ● ●

YIELD: 20 PEPPER HALVES
(ABOUT 1 QUART)

EAT: WITHIN 1 YEAR

8–10 red peppers

YOU WILL NEED

Cold smoker or smoke maze

Oak chips

Dehydrator

These started as an experiment inspired by chipotle peppers. They are now a must-have in my pantry. The recipe was a collaboration with our friends Aaron and Kelly, and is one of the most unique. The peppers add instant smoke and richness to any dish. I often put 1–2 in the slow cooker when pulling beef or making stew. The peppers melt into the dish and their smoky flavor penetrates the entire meal.

Remove the stems and cut the peppers lengthwise into two or three pieces. Place in a smoker flesh side down. Cold smoke over oak for 6 hours (see page 66 to create your own smoker from your BBQ). Place on a dehydrator, skin side down, and dry at 125°F until brittle, 8–10 hours.

Pickled Sweet Cherry Peppers

WATERBATH

LEVEL: ● ● ○

YIELD: 8 HALF-PINT JARS

EFFORT: 30 MINUTES

ELAPSED: 2 HOURS

EAT: AFTER 6 WEEKS

    AND WITHIN 1-2 YEARS

4 lb cherry peppers

1½ cups granulated sugar

1½ cups white vinegar

1 large onion, shaved into rounds

4 cloves garlic, sliced into thin disks

¼ cup mustard seeds

2 tsp celery seeds

2 tsp canning or pickling salt

Cherry peppers are circular and the size of a large plum. There are sweet and spicy varieties, and they look nearly identical, so make sure to pick carefully and label your jars!

The first time I saw a jar of these was at a restaurant owned by Canadian chef and champion of local food and preserving Jamie Kennedy. The peppers looked like jewels encased in glass. To this day I think they are by far the most beautiful preserve in the world.

1 Prepare your canning pot and rack, and sterilize your jars and lids (see page 17).

2 Poke three or four holes in each pepper to allow the brine to penetrate them. You can hide the holes near the stems.

3 Place the sugar, vinegar, and 1½ cups water in a large pot, mix to combine, and bring to a boil over high heat for 1 minute. Add the peppers, onion, garlic, mustard seeds, celery seeds, and salt and bring to a hard boil for 1 minute.

4 Remove the jars from the canner and turn the heat to high.

5 Fill the jars with peppers then ladle brine overtop, leaving ½ inch headspace and process for 10 minutes (if you live higher than 1,000 feet above sea level, refer to the Adjust for Altitude chart on page 17 for additional processing time).

6 Remove the jars and allow them to cool.

VARIATIONS: To each jar add any of the following: 1 tsp cumin, 1½ tsp minced ginger, or 1 Tbsp of chili flakes for some heat!

CENTER OF THE PLATE: These are awesome on sandwiches and can be a great addition to a pile of nachos (chop them, drain well, and add to the nachos before baking).

Pickled Peppers

Slice 2 peppers into long strips (8-10 slices per pepper) and place in a pot with ½ cup of white wine (or cider) vinegar, ¼ cup water, 1 Tbsp honey, and 10 black peppercorns. Bring to a hard boil over high heat for 3 minutes. Remove the pepper-corns and add ¼ cup chopped chives or fresh parsley. Stir everything together and allow the mixture to cool. Store in the fridge. Add these to fish, cured meats, or salads, or as a contrast to roasted vegetables.

 # Giardiniera

CELLAR

This is a twist on a traditional Italian giardiniera, a pickle that is often eaten as a relish or condiment. While some recipes waterbath giardiniera, I prefer to make a version for the fridge, which will remain crunchy and vibrant as there's no cooking involved.

LEVEL: ● ● ○
YIELD: 1–1½ QUARTS
EFFORT: 30 MINUTES
ELAPSED: 2½ DAYS
EAT: WITHIN 1 MONTH

DAY 1:

2 red peppers, diced
2 green peppers, diced
1 medium zucchini, diced with skin on
½ cup fennel, chopped
1 cup chopped cauliflower
6-8 green onions, chopped
3 cloves garlic, minced
2 jalapeños, diced
¼ cup coarse salt

DAY 2:

3 Tbsp fresh lemon juice (about
　1 lemon)
¼ cup mustard seeds
1 Tbsp dried oregano
1 tsp smoked paprika
½ tsp black pepper
1 cup olive oil
1 cup vinegar
2 Tbsp honey

DAY 1:

1 Mix all the Day 1 vegetables with the salt in a large, non-reactive bowl. Cover loosely with a cloth and leave on counter for 6–18 hours, or overnight.

DAY 2:

2 Drain and rinse the vegetables thoroughly in cold water. Taste them after rinsing, and see what you think—you can soak them in cool water for a few hours, changing the water a few times, to reduce their saltiness.

3 Add the lemon juice, mustard seeds, oregano, paprika, and black pepper with the oil, vinegar, and honey. Place in an airtight container with a lid and refrigerate for at least two days before eating. Store this in the fridge. The flavors will develop over time and it will keep for months.

VARIATIONS: You can swap many of the ingredients according to what's available. I often make with the end-of-harvest vegetables from the garden in the fall. I like to think of it as a "kitchen sink pickle." You can even dye the entire batch purple by adding a cubed beet!

CENTER OF THE PLATE: The liquid from this is great for cooking or seasoning a brine, while the vegetables can be eaten a million different ways. They are particularly great with white fish or fatty meats, stirred into mashed potatoes right before serving, or eaten straight off a spoon.

Slow-Cooked Pulled Beef with Preserved Peppers

3-4 lb lean roast (chuck or round is fine), trimmed of any excess fat

Salt

Black pepper

Oil or tallow for searing

1½ cups beef stock (page 236)

1 cup marinated roasted red peppers without oil (page 280) or ¾ cup frozen red pepper puree (page 281)

1 dried hot pepper (page 174)

1-2 smoke-dried peppers (page 281) (optional but recommended)

YOU WILL NEED

Slow cooker

Pulled meat is immensely reusable, freezes well, and goes a long way. Pull a roast on Sunday and use it as an ingredient throughout the week by adding it to sandwiches, stir-fries, salads, chili, pasta sauce, stews . . . the list goes on!

When searing meat in a frying pan, avoid placing it in the center. By searing the meat on one side of the pan, you can alternate sides when flipping and are more likely to retain the heat through the process.

1 Heat a large frying pan on medium-high heat.

2 Pat the roast dry, then season it liberally with salt and pepper.

3 Add fat to the pan. When it just begins to smoke, place the roast on one side of the pan. Sear until browned on all sides, about 3 minutes per side.

4 Puree the stock and peppers in a blender until smooth.

5 Add the roast, pepper puree, hot pepper, and smoke-dried pepper (if using) to the slow cooker. Set it on low, checking occasionally to ensure there's ample liquid. Cook until the beef easily falls apart with a fork, 6–8 hours.

6 Shred the beef into a large bowl. Add as much of the liquid (and hot pepper) as you'd like. Season to taste with salt and pepper.

PANTRY RAID: Replace the stock with the liquid from any pressure canned vegetables, or add dried herbs (page 227) or mushroom or tomato powder (pages 251 and 332). If you have smoke-dried peppers, make sure to add 2 big pieces of them in at the start of cooking.

Pasta with Olive Oil, Garlic, and Roast Pepper Puree

SERVINGS: 2 JOEL-SIZED SERVINGS
(3–4 FOR EVERYONE ELSE)

EFFORT: 15 MINUTES

ELAPSED: 30 MINUTES

1 lb dried pasta (or ¾ lb fresh pasta)

3 Tbsp olive oil

3 garlic cloves, minced

1 Tbsp capers

Black pepper

¼ cup red pepper puree (page 281)

Juice of half a lemon

½–¾ cup loosely packed
Parmigiano-Reggiano, finely
grated then measured

This is an easy dinner that can be made with any pasta shape you choose. This looks like a lot of olive oil but it isn't just for cooking—it's added as part of the flavor here. Aged cheddar can be substituted for the Parmigiano-Reggiano. I like to grate either with a rasp that makes a small amount of cheese seem like a whole lot!

1   Place a large pot of heavily salted water on high heat to cook the pasta. Cook the pasta until al dente.

2   In a frying pan, gently warm the olive oil on medium heat until hot. Add the garlic, capers, and lots of black pepper. Cook for 90 seconds, stirring constantly. Remove from the heat and add the pepper puree and lemon juice.

3   Drain the pasta and toss it with the sauce. Season with salt and black pepper if needed. Plate and top with Parmigiano-Reggiano to finish.

PANTRY RAID Flavored salts (pages 175 and 229), sundried tomatoes, or chunks of pressure canned tuna (page 208) can all be fun ways to extend this dish.

TIP: VINTAGE JARS ARE USEFUL

Many preservers swoon over glass. We love funky jars and cool relics of the past but realize that, in most cases, they can't be safely used for canning (page 16). There are many reasons why they can't, but most boil down to out-dated technology such as swing-top jars, out-dated gaskets, or jars requiring paraffin wax to form a seal. These jars are, however, very useful when it comes to storing dehydrated or fermented food, and we use them for both.

Plums

I've been a sauce dude my whole life. Dana's brother, Kevin, once called me on it. "I don't understand how a guy puts so much care into what he cooks then drowns it in sauce."

Plum sauce is one of the first condiments I remember eating. It was this amazing balance of sweet and sour and I thought it made everything it touched taste better. It was frequently slathered on pork, chicken, rice, and anything else that landed on my plate. I'm still a fan of plum sauce, though I'm slightly more restrained now.

It took me years to figure out that plum sauce was actually made from plums. I imagine that sounds odd, but I think a lot of us overlook the humble plum as a cooking ingredient. Plums (and any form of plum puree) can be sweetened, spiced, soured, or made savory. They are a fruit that easily transcends dessert and, when preserved, a versatile ingredient that can be used in a nearly infinite combination of ways.

PRESERVING NOSE-TO-TAIL

Like grapes and apples, there are many plum varieties in the world today. They range from sweet to acidic, and I encourage you to taste different varieties to see what you like before deciding to preserve with them.

Any plum can be preserved, but the most sought-after tend to be damson, a clingstone variety that is quite acidic, and the Italian plum, also referred to as the Italian prune plum or empress. Damsons are circular and almost look like gigantic blueberries, while Italian plums tend to be much more elongated and have a higher flesh-to-pit ratio.

You can peel a plum by blanching it like you would a peach or tomato (page 261). Another way to remove the skins is to cook plum halves on high heat with ½ cup of water. As the flesh begins to fall off, you can remove the fruit and peel off the skins. The skin is slightly bitter and can be dried on its own, but I usually leave it on when preserving and save myself the hassle of removing it.

The pits of plums, like those of apricots, cherries and peaches, can be toxic in large amounts (page 91). And like peaches, plums come in both clingstone and freestone varieties. if you're trying to preserve plums, you'll want to find freestone varieties for easiest removal of the pits.

continued . . .

CHILLED
Frozen in slices or as a freezer jam.

CANNED
Plum sauce, jam, juice, chutney, and chunks of whole fruit in simple syrup.

DEHYDRATED
Dried into prunes, fruit leather, or chunks of dried fruit.

FERMENTED
Japanese chefs ferment a special form of dried plum to make umeboshi vinegar.

INFUSED
Plums can be infused in vinegar or booze.

1 Damson Plum Gin
2 Roasted Spiced Plum Fridge Jam
3 Sweet and Sour Plum Sauce
4 Dehydrated Plums (Prunes)
5 Plum Leather
6 Plum Jam with Cinnamon and Orange

TIPS FOR STORING

Unripe plums should not be stored in the fridge as they will soften but not develop in flavor. The quickest way to ripen them is to place them in a sealed brown paper bag containing an apple. Store them on the counter, out of direct sunlight, and with space between them.

Ripe plums can be stored in the fridge, with space between them, to maintain their texture for a few days. Keep small plums in egg cartons. If they begin to soften, you can save them by pureeing them and then mixing 1 part cider vinegar and 1 part honey to 8 parts plum puree. This quick sauce will keep for a week or longer and can be eaten as is, used to baste meat, or reduced and thickened on the stove when you're ready to eat.

Damson Plum Gin

The damson plum has a cult-like following. It's acidic, tart, and dense in texture so it holds flavor well. The firm texture of the damson makes it an ideal fruit for infusing. Wash and quarter ten to twelve plums, discard their pits, and cover with good gin. Remove enough gin from a 26 oz (750 mL) bottle to accommodate the plums or pour both ingredients into a 1-quart Mason jar. Place a lid on either container and store out of direct sunlight for six months. The plums will be edible and the gin will be fantastic as a sipper or sweetened to taste with a 25:75 mixture of honey and water (make it sweeter if you prefer).

Sweet and Sour Plum Sauce

WATERBATH

LEVEL: ● ● ○

YIELD: 3-4 HALF-PINT JARS

EFFORT: 45 MINUTES

ELAPSED: 1½ HOURS

EAT: WITHIN 1-2 YEARS

2½ lb plums

½ cup cider vinegar

½ cup honey

¼ cup dark rum

¼ cup soy sauce

4 garlic cloves, minced

1½ inches ginger, minced

½ tsp ground cinnamon

½ tsp cayenne pepper

¼ tsp ground cloves

1 Puree the plums in a blender and then pour them into a large pot set over medium heat.

2 Add ½ cup water, vinegar, honey, rum, and soy sauce. Then add the garlic, ginger, cinnamon, cayenne, and cloves. Bring to a boil on high heat before lowering to a simmer until the sauce thickens to the desired consistency. I let it simmer for 12–15 minutes.

3 Prepare your canning pot and rack, and sterilize your jars and lids (see page 17).

4 Remove the jars from the canner and turn the heat to high.

5 Ladle the sauce into the jars. Wipe the rims of the jars, apply the lids, and process for 20 minutes (if you live higher than 1,000 feet above sea level, refer to the Adjust for Altitude chart on page 17 for additional processing time). Remove the jars and allow them to cool.

VARIATIONS: You may want to add an additional ½ cup of honey or replace all of the honey with 2–2½ cups of brown sugar.

CENTER OF THE PLATE: Use this as you would plum sauce, but don't be afraid to cook with it. Add a 50:50 mixture of this sauce and goat cheese or ricotta to a stuffed chicken or a pork tenderloin.

TIP: SAVE BOXES FROM SCOTCH AND CRAFT BEER BOTTLES

If you happen to drink Scotch or craft beer, you'll know that many of these bottles come inside attractive boxes. The boxes aren't just for packaging—they allow you to store the bottle out of direct sunlight. So save your left-over boxes to store fruit wine and other ferments that require the same care.

Batch-It

Plum Jam with Cinnamon and Orange

WATERBATH

LEVEL: ● ● ○

YIELD: 4 HALF-PINT JARS

EFFORT: 45 MINUTES

ELAPSED: 2 HOURS

EAT: WITHIN 1–2 YEARS

2½ lb Italian plums

¾ cup honey

⅔ cup orange juice

2 Tbsp fresh lemon juice

¼ tsp ground cinnamon

Plum Leather

DEHYDRATE

LEVEL: ● ○ ○

YIELD: 1 18- X 18-INCH SHEET

EFFORT: 10 MINUTES

ELAPSED: 8-12 HOURS

EAT: WITHIN 6 MONTHS

1½ lb Italian plums

¼ cup honey

1 Tbsp balsamic vinegar

½ tsp black pepper

YOU WILL NEED

Dehydrator

Jam doesn't have to be candy-sweet. I prefer it on the tart side as I find it makes a more diverse cooking ingredient. And individual jars can easily be sweetened to taste by adding liquid honey after opening.

I make the leather while the jam processes and still have enough time to clean the kitchen before the jam is done. This is a partly savory leather that is an unexpectedly versatile ingredient. Add small amounts to rice, stir-fries, or tea!

MAKE THE JAM:

1 Cut the plums into chunks, discarding the pits.

2 Prepare your canning pot and rack, and sterilize your jars and lids (see page 17).

3 Place the plums in a large pot with the honey, orange juice, lemon juice, and cinnamon. Bring to a boil on high heat before lowering to a simmer. Skim any foam that appears until the jam passes the freezer test (see page 13). This will take about 10–15 minutes depending on the size of your pot.

4 Remove the jars from the canner and turn the heat to high. Fill the jars with the plum jam, leaving ¼ inch of headspace. Use the handle of a spoon to release any air bubbles. Wipe the rims of the jars, apply the lids, and process for 15 minutes (if you live higher than 1,000 feet above sea level, refer to the Adjust for Altitude chart on page 17 for additional processing time). Remove the jars and allow them to cool.

MAKE THE LEATHER:

5 While the jam processes, puree the plums in a food processor. Once it's smooth, add the honey, vinegar, and black pepper and process for another few seconds.

6 Pour the mixture in a thick layer onto parchment paper or a Silpat mat. Dry in the dehydrator at 125°F, checking after 4 hours. Remove from the parchment paper when it easily separates and continue to dehydrate until dry but not brittle, about 6 hours. Cut it into slices, separate them with parchment paper, and store in the fridge in a glass container.

10 Minutes or less

Dehydrated Plums (Prunes)

DEHYDRATE

LEVEL: ● ○ ○

YIELD: 1 QUART

EAT: WITHIN 1 YEAR

3 lb plums

You can dehydrate plums whole by poking several holes with needles, but I far prefer to cut them in half when drying for time's sake. Choosing freestone plums and cutting along the crease of the plum will make the pit easier to remove.

Wash and pit the plums. Using your thumb, turn the plum inside out by pushing against the outside. Place the fruit on dehydrator trays skin side down and dehydrate at 135°F until dry, 12–18 hours.

Roasted Spiced Plum Fridge Jam

CELLAR

LEVEL: ● ○ ○

YIELD: 1 CUP

EAT: WITHIN 3-6 MONTHS

6 plums

¼ cup brown sugar, lightly packed

2 tsp chili flakes

¼ tsp ginger powder (or ¾ inch piece fresh ginger, minced)

2 Tbsp lemon juice (about ½ lemon)

2 Tbsp orange juice

My grandmother made a lot of fridge jam using whatever fruit she had on hand. I often roast plums when cooking other meals and find time to make jam like this when I'm waiting for dinner to cook. Yes, it's just that easy!

Turn the broiler on maximum. Halve and pit the plums, turning them inside out by pushing against the outside. Toss them in a bowl with the chili flakes, ginger, and lemon juice as you cut them. Once you've finished cutting all the plums, drain any excess liquid from the bowl and add the brown sugar. Lay the plums on a rimmed baking tray, skin side down, and place under the broiler on the top rack of the oven. Watch them closely until they start to brown, no more than 2 minutes. Remove from the oven, roughly chop the plums, and put them in a small pot with the orange juice. Simmer over medium heat until gelled, about 5 minutes. Taste as you go, and add additional brown sugar to sweeten, if desired.

Slow-Cooked Steel-Cut Oats

SERVINGS: 2-3

EFFORT: 5 MINUTES

ELAPSED: 8-9 HOURS

1 cup steel-cut oats

¼ cup dried plums (page 293), measured then chopped into small cubes

1 Tbsp unsalted butter, chilled

2 tsp maple syrup

Ground cinnamon

2-4 Tbsp plum jam (page 292)

YOU WILL NEED

Slow cooker

For all of my childhood, my parents cooked a warm breakfast for me. As an adult, I am notorious for missing my morning meal. But there's no excuse for missing breakfast with this simple recipe that will cook itself while you sleep. It comes with an added bonus: the most glorious smells wafting through your house as you wake up.

1 Place 4 cups water in a slow cooker and add the oats, plums, butter, maple syrup, and a pinch of cinnamon. Cook on low heat for 8–9 hours.

2 Serve with jam stirred in!

PANTRY RAID: Any dried fruits or jams are obvious additions (pages 132, 164, and 219). You may also want to add a slice or two of dried lemon a few minutes before serving to incorporate some citrus flavor and add a touch of bitterness to contrast with the jam and fruit.

Baked French Toast with Plum Preserves

SERVINGS: 4

EFFORT: 20 MINUTES

ELAPSED: 12 HOURS

½ cup unsalted butter, chilled

½ cup brown sugar, lightly packed

¼ cup honey

¾ cup plum jam (page 292)

12 slices sandwich bread

6 eggs

½ cup whole milk

Ground cinnamon

Coarse salt

YOU WILL NEED

A 9- x 12-inch baking dish with
   2-inch-deep sides

Many years ago, I was helping my dad and our friend Frank build a cottage. Frank's wife, Kyra, assembled a French toast casserole as we unwound by the fire after a long day of work. She baked it the next morning and I fell in love with the idea and the results! This recipe can be scaled up or down and is ideal when you have company or you need to cook breakfast for a large group. Note that you need to start this the night before you plan to eat it.

12–18 HOURS BEFORE EATING:

1 In a small pot on low heat, melt the butter. Remove from the heat and add the sugar and honey. Pour it into the baking dish, using a spoon to lightly grease the sides.

2 Make 6 sandwiches by spreading the plum preserves across half the bread and topping with a second slice. Lay these in your baking dish in a single layer. Wedge them in tightly, cutting the bread if necessary.

3 Beat the eggs. Add the milk, ½ tsp cinnamon, and a pinch of salt to them and stir to combine. Pour this over the bread.

4 Cover the dish and refrigerate overnight or up to 18 hours.

30–45 MINUTES BEFORE EATING:

5 Preheat the oven to 350°F.

6 Bake the bread, uncovered, until golden brown, about 30 minutes.

7 Serve as you would cake, making sure each portion has a slice from both the top and bottom.

PANTRY RAID: Small pieces of fruit leather (page 272), infused maple syrup (page 132), a touch of peach crème fraîche (page 263), or dried fruit can all be added between the pieces of bread before baking.

Raspberries

My mother grew up in a small fishing community in Cape Breton, Nova Scotia. Foraging was one of her chores as a child; she used to pick blueberries for 10 cents a pound to raise money for school supplies. Mom had a reputation as a masterful picker. She seemed to have a gift for finding the greatest spots to harvest and could fill her basket twice as fast as anyone else.

The first time I saw my mom pick a wild fruit other than a blueberry was on a long hike in Nova Scotia. As she walked along the trail in front of me, she plucked a fruit from a bush and began to chew. I asked how she knew she was being safe. For the next 90 minutes she walked along the trail, showing me which berries and plants she picked as a child and which ones to avoid. She knew the names of every one of them and shared tips on how her family used to preserve them. I was shocked!

She's returned to foraging in the last few years at our hunting cabin. There are patches of blackberries, wild leeks, blueberries, raspberries and more. She harvests each on early morning walks or late afternoon ATV rides (yes, she has her own) before heading back to our cabin and making jam on a propane powered stove.

My mother's foraged jams are my favorite preserves in the world.

PRESERVING NOSE-TO-TAIL

Most people preserve raspberries whole but it is possible to separate them into two parts: the juice and the seeds/skin.

Separating the two is an easy process but requires patience: strain the crushed fruit through a sieve or cheesecloth, or process with a food mill. You can also cook the berries and then strain them. The juice can be consumed as is, added to other preserves, transformed into jelly, or processed by a waterbath.

Raspberry seeds have many health benefits but are often discarded when people make jelly or other seed-free preserves. Dry them on low in a dehydrator, or spread them on parchment paper for a few days, and you'll be left with seeds that can be added to baking, smoothies, or fruit salads.

continued . . .

FILLING THE PANTRY

CHILLED

Fridge and freezer jams or frozen whole.

CANNED

Jam and jelly.

DEHYDRATED

Because of the seeds, whole berries are not ideal candidates for drying. Mix strained raspberry juice into applesauce and dry to make a raspberry-apple fruit leather.

FERMENTED

A common ingredient in homemade sodas, fruit wine, beer, and sour beer.

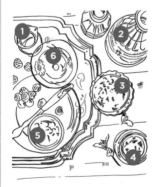

1 Raspberry Wine Vinegar
2 Raspberry Brandy
3 Mint-Maple Fridge Jam
4 Fermented Raspberries
5 Raspberry Jam
6 Raspberry-Apple Hard Cider

Fresh raspberries from the field or farm can go soft and turn moldy 24–48 hours after they enter your house. Some may even bruise during the shortest of commutes. Raspberries do not ripen after harvesting, so buy them as fresh as possible or pick your own for the best results.

Raspberries have a lot of surface area, which makes them fantastic collectors of yeast spores. This means that they're easy to ferment but they can quickly become overripe. If you're not fermenting them, the best way to prolong their life is to use the vinegar trick or thermotherapy (see page 54).

10 Minutes or less

Raspberry Wine Vinegar

INFUSE

LEVEL: ● ○ ○

YIELD: 1 PINT

EAT: WITHIN 1-2 YEARS

1¼ cups red wine vinegar
1 cup raspberries

This simple preserve is one of my favorite winter ingredients. White wine vinegar would also work for this.

Heat the vinegar in a pot over medium heat and bring to a low simmer. Crush the berries and place them in a clean 1-pint Mason jar. Pour the vinegar over the berries, stir, cover with an airtight lid, and store in a cool, dark place. Shake every day for the first week (don't worry if you forget one day) and open the jar over the sink to release any pressure. Shake occasionally and taste as it ages. The longer it ages, the more complex it becomes. Strain the raspberries within three months to prevent them from growing mold. Use as is or strain into a clean, airtight jar. It will last longer if strained. Store on a cool, dark shelf in your kitchen.

Raspberry Jam

WATERBATH

LEVEL: ● ● ○

YIELD: 5–6 HALF-PINT JARS

EFFORT: 30 MINUTES

ELAPSED: 2 HOURS–2 DAYS

EAT: WITHIN 1–2 YEARS

4 cups raspberries

3 cups granulated sugar

¼ cup fresh lemon juice

20 whole peppercorns

¼ cup brandy (optional)

YOU WILL NEED

Cheesecloth

Mint-Maple Fridge Jam

Place 2 cups raspberries and 1 Tbsp balsamic vinegar in a large bowl. Crush the berries and add 3 Tbsp maple syrup. Crush a handful of mint, wrap it in a piece of cheesecloth or jelly sack, and add it to the bowl. Loosely cover with a clean towel and leave on the counter for 24 hours. Lightly simmer for 10 minutes, taste, and add more maple syrup if needed. Store in an airtight container in the fridge for two to three weeks or in the freezer where it will keep for three to four months.

Alcohol is an interesting ingredient to add to a jam. The addition is for flavor; if you're cooking the booze with the fruit, your final jam will contain little (if any) alcohol at all. The jam will taste fine without it, but I like the warmth that brandy adds, and I find that it transforms the jam from a sweet condiment to a balanced ingredient suitable for wider range of cooking.

1 Crush the raspberries with the sugar and lemon juice in a large non-reactive bowl. Cover loosely with a clean towel and place on the counter for 1–2 hours or in the fridge for up to two days.

2 Prepare your canning pot and rack, and sterilize your jars and lids (see page 17).

3 Create a jelly sack with the cheesecloth and place the peppercorns inside it.

4 Put the jelly sack in a pot with the raspberries and their liquid. Add the brandy and bring to a boil over high heat before lowering to a simmer. Skim off any foam and simmer until the gelling point, about 10–15 minutes. See the freezer test on page 13 if you're not sure when to stop cooking.

5 Remove the jelly sack from the pot.

6 Remove the jars from the canner and turn the heat to high. Ladle the jam into the hot jars, wipe the rims, and apply the lids. Process for 10 minutes (if you live higher than 1,000 feet above sea level, refer to the Adjust for Altitude chart on page 17 for additional processing time). Remove the jars and allow them to cool.

VARIATIONS: Replace the brandy with Grand Marnier or dark rum, or replace half of the raspberries with strawberries. Or make the jam without the brandy and add 2 tsp of booze to each jar before ladling in the jam. Use a Sharpie marker to label the lids (it will withstand the waterbath) and you can make four or five variations of the same jam at the same time!

CENTER OF THE PLATE: Add a shot glass of brandy (or the raspberry brandy) and 2–4 Tbsp of this jam to a vanilla milkshake!

Batch-It

Fermented Raspberries

FERMENT

LEVEL: ● ○ ○

YIELD: 1 QUART

EFFORT: 5 MINUTES

ELAPSED: 24–72 HOURS

EAT: WITHIN 30 DAYS

3½ cups organic raspberries

½ cup granulated sugar

Raspberry-Apple Hard Cider

FERMENT

LEVEL: ● ● ●

YIELD: 1 GALLON

EFFORT: 15 MINUTES

ELAPSED: 4–6 WEEKS

DRINK: BEST AFTER AGING 1–2 YEARS, BUT CAN BE DRUNK ANY TIME

2 cups fermented berry puree

1 gallon apple cider

YOU WILL NEED

Airlock

5 26 oz (750 mL) wine bottles with corks and bottling supplies (refer to page 48 for an overview of bottling)

Fermented berries contain a small amount of sugar to feed the wild yeasts. Any time you ferment with sugar you run the risk of creating alcohol as the yeast converts sugar into carbon dioxide and ethyl alcohol. This is a good thing if it's your intention; not so great if you do it unintentionally. In this recipe, I specify organic berries because they contain more wild yeast than non-organic.

The cider is non-carbonated and is the definition of micro-brewing—you're making hard cider a gallon at a time! Most apple cider has been pasteurized and needs additional yeast to help it ferment in order to turn into alcohol. By using fermented raspberries as a starter, we can avoid commercial yeast.

NOTE: Most store-bought cider is pasteurized, which will kill wild yeast. Some farmers will sell unpasteurized cider if you ask discreetly at a local farmers' market.

DAY 1: FERMENT THE BERRIES:

1 Crush the berries and sugar together in a clean jar or other container. Place in a dark, warm spot in your kitchen. Cover loosely with a clean towel.

2 Taste after 12 hours, and every 6–12 hours thereafter. It starts off very sweet before becoming almost savory and slightly sour at the end. Don't be alarmed if you notice small pockets where air bubbles have surfaced through the thick puree.

3 Fermenting is done when you are happy with the taste (this usually takes two to three days for me). Cover tightly and store in the fridge to slow or stop fermentation. This will keep for weeks or use it to make the cider!

DAY 3 OR 4: START THE CIDER:

4 Using a funnel, pour 2 cups fermented berry puree into a sterile 1 gallon jug. Add cider until the liquid reaches the point where the jug neck just begins to narrow. Secure with the airlock. Place the jug on a plate in case any of the liquid overflows and store in a dark, warm place where it won't be disturbed. Leave for ten days.

DAY 13 OR 14: RACK THE CIDER:

5 Syphon the liquid from the jug into a clean container. Clean the jug and add the cider back to it, topping up with enough fresh cider so that the liquid reaches into the narrow part of the neck.

6 Secure with an airlock and age for four to six weeks, checking to ensure the airlock has enough water to seal it. Write the date on a piece of tape on the bottle.

7 After four weeks, taste your cider. If you like it, it's ready to go! If it's too sweet, let it ferment longer. If it's not sweet enough, add a bit more sugar and let it ferment longer. Don't let it ferment for longer than six weeks.

8 Strain the ferment through a fine sieve, chill, and serve. You can also bottle and age the cider. I like to wait two years (see the note on page 134 about brewing double batches) and I find it becomes smoother with time.

> ### TIP: ALTERNATE YOUR LIDS
>
> One of the common frustrations of using two-part lids in canning happens as you bathe the seals in hot water before jarring your final product; seals can become stuck to one another by a thin layer of water. Avoid this by stacking lids in alternate directions (top side to under side) before tossing them in the water.

10 Minutes or less

⊕ Raspberry Brandy

INFUSE

LEVEL: ● ○ ○

YIELD: 1½ PINTS

DRINK: AFTER 1 MONTH BUT BETTER AFTER A YEAR. ONCE STRAINED WILL LAST INDEFINITELY WITHOUT AN AIRLOCK.

4 cups raspberries
1 cup granulated sugar
2 cups brandy

YOU WILL NEED
1-quart Mason jar with airlock

Most infusions are very short. I decided to try a long infusion and waited a year with this one—I was instantly convinced of its worthiness. If you're willing to wait, you'll find that the brandy has transformed from a thin liquid to a near syrup that is sweet with a slight bitterness from the seeds. It is impossible to resist, and worth the wait.

Crush the berries and the sugar in a bowl. Loosely cover with a clean cloth and leave on the counter for 1–2 hours. Pour the berries into a clean jar and cover with brandy. Place an airlock on top and age for one to twelve months, topping up the airlock with water as needed. Strain and store in a clean jar or bottle. Store out of direct sunlight.

Venison, Moose, or Grass-Fed Beef with Brandy Raspberry Reduction

SERVINGS: 2–4

EFFORT: 20 MINUTES

ELAPSED: 40 MINUTES

10 peppercorns

5 juniper berries

3 sprigs thyme

2 bay leaves

2 game or grass-fed beef steaks,
   1 inch thick (6–12 oz each),
   at room temperature

Salt

Black pepper

¾ cup veal or beef stock, divided

1 small sweet onion, finely chopped

¼ cup raspberry brandy jam
   (page 301)

I grew up eating deer and moose hunted by the camp that I now run. I find that most people overcook game and confuse bad cooking with the term "gamey." Game meat tends to be lean; it's best served medium-rare and it must be allowed to rest after cooking. When venison and moose are cooked properly, most people can't tell the difference between them and grass-fed beef. My mother forages wild raspberries on the property that we hunt; the moose eat the same berries and make this sauce a natural pairing.

1 Turn your burner to high and heat a cast iron pan on it for 5 minutes. It must be ridiculously hot. There is no need to add fat or oil.

2 While the pan is heating, create a jelly sack with a piece of cheesecloth. Add the peppercorns, juniper berries, thyme, and bay leaves and seal the sack.

3 Season the meat generously with salt and pepper.

4 Place the steaks carefully in the pan. Don't touch them. Time 2 minutes exactly, then flip the steaks. Wait two more minutes, without touching.

5 Remove the meat and let it rest on a plate, loosely tented with aluminum foil.

6 Deglaze the pan with ¼ cup of the stock, stirring to remove any bits stuck to the pan. Turn down the heat to medium-high and cook the onion until translucent, stirring constantly, for about 3 minutes.

7 Add remaining stock and the jelly sack and return to a boil. Reduce the stock by half, about 6–10 minutes, remove the jelly sack and turn down the heat to a simmer.

8 Remove stock from heat, stir in the jam, and taste. Adjust the flavor by adding some of the remaining stock, salt, or pepper.

9 Slice the meat across the bias, spoon the sauce over top, and allow it to rest for 3 additional minutes before serving.

PANTRY RAID: Add herbes salées (page 229) instead of salt or dress with mushroom powder (page 251) and flavored salt (such as the chili salt on page 175).

Apple-Raspberry Shrub

SERVINGS: 3–4

EFFORT: 5 MINUTES

ELAPSED: 5–7 DAYS

3–4 sweet apples (about 2 cups), peeled and grated

¾ cup raspberry-wine vinegar (page 300), strained or unstrained

1 cinnamon stick

⅓–½ cup honey, plus more to taste

A shrub is also known as a drinking vinegar. Don't be fooled, though: it's as refreshing as lemonade!

I make this in the winter when I'm craving a taste of summer. You can drink it as is, use it in cocktails or marinades, or add to carbonated water. It's generally served chilled but it's delicious when warmed and served with bourbon, too.

1 Place the all ingredients into a clean 1-quart Mason jar.

2 Cover the jar with its lid and place it in the back of your fridge for four to five days.

3 Taste the shrub; if you're happy with it, strain it and serve. Or you can store in the fridge where it will continue to mature. If it's too sour for you, add honey to taste. Drink as is or mix 2–3 Tbsp into every cup of still or sparkling water.

PANTRY RAID: Add frozen fruit as ice cubes, sweeten with jam instead of honey, rim the glass with dried mint, or spike with a touch of raspberry-apple cider (page 302).

Rhubarb

I was so lucky to spend the first five years of my life in the country. I've never really left it behind and often catch myself daydreaming about going back.

My parents had a large garden that was secured from predators by a large fence. I have vivid memories of them working in the garden picking carrots and digging for potatoes, as I watched the corn reach higher into the sky with each passing summer day.

Rhubarb was one of the few ingredients that my parents grew outside of the fenced garden. I can't remember them cooking with it, but I do remember that I was allowed to eat as much of it as I wanted. I loved the overwhelming rush that came with biting into a sour stalk freshly pulled from the garden. My memories of wielding a stalk of rhubarb while being chased around the yard by our dog, Flip, are some of my most cherished.

PRESERVING NOSE-TO-TAIL

Rhubarb is generally preserved unpeeled but it can be easily peeled with a paring knife if you wish. Simply trap an end of the peel between the knife and your thumb and pull.

The peels tend to be the most colorful part but are stringy compared to the rest of the stalk. If you do peel your rhubarb, use the peels to make a bitter infusion.

Using a steam juicer you can extract the water from rhubarb stems to make juice that can be used for wine, jelly, and more (about 5 pounds makes a quart/4 cups).

It is worth noting that the leaves are toxic and the roots, which are not often dug up, are sometimes used in Chinese medicine.

TIPS FOR STORING

Remove any leaves and chop the stalks into small cubes or 1-inch pieces. Store in an airtight container in the fridge.

If your rhubarb is starting to soften, you can add ½ cup of granulated sugar per quart of rhubarb to the container. Shake the rhubarb three or four times in the 24 hours following the addition of sugar and it will keep for another week or more with only a minor loss in texture.

FILLING THE PANTRY

CHILLED
Frozen stalks.

CANNED
Jam, chutney, pickled or preserved as chunks in simple syrup.

DEHYDRATED
I love dehydrated rhubarb. Eat whole pieces or blend into a powder for beverages, rubs, or sweet sauces.

FERMENTED
Rhubarb wine is a common country wine that ages particularly well.

1 Strawberry-Rhubarb Honey Wine
2 Roasted Rhubarb Jam
3 Rhubarb Soda
4 Rhubarb Sour "Candies"
5 Rhubarb Salt

Batch-It

Roasted Rhubarb Jam

WATERBATH

LEVEL: ●●○

YIELD: 3 HALF-PINT JARS

EFFORT: 45 MINUTES

ELAPSED: 2 DAYS

EAT: WITHIN 1–2 YEARS

2 lb rhubarb

1½ cups brown sugar, lightly packed

1 Tbsp whole black peppercorns

1 Tbsp candied ginger, diced then measured

1 tsp whole cloves

1 Tbsp fresh lemon juice

Zest of 1 lemon, chopped fine

½ tsp pure vanilla extract

YOU WILL NEED

Small piece of cheesecloth

Rhubarb Sour "Candies"

DEHYDRATE

LEVEL: ●●○

YIELD: 1 CUP

EFFORT: 20 MINUTES

ELAPSED: 10–12 HOURS

EAT: WITHIN 1 YEAR

1½ lb rhubarb

2 Tbsp maple syrup

YOU WILL NEED

Dehydrator

Anytime I waterbath I know that I'm going to have some free time while I wait for water to boil, jam to set, or jars to process. Whenever I waterbath I almost always make a quick preserve at the same time. In these recipes, I'll show you how to create a roasted rhubarb jam (the oven adds a rich sweetness that you wouldn't otherwise get), while finding time to make rhubarb sour "candies" that bring me back to my youth when I adored sucking on sour candies that made my mouth turn inside out!

MACERATE THE RHUBARB FOR THE JAM:

1 Wash the rhubarb and chop it into ½-inch pieces. Place the pieces in a bowl and toss with 1 cup of the sugar. Cover tightly and refrigerate overnight (and up to 36 hours). A natural syrup will form.

DEHYDRATE THE RHUBARB FOR THE CANDY:

2 Bring a large pot of water to a rapid boil. Prepare an ice bath.

3 Clean the rhubarb and then use a mandolin to cut it into ¼-inch-thick pieces.

4 Blanch the rhubarb for about 30 seconds, drain, and cool immediately in the ice bath.

5 Spread the rhubarb onto dehydrator trays. Dehydrate at 125°F for 6–8 hours.

MAKE THE JAM:

6 Prepare your canning pot and rack, and sterilize your jars and lids (see page 17).

7 Preheat the oven to 400°F.

8 Remove the rhubarb from the fridge and scatter it on a rimmed baking tray, reserving the liquid. Bake until soft and slightly brown, about 20 minutes.

9 Remove the jars from the canner and turn the heat to high.

10 Wrap the peppercorns, ginger, and cloves in a piece of cheesecloth and secure tightly. Place the cheesecloth in a pot with the roasted rhubarb and add the lemon juice and zest. Bring to a low simmer on medium-high heat, skimming off any foam as you go. The jam will slightly reduce and thicken

in 10 minutes. Turn down the heat and test if it's ready (see page 13).

11 Stir the vanilla into the jam mixture right before canning.

12 Pour the jam into the jars, wipe the rims of the jars, apply the lids, and process for 15 minutes (if you live higher than 1,000 feet above sea level, refer to the Adjust for Altitude chart on page 17 for additional processing time). Remove the jars and allow them to cool.

FINISH THE CANDY:

13 Place the maple syrup in a pot and bring to a boil on high heat before reducing to a simmer.

14 Toss the dehydrated rhubarb into the syrup, stirring to coat. Cook for 90 seconds and remove from heat. It will look slightly plump.

15 Use a spoon to spread small clumps of the rhubarb on a dehydrator tray and dry at 125°F for 6–8 hours. The pieces should be completely dry but sticky on the surface. Store the candy in a Mason jar on a shelf. Any pieces that touch each other will be almost impossible to separate when dry, so keep any clumps small.

TIP: RE-DEHYDRATION

"Re-dehydration" was a silly term we coined in 2011. The process is simple: dehydrate food, rehydrate it with warm liquid, and dehydrate it again. The dried food absorbs new flavors, which are concentrated as they dehydrate further. Our first experiments were with strawberries and 25-year-old balsamic vinegar and we've been experimenting ever since.

---

10 Minutes or less

Rhubarb Salt

SALT

LEVEL: ● ○ ○

YIELD: 1 CUP

EAT: AFTER 10 DAYS
    AND WITHIN 1–2 YEARS

¼ cup rhubarb, diced then
    measured (about ½ a stalk)

1 cup coarse salt

Bitter salt becomes magic around the rim of a glass! Use just this salt or make a 50:50 combination of it and maple sugar.

Chop the rhubarb as thinly as possible. Place it in a clean jar with the salt and secure the lid. Shake until the ingredients are thoroughly mixed. Shake daily for ten days. Store on a shelf.

Strawberry-Rhubarb Honey Wine

FERMENT

LEVEL: ● ● ●

YIELD: 1 GALLON/5 26 OZ (750 ML)
    BOTTLES

EFFORT: 2 HOURS

ELAPSED: 5 MONTHS

DRINK: YOU CAN DRINK RIGHT AWAY BUT
    BEST AFTER 1–2 YEARS OF AGING

2 lb strawberries, rinsed, hulls
    removed, and lightly mashed

1 lb rhubarb stalks, chopped into
    1-inch pieces

3 lb honey

16 cups (4 quarts) filtered water

1 Campden tablet (see note)

1 package champagne or ale yeast

½ tsp yeast nutrient

YOU WILL NEED

2 1-gallon fermenting vessels (jugs,
    available at home-brew stores,
    are most common)

Funnel that fits the jug

Sanitizer

Airlock

Syphoning hose

5 26 oz (750 mL) wine bottles

Corks and corker

Fruit wines are common ferments that were often made at the end of a growing season. Farmers who had leftover crops would transform the food into alcohol. My recipe departs from tradition and is a hybrid of mead and fruit wine. It was inspired by T'ej (a slightly bitter Ethiopian honey wine) and my love of bitter beer. If you don't love bitter beer, don't worry—although the rhubarb is noticeable it's also subtle.

If you haven't bottled before, I recommend a visit to your local wine-brewing store which will help you source what you need and learn how to use it (there is an overview of the bottling process in the fermenting chapter).

DAY 1: START THE FERMENT

1 Place the strawberries, rhubarb, honey, and 2 cups of the water in a large pot and simmer over medium heat for 10 minutes. Mash everything finely enough for it to fit through the funnel. Remove from the heat, add 4 cups of the water, stir to combine, and allow to cool to room temperature.

2 Clean and sanitize the fermenting jug and airlock.

3 Crush the Campden tablet and add it to the jug. Using a funnel, pour the rhubarb mixture into the jug. Top with water if needed to raise the level of the water until it reaches the point a few inches below the start of the neck. This will leave room for it to ferment. Attach the airlock and wait 24 hours.

DAY 2: ADD THE YEAST

4 Add the yeast and yeast nutrient, and re-attach the airlock.

5 Place the jug on a deep plate or rimmed baking tray in case the ferment bubbles over. Store out of direct sunlight (60°F–75°F is ideal; it will ferment faster in hotter temperatures).

6 Gently jostle the jug each day to mix the contents. Fermenting will begin slowly but will eventually be easy to see as it rolls and bubbles. Once it stops visibly fermenting, after two to four weeks, move to the next stage.

2-4 WEEKS LATER: RACK THE MEAD AND SECOND FERMENT

7 Sanitize the second jug and rack the mead from the first jug into the second jug. You do this by syphoning the first jar into the second and leaving as much sediment and solids behind as possible. This will result in a clearer mead. You may wish to do this a few times for maximum clarity.

8 Sanitize the 1-gallon jug and transfer the liquid back to it. Top with more filtered water until the liquid just touches the base of the neck. Too much headspace or air can turn your mead into vinegar. Sanitize and attach the airlock, then set the jug out of direct sunlight for two to three months. Check the airlock every few days (and more often if it's warm in your kitchen) to ensure it doesn't dry out and top with water.

2-3 MONTHS LATER: RACK AND BOTTLE THE WINE

9 Sanitize the bottles, corks, and bottling equipment. Make sure the ferment has stopped completely (there should have been no visible signs of bubbles for weeks). Fill the bottles equally, topping them up with filtered water if necessary. The liquid should reach into the neck to reduce oxygen contact. Best stored in a cool, dark place.

10 Make sure the ferment has stopped completely (there should have been no visible signs of bubbles for weeks). Bottle and age; you can drink immediately but it will be better after one or two years. Young wine will have edges that can be smoothed by decanting for a few hours, or up to a day. See the bottling overview (page 48) for more details.

VARIATIONS: If you really want to capture the essence of the fruit, juice some of the rhubarb and/or strawberries from the recipe and freeze a cup of the juice. Add this after the first racking.

NOTE: Campden tablets and yeast nutrient are available at wine-making shops. You need Campden tablets to kill any wild yeasts that could alter the flavors you're cultivating with the champagne or ale yeast. This recipe uses one to create a consistent, repeatable flavor.

Frozen Rhubarb

Clean the stalks, cut them into ½-inch pieces, steam for 2 minutes or blanch in boiling water for 30 seconds, and then cool in an ice bath. The leftover water from blanching will be bitter and can be mixed with honey for a great fake lemonade. Spread the pieces on a rimmed baking tray to prevent clumping and freeze for 3 hours before transferring the rhubarb to a sealed container or freezer bag. Remove as much air as possible and store in the freezer.

Rhubarb Soda

LEVEL: ● ● ○

YIELD: 2 26 OZ (750 ML) BOTTLES

EFFORT: 15 MINUTES

ELAPSED: 1–2 DAYS

DRINK: WITHIN 1 MONTH

2–3 lb rhubarb, cleaned and
   chopped into 1-inch pieces

¾ cup honey

6 cups filtered water

1 tsp fresh lemon juice

½ tsp pure vanilla extract

Salt

⅛ tsp champagne yeast

YOU WILL NEED

2 reusable plastic pop bottles
   designed for home brewing (see
   the note on page 47)

A cross between lemonade and sour candy, rhubarb soda is surprisingly refreshing and awesome on a warm spring day. Our friend Paul loves rhubarb as much as I do; this drink was inspired by our friendship and my childhood memories of pink soda pop.

1   Place the rhubarb and honey in a large pot with 3 cups filtered water. Bring to a boil on high, lower the heat, and simmer vigorously for 10 minutes.

2   Mash the rhubarb slightly and allow it to cool.

3   Puree the mixture in a blender. Strain it through a fine sieve into a large bowl. Squeezing it will add flavor but result in a cloudier product.

4   Add the lemon juice, vanilla, a pinch of salt, and the yeast, stir, and divide into sanitized plastic bottles. Top each bottle with remaining filtered water, leaving 1 inch of headspace. Taste and add additional honey if desired.

5   Place the caps on the bottles and leave them in a warm, dark place in your kitchen. Squeeze daily to test for carbonation. When the bottle is hard to squeeze, it's done. This should take 12–48 hours. Store in fridge to help stabilize the pressure and slow fermentation. Open slowly over a bowl as this can be a little volatile!

VARIATIONS: Replace the honey with maple syrup, substitute blood orange for the lemon, or add ½ cup chopped fresh ginger to the rhubarb while it cooks.

CENTER OF THE PLATE: Drink as is, reduce to make an interesting salad dressing ingredient or pour over pie, or add a touch of Grand Marnier just because.

Maple Cream Fudge with Rhubarb Salt

SERVINGS: 8- x 8-INCH TRAY OF
FUDGE

EFFORT: 20 MINUTES

ELAPSED: 2 HOURS

3 cups brown sugar, lightly
packed

¾ cup unsalted butter, chilled

½ cup whole milk

¼ cup maple syrup

2 cups icing sugar

½ cup all-purpose flour

1 tsp pure vanilla extract

2 tsp rhubarb salt (page 311)

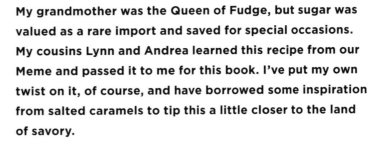

My grandmother was the Queen of Fudge, but sugar was valued as a rare import and saved for special occasions. My cousins Lynn and Andrea learned this recipe from our Meme and passed it to me for this book. I've put my own twist on it, of course, and have borrowed some inspiration from salted caramels to tip this a little closer to the land of savory.

1 Grease an 8- x 8-inch baking pan with butter.
2 Place the brown sugar, butter, milk, and maple syrup in a large pot and bring to a gentle boil over medium heat. Cook for 4½–5 minutes, stirring frequently, then remove from the heat.
3 Add the icing sugar, flour, and vanilla. Stir quickly to incorporate all the ingredients and pour the mixture into the baking pan.
4 Let the fudge rest for 5 minutes then scatter rhubarb salt (and pieces of dried rhubarb from it) across the surface.
5 Allow the fudge to cool while you lick the pot.
6 Once it has cooled completely, it can be stored in an airtight container in the fridge. Best served at room temperature. It will last indefinitely but become harder with time. If it becomes too hard, dilute fudge in a small amount of boiling water and pour over ice cream.

PANTRY RAID: Toss dried strawberries or dried cherries (pages 320 and 164) overtop while it's cooling, serve with a touch of jam (pages 92, 133, and 320), or a top with chili salt (page 175) for contrasting flavors.

Brined Pork Loin Roast with Maple-Rhubarb-Cornmeal Crust

SERVINGS: 6–8

EFFORT: 30 MINUTES

ELAPSED: 32 HOURS

PORK AND BRINE

3–4 lb boneless lean pork loin roast

Scant ½ cup kosher salt

2 Tbsp whole peppercorns

2 Tbsp mustard seeds

2 bay leaves

¼ cup honey

CRUST

¾ cup cornmeal

GLAZE

½ cup rhubarb jam (page 310)

¼ cup orange juice

Zest of ½ orange, finely grated

1 Tbsp cider vinegar, homemade
   (page 82) or store-bought

1 Tbsp maple syrup

Coarse salt

My dad started roasting peameal bacon as a whole roast in order to feed the guys at our hunting camp. It was more efficient than grilling the meat and the results were far superior. Although this recipe will work with peameal bacon, I like to start with a pork loin roast, which is often larger and juicier after brining.

You can serve this in slices for breakfast or stack it high on a bun with pickled hot peppers and shredded cheddar for a great sandwich.

BRINE THE PORK:

1 In a container just large enough to hold the pork snugly, dissolve the salt in 1 cup of boiling water. Add 2 quarts water (or enough to completely submerge the roast), salt, peppercorns, mustard seeds, bay leaves, and honey. Mix to combine then submerge the pork in the liquid. Cover tightly and refrigerate for 24 hours.

COOK THE PORK:

2 Preheat the oven to 225°F. Place a rack on top of a roasting pan.

3 Remove the pork from the brine, pat dry, and dredge in the cornmeal.

4 Place the pork on the rack and roast, uncovered, for 2 hours, or until it just starts to brown.

PREP THE GLAZE:

5 While the pork is cooking, place the jam, orange juice and zest, vinegar, maple syrup, and a pinch of salt in the blender and make the glaze.

6 At the 2-hour point, spoon glaze over the pork to baste and put it back in the oven for 7 minutes. Baste and then cook for another 7–8 minutes. Check it often to ensure it doesn't burn.

7 Remove the pork from the oven and let it rest for at least 10–12 minutes before cutting.

PANTRY RAID: Serve with applesauce (page 82), apple gastrique (page 86), or chili salt (page 175), or finish with herbes salées (page 229).

Strawberries

When I was a child, my family would visit pick-your-own strawberry farms in the summer. We'd go early in the morning, and my parents would make jam when we returned home.

I hadn't preserved in years when I called my dad and declared that Dana and I wanted to come to his house to learn how to make jam. I was shocked to see that the entire process took about an hour.

Dana and I call strawberry jam the gateway drug to preserving because it's a starting point for so many people. It's strange, because strawberry jam requires a little more diligence than jam made from other fruit with more seeds, like raspberries, or thicker skins, like plums.

Once we learned how to make jam, strawberries became the first fruit we ate only when they're in season. Like our experience with asparagus (page 101), the change happened almost by accident, but a case of jam made the choice an easy one. Homemade jam is better than any berry that can survive a drive across the continent.

PRESERVING NOSE-TO-TAIL

Strawberries are generally preserved by cooking the fruit into jam or jelly, but they can actually be broken down further. Strawberry juice can be extracted with a steam juicer, seeds can be removed by straining through a sieve or jelly sack, and the hulls can be dried with some flesh attached to flavor tea or tossed over coals to make BBQ smoke.

TIPS FOR STORING

There is no replacement for a locally grown strawberry. However, compared to their flavorless counterparts that are shipped across the country, most local strawberries will begin to soften within a day or two. You can extend the life of strawberries by neutralizing some of the wild yeast on the surface: lightly toss them in a tablespoon of cider vinegar before storing them and rinse them before cooking or eating.

If you still have too many berries on the cusp of spoiling, remove their stems, chop them coarsely, and add one-eighth to one-quarter of their volume in granulated sugar. Place them in an airtight container and refrigerate. You'll lose some texture and have increased the sugar content, but you'll be left with semi-firm berries and sauce that will last for five days or longer.

FILLING THE PANTRY

CHILLED
Freeze whole or cook into a freezer jam with any amount of sugar or honey.

CANNED
Jam, jelly, juice, and whole berries in simple syrup. You can also pickle green strawberries.

DEHYDRATED
Strawberries dry really well, either in slices or whole.

FERMENTED
Wonderful additions to fruit wine and mead.

INFUSED
Rumtopf is my favorite, though you can infuse almost any alcohol or vinegar with berries.

1 Strawberry Balsamic Jam
2 Rumtopf
3 Strawberry Hops Bitters
4 Strawberry Ginger Leather
5 Dried Strawberries and Hulls Infused with Vanilla

Batch-It

Dried Strawberries and Hulls Infused with Vanilla

DEHYDRATE

LEVEL: ● ○ ○

YIELD: 1½–2 CUPS DRIED STRAWBERRY
  SLICES, 1 CUP HULLS

EFFORT: 10 MINUTES

ELAPSED: 7–10 HOURS

EAT: WITHIN 1 YEAR

12 cups (6 pints) whole strawberries
  with hulls on

1 Tbsp pure vanilla extract

Strawberry Balsamic Jam

WATERBATH

LEVEL: ● ● ○

YIELD: 3 HALF-PINT JARS

EFFORT: 55 MINUTES

ELAPSED: 2 DAYS

EAT: WITHIN 1–2 YEARS

Reserved berry tops from the
  dehydrated strawberries

2 cups brown sugar, lightly packed

30 whole peppercorns

1 large bunch basil, including stems

4½ Tbsp fresh lemon juice

Zest of 1 lemon, finely chopped

3 Tbsp balsamic vinegar

YOU WILL NEED

Dehydrator

Cheesecloth

This was the first batch-style recipe we ever made, and it inspired this book. Use a mandolin to slice the strawberries in preparation for dehydrating them. When you feel like the blade is getting too close to your fingers, stop slicing and chop the hulls off and use the tops. Dehydrate the hulls and use the unsliced berries for jam. I've been doing this for years and it's been a great way to get the most out of the fruit. You end up with three preserves (jam, dried slices, and dried hulls) in only slightly more time than it would take just to make jam.

DEHYDRATE THE BERRIES AND HULLS:

1 Carefully hold the hull of the strawberry and use a mandolin to slice off the tips of the berries. Place these on a dehydrator tray, leaving space between the slices. As you slice the berries, your fingers will come closer to the blade—stop before you become uncomfortably close. You will be left with a hull and half a berry (or more) in your fingers.

2 With the remaining top of the berry, remove the hull with a paring knife, leaving some flesh attached to it, and set that on another dehydrator tray. Toss the remaining berry (you will be left with about half of the original berry) into a large bowl to make jam.

3 Dehydrate the slices and hulls at 135°F for 4–6 hours, until dry and brittle.

PREP THE JAM:

4 Clean the reserved berry tops, place them in a pot, and lightly crush them. Add the sugar and mix to combine. Cover tightly and refrigerate for 1–24 hours, stirring occasionally.

MAKE THE JAM:

5 Prepare your canning pot and rack, and sterilize your jars and lids (see page 17).

6 Tie the peppercorns and basil into a piece of cheesecloth. Use several layers if necessary to ensure the peppercorns don't escape.

7 Put the cheesecloth in a wide pot and add the strawberry-sugar mixture. If you have soda water, use it to rinse the bowl the berries have been in and pour it into a glass for a quick beverage.

PROCESS THE JAM:

8 Turn the heat to high and raise to a boil before lowering to a light simmer until the jam mixture reduces by half, 15–20 minutes.

9 Add the lemon juice and zest and the vinegar. Simmer the jam until it sets (see page 13), skimming off any foam into a bowl (you can eat it right away or store in fridge). It should take 15–30 minutes.

10 Remove the cheesecloth bag from the pot.

11 Remove the jars from the canner and turn the heat to high.

12 Using a spoon and funnel, fill the jars with jam, leaving ¼ inch of headspace. Gently jostle the jars or use the handle of a spoon to release any air bubbles. Wipe the rims of the jars, apply the lids, and process for 10 minutes (if you live higher than 1,000 feet above sea level, refer to the Adjust for Altitude chart on page 17 for additional processing time). Remove the jars and allow them to cool.

FINISH OFF THE DEHYDRATED BERRIES:

13 Transfer the dehydrated berries to a large bowl.

14 In a small pot, bring the vanilla to a boil over high heat before lowering to a simmer. This will happen quickly, so monitor it constantly. Pour it over the dehydrated berries and stir to combine. Place the strawberries back on the dehydrating tray and dehydrate them at 135°F until dry, about 5–7 hours.

15 If you like, you can repeat step 14 with the hulls.

16 When the berries are completely dry, they are ready. Store them in an airtight jar on a shelf.

> **TIP: MULTIPLE SIEVES**
> Using a sieve or a colander to strain ingredients can lead to a common frustration: the holes get clogged and straining takes forever. To prevent this, I use different strainers (starting with large holes and ending with small ones) to reduce clogging and speed things along.

10 Minutes or less

Strawberry Hops Bitters

INFUSE

LEVEL: ● ○ ○

YIELD: 3 HALF-CUPS

DRINK: AFTER 1–12 MONTHS

    AND WITHIN 2–3 YEARS

1½ cups vodka or grain alcohol

½ cup hop leaves

¼ cup dried strawberries

YOU WILL NEED

3 half-pint Mason jars,
    lids and rings

This is actually three preserves: alcohol is infused with strawberries in one jar, another jar of vodka is turned bitter with hops, and a final jar includes a combination of the two to make strawberry bitters. I'm a big fan of making bitters separately like this, as it gives you the greatest control of the final flavor. They are ready within a month but you can age them for up to a year for a more intense final product.

Pour the vodka into a small pot over medium heat. Heat to just under a simmer. While the vodka is heating, clean 2 half-pint Mason jars. Place the hops in one and the strawberries in the other. Evenly divide the warm vodka between the two jars, place their lids loosely on top, and allow them to cool. If the lids seal, open the jars before placing the lids back on top and securing with the jar rings.

Place in a dark, relatively cool place in your kitchen. Taste the liquids occasionally after one month and let them age for two to twelve months. When you are happy with the intensity of the flavors, strain off the solids. Pour some of the strawberry bitters into a third clean jar and, using a teaspoon, add small amounts of the hop bitters to it. Stir and taste. Continue to do so until you are happy with the flavor. Store in Mason jars with lids out of direct sunlight, where they will last indefinitely.

Frozen Strawberries

Strawberries freeze really well, and it's simple to do. Gently clean and dry the berries, spread them out on a rimmed baking tray, and leave them in the freezer overnight. The next day, transfer them to a freezer bag. Remove as much air as you can, but don't be overly concerned. Label, including the date, and leave in the freezer for up to six months.

10 Minutes or less

Rumtopf

INFUSE

LEVEL: ● ○ ○

YIELD: 1 PINT

DRINK: AFTER 6 MONTHS
AND WITHIN 1–2 YEARS

1 lb strawberries and other fruit

½ lb sugar

1–2 cups dark rum (enough to
cover the fruit)

YOU WILL NEED

1-gallon glass jar

Kitchen scale

Rumtopf is a traditional German preserve made with different types of fruit, sugar, and rum. It generally starts with strawberries, as they are the first fruit of the season, but you can use other fruits as the summer progresses (just add more fruit, sugar, and rum as you go). We make a gallon every summer by combining strawberries, blueberries, pitted cherries, slices of apricots, peaches, plums, raspberries, and blackberries in a 1-gallon cookie jar. For best results, you should weigh the ingredients in this recipe as it's the only reliable way to balance the flavors.

Clean the fruit and remove hulls or pits. Place it in an airtight container, cover with the sugar, and gently mix. Refrigerate overnight. Lots of liquid will appear. Place the fruit mixture in a clean jar, cover with rum, and close the jar tightly. Each time a new fruit comes into season, repeat these steps and add more fruit to your jar. Let the fruit and alcohol rest for several months, then drink the syrup and eat the fruit. We open it at Christmas, and spoon it over ice cream or in cocktails.

Strawberry Ginger Leather

DEHYDRATE

LEVEL: ● ○ ○

YIELD: 1 SQUARE FOOT

EAT: WITHIN 1–3 MONTHS

4 cups (2 pints) whole strawberries,
hulls removed

1 Tbsp balsamic vinegar

1-inch piece ginger, minced

¼ cup honey (optional)

YOU WILL NEED

Dehydrator

You don't need a high-speed blender for this recipe, but it helps to pulverize the ginger and strawberry seeds into a consistent mixture.

Place the berries, vinegar, and ginger in a blender and blend to liquefy. Taste and sweeten with honey if desired. Line a dehydrator tray with parchment paper. Pour on liquid to about ⅛ inch thick and use a spoon to cover over any "holes" that appear in the surface. Dehydrate at 135°F for 6–8 hours, until slightly pliable and sticky. You should be able to pull it off the sheet fairly easily (though I leave the sheet on the bottom for storage). Cut to your preferred size, stack in an airtight container with parchment separating the layers, and store in the fridge.

Strawberry Sundae with Balsamic and Honey Caramelized Apples

SERVINGS: 2

EFFORT: 10 MINUTES

ELAPSED: 10 MINUTES

2 apples ("pie" varieties are best)

1 Tbsp honey

1 Tbsp unsalted butter

¼ cup strawberry balsamic jam (page 320)

Vanilla ice cream, for serving

1 tsp aged balsamic vinegar

Fresh mint, for garnish

My dad is an ice cream monster and I love any dessert that includes apples. The additional step of cooking the apples is well worth the effort—the combination of hot apples melting into the cold ice cream elevates this to something phenomenal.

If you don't have access to aged balsamic vinegar, make a glaze by simmering 1 cup of balsamic vinegar until it reduces to ¼ cup of glaze.

1 Peel and core the apples, and then cut each apple into eight pieces. Toss them in the honey.

2 Heat a pot on medium-high. Melt the butter and cook the apples until brown and caramelized on all sides.

3 Remove the pan from heat, add the jam and 2 Tbsp water, and toss to combine with the apples.

4 Pour the apple mixture over ice cream. Drizzle with balsamic and garnish with mint.

PANTRY RAID: Add 1–2 Tbsp chopped dried fruit (pages 132 and 271) or pieces of fruit leather (pages 272 and 292), use a touch of fruit juice or fruit booze in place of the water, or add a small pinch of peach salt (page 263)!

Winter Salad

SERVINGS: 4 SIDES OR 2 MAINS

EFFORT: 5 MINUTES

ELAPSED: 20 MINUTES

¼ cup almonds, chopped
   then measured

Black pepper

2 Tbsp white wine vinegar

1 Tbsp honey

Coarse salt

½ red onion, cut into thin strips

6 cups spinach, kale, or any green
   other than arugula

2–3 Tbsp dried strawberries
   (page 320)

½ cup ricotta cheese

6 Tbsp olive oil

2 Tbsp strawberry jam (page 320)

2 Tbsp balsamic vinegar

Jam is a frequent flavor-booster for salad dressings in our house. I have a standard ratio of jam that I mix into any dressing, but I tend to change the vinegar based on the fruit. Raspberry is great with red wine vinegar, peaches love white wine vinegar, and strawberries are a natural complement to balsamic.

Sometimes I mix powdered dehydrated fruit into the dressing. Reserve a few of your dehydrated strawberries, pulverize them, and add them, a little at a time, at the end.

1   Place a small pot on medium-high heat. Add the almonds and as much black pepper as you like. Toast for a few minutes, stirring frequently so the nuts don't burn. Place the nuts on a plate to cool and return the pot to the heat.

2   Quick pickle the onions. Turn the heat to high and add the vinegar, honey, and a pinch of salt and pepper to the pot. Add the onion as soon as the liquid starts to boil. Stir constantly for 30 seconds before removing from the heat. Allow to cool for a few minutes.

3   Strain out the onion mixture and discard the liquid.

4   Mix the greens with the almonds and dried strawberries on a serving platter, and scatter the ricotta over top.

5   Whisk the olive oil with the jam to loosely combine.

6   Drizzle balsamic vinegar and oil-jam mixture across the salad. Allow it to rest for a few minutes before serving.

PANTRY RAID: Add pickled beets (page 124) or pressure canned (or pickled) mushrooms (page 250), use any of the homemade or infused vinegars instead of the balsamic, or add a tiny bit of thyme-infused honey (page 229).

Tomatoes

My parents discovered the joy of canning tomato sauce from friends. They used a number of hand-grinders for years, and the work was back-breaking. I'll never forget my father's pride when he modified a hand-crank tomato press by removing the handle and attaching the machine to a furnace motor.

By the time I started canning tomatoes with my parents, they had acquired a proper motorized press and had a small inventory of preserving equipment that allowed us to produce an amazing yield. Now, each fall, Dana and I head to their place and can process up to 8 bushels (almost 400 lb) of tomatoes in a single day, though we normally split it over two days.

We've also begun to include friends in our sauce-making days, and this fall tradition feels more like a party than a chore. Opening each jar transports me through more than a decade of memories of making sauce with family and friends. It connects me to who I am and the people I value most.

PRESERVING NOSE-TO-TAIL

A tomato breaks down into five components:

- **SKIN** The most bitter part. It can be removed by blanching.
- **SEEDS** Although they can be removed with a spoon, it's easiest to use a food mill or press, especially for larger amounts.
- **FLESH** Easily transformed into sauce and can be dried.
- **WATER** Tomato water is the clear liquid that you see on your cutting board after slicing many tomatoes. You can extract it with a steam juicer.
- **LEAVES** Tomato leaves have the most aroma and many chefs add them during the final stages of cooking sauce.

TIPS FOR STORING

Storing tomatoes in the fridge destroys their flavor. For short-term storage, keep them on the counter, out of direct sunlight, stem side down. If they get too soft, make a quick sauce and refrigerate.

My parents individually wrap the last of their homegrown tomatoes in ink-free newsprint and store them in the garage in the fall. Keep them in a single layer and ripen them on a sunny windowsill when needed. They will store for six to eight weeks like this and will retain much of their flavor.

FILLING THE PANTRY

CHILLED
Tomatoes freeze well.

CANNED
Sauce, salsa, soup, tomato jam, and tomato juice.

PRESSURE CANNED
Some people pressure can tomatoes because they are relatively low-acid. Pressure canning eliminates the need to add lemon juice or citric acid.

DEHYDRATED
Sundried tomatoes are easy to make.

INFUSED
Small amounts of olive oil can be infused with dehydrated tomatoes but should be kept in the fridge and only for short periods of time.

1 Tomato Skins (for Powder)
2 Canned Tomatoes
3 Tomato Sauce
4 Dehydrated Tomatoes
5 Tomato Salsa

Batch-It

Tomato Salsa

WATERBATH

LEVEL: ● ● ○

YIELD: 6 HALF-PINT JARS

EFFORT: 1 HOUR

ELAPSED: 2 HOURS

EAT: WITHIN 1–2 YEARS

2½ lb plum tomatoes

1 lb jalapeño peppers

½ lb onions

½ cup white vinegar (5% or higher)

1 tsp salt

1 tsp black pepper

1 tsp ground cumin

1 tsp dried oregano

½ tsp celery seeds

½ tsp dried thyme

Frozen Tomatoes

CELLAR

LEVEL: ● ○ ○

YIELD: 2 LB TOMATOES

EFFORT: 15 MINUTES

ELAPSED: 6 HOURS

EAT: WITHIN 6–9 MONTHS

4 lb plum tomatoes

When you make salsa you'll find that there is a lot of dead time. I use that time to prep a large bowl of tomatoes that can be easily frozen and used for cooking through the winter. For thicker salsa, my friend Kaela, of *Local Kitchen* blog, recommends straining it after opening and reducing it before serving. The ingredients of this salsa should be weighed as that will help ensure you have enough acidity for the waterbath.

MAKE THE SALSA:

1 Peel the tomatoes for the salsa (see page 261).

2 Coarsely chop the tomatoes, jalapeños, and onions. Place them in a large pot with the vinegar and the salt, pepper, cumin, oregano, celery seeds, and thyme. Bring to a boil on high heat then lower to a simmer, uncovered, for 10 minutes.

3 Prepare your canning pot and rack, and sterilize your jars and lids (see page 17).

4 Remove the jars from the canner and turn the heat to high.

5 Fill the jars, leaving ½ inch of headspace. Gently jostle the jars or use the handle of a spoon to release any air bubbles. Wipe the rims of the jars, apply the lids, and process for 15 minutes (if you live higher than 1,000 feet above sea level, refer to the Adjust for Altitude chart on page 17 for additional processing time). Remove the jars and allow them to cool.

PREPARE THE FROZEN TOMATOES:

6 While the salsa is processing, wash and dry the tomatoes you're planning to freeze.

7 Remove the stems and stem scars with a paring knife by cutting a cylinder around them.

8 Place the tomatoes on a rimmed baking tray, scar side facing up. Ensure there is space between each tomato. Freeze for 6 hours.

9 Transfer the tomatoes to airtight bags or containers and put them back in the freezer.

10 Minutes or less

Dehydrated Tomatoes

DEHYDRATE

LEVEL: ● ○ ○

YIELD: 1 CUP DRIED TOMATOES

EAT: WITHIN 1 YEAR

2 quarts (4 pints) cherry tomatoes

2 cloves garlic, minced

1 Tbsp balsamic vinegar

1 Tbsp maple syrup or honey

¼ cup fresh basil, measured then roughly chopped

Coarse salt

½ tsp black pepper

YOU WILL NEED

Dehydrator

Many commercial sundried tomatoes are treated with chemicals and dried in large dehydrators instead of the sun. If you feel cheated by this, you're not alone.

Chop all the tomatoes in half. Toss them with the garlic, vinegar, maple syrup, basil, ½ tsp salt, and the pepper. Remove the tomatoes from the liquid, and scatter them across dehydrating trays, leaving space between. Dry at 125°F until brittle, anywhere from 8 to 20 hours, depending on the size of your tomatoes (some heirloom varieties can be rather large). This recipe will also work well with plum tomatoes.

TIP: MONSTER BATCHES

My family slowly built a collection of preserving tools dedicated to tomato sauce over fifteen years. The key pieces include:

- **1 MOTORIZED TOMATO PRESS ($400+).** A motorized food mill that separates skins and seeds from the pulp. It can process 100 lb of tomatoes or more in an hour and also works on apples. We also have a meat grinder attachment for it.
- **2 OUTDOOR BURNERS ($100).** These are propane-powered burners that can be used for cooking or waterbathing.
- **2 OVERSIZED POTS ($80+).** We use massive pots that hold 18 or 19 quart jars of sauce while waterbathing.
- **GIANT SPOON ($20).** It's the size of a small canoe paddle!
- **FOOD-SAFE BUCKETS ($0–$10).** These make transferring a large amount of tomato pulp or seeds and skins a breeze.

All this equipment can be purchased online, at a restaurant supply store, or at a European grocery store during harvest season.

 # Tomato Sauce

WATERBATH

LEVEL: ● ○ ○

YIELD: 4-5 QUART JARS

EFFORT: 4-5 HOURS

ELAPSED: 1-2 HOURS

EAT: WITHIN 1-2 YEARS

¼ bushel plum tomatoes
   (about 13 lb)

2 Tbsp bottled lemon juice per
   quart jar (8–10 Tbsp total)

YOU WILL NEED

Food mill or tomato squeezer

The quality of your mill or tomato squeezer will vastly affect your yield—the more liquid you can extract, the more sauce you'll get. We process tomatoes through the squeezer three or four times to get as much juice as possible from them.

Tomatoes are relatively low in acid and so many people recommend pressure canning them. We add additional acid—bottled lemon juice—for safety. It is not detectable in the finished product. You should not add other low-acid ingredients such as herbs, garlic, or meat.

1   Wash and cut the tomatoes in half, discarding any soft or black spots.

2   As you chop them, transfer them to a large pot containing a ½-inch layer of water to prevent initial burning. Bring to a boil and reduce to a simmer, stirring often, to soften.

3   When all tomatoes are soft enough to easily crush with a spoon, process through a food mill.

4   Return the tomatoes to the pot, add the lemon juice, turn heat to high and bring to a boil before immediately lowering to a gentle simmer, uncovered, until the sauce becomes thick, about 1–1½ hours. It will turn pink and frothy before thickening. Stir occasionally to prevent burning.

5   Prepare your canning pot and rack, and sterilize your jars and lids (see page 17).

6   Fill the jars, leaving ½ inch of headspace. Gently jostle the jars or use the handle of a spoon to release any air bubbles.

7   Remove the jars from the canner and turn the heat to high.

8   Wipe the rims of the jars, apply the lids, and process for 35 minutes (if you live higher than 1,000 feet above sea level, refer to the Adjust for Altitude chart on page 17 for additional processing time). Remove the jars and allow them to cool.

VARIATIONS: Add up to 1 tsp salt per jar, but no other ingredients should be added or removed.

CENTER OF THE PLATE: Break out from pasta. This is an amazing addition to soup or a braising liquid.

Tomato Powder

The leftover seeds and skin from your tomato sauce, salsa, or frozen tomatoes can—should!—be used to make dehydrated tomato powder, which can usually take the place of tomato paste (in volume and taste). Spread tomato scraps onto drying racks and dehydrate at 125°F for 6–8 hours, until completely dry. Store in jars and blitz small amounts into a powder as needed.

Canned Tomatoes

WATERBATH

LEVEL: ● ● ○

YIELD: 6–7 PINT JARS

EFFORT: 45–60 MINUTES

ELAPSED: 2 HOURS

EAT: WITHIN 1–2 YEARS

10 lb plum tomatoes such as
   San Marzanos

Coarse salt

6–7 Tbsp bottled lemon juice

It took me more than 20 years to appreciate how fantastic home-canned tomatoes are. They have a higher water content than tomato sauce and add a wonderful texture to food when added at the final stage of cooking. I sometimes chop them and add them to pasta after I've plated it. Don't toss out the liquid—it's awesome!

1 Prepare your canning pot and rack, and sterilize your jars and lids (see page 17).

2 Bring a large pot of water to a boil.

3 Peel the tomatoes (see page 261) and place them in a large bowl.

4 Remove the jars from the canner and turn the heat to high.

5 Add ½ tsp salt and 1 Tbsp lemon juice to each jar.

6 Add the whole tomatoes to the jars and top with boiling water, leaving ½ inch of headspace. Gently jostle the jars or use the handle of a spoon to release any air bubbles. Wipe the rims, apply the lids, and process for 40 minutes (if you live higher than 1,000 feet above sea level, refer to the Adjust for Altitude chart on page 17 for additional processing time). Remove the jars and allow them to cool.

VARIATIONS: If you want to skip the lemon juice, pressure can for 15 minutes with 5 lb of pressure. The National Center for Home Food Preservation claims this will better preserve the flavor and nutritional values but I continue to waterbath them. Do not add additional ingredients (such as herbs or oil) which would lower the acidity.

CENTER OF THE PLATE: Use this like store-bought canned tomatoes, except these are much better! Add to chili at the last minute or lightly crush, drain the juice, and mix the flesh with olive oil to make an amazing pizza sauce.

Joel's mom, Ruth

Mussels Steamed in Tomato Sauce

SERVINGS: 4

EFFORT: 10 MINUTES

ELAPSED: 30 MINUTES

1 Tbsp unsalted butter, chilled

1 Tbsp olive oil

2 cloves garlic, minced

2 tsp chili flakes, or more to taste

1 cup onion, diced small
   then measured

½ cup celery, diced small
   then measured

½ cup carrot, diced small
   then measured

Coarse salt

Black pepper

1 quart (4 cups or 32 oz) tomato
   sauce (page 332)

2 bay leaves

4–5 lb mussels

¼ cup flat-leaf parsley, measured
   then chopped

Finely grated Parmigiano-Reggiano
   or pecorino cheese, for garnish

Mussels are one of the easiest, cheapest, fastest, and most delicious meals you can serve at home. There are two tricks to buying mussels:

The shells must be closed or must close when lightly tapped on a hard surface. This is an indicator that they are alive.

They should not be stored in a plastic bag for a prolonged period of time. Instead, pour them into a container and store in your fridge (for large amounts pour them directly into your crisper). This will increase their life expectancy dramatically.

This recipe is entirely scalable. We've made 8–10 lb at a time for large dinner parties. If you've never cooked mussels before, don't be scared! It's almost as easy as boiling pasta.

1   Preheat a large pot (one that has a tight-fitting lid) on medium-high heat. Add the butter and oil.

2   Add the garlic and chili flakes and cook for 3 minutes, stirring frequently.

3   Add the onion, celery, and carrot. Season liberally with salt and pepper. Cook until the onion softens and is translucent, stirring occasionally.

4   Add the tomato sauce with the bay leaves and turn the heat to high. As you wait for it to reach a simmer, check each mussel for signs of life.

5   Once the sauce is simmering, add the mussels. Place the lid on top and cook until all mussels are open, about 5 minutes.

6   Stir the mussels and then spoon them into serving bowls. Make sure to add some of the cooking liquid. Garnish with parsley and cheese, and eat at once!

PANTRY RAID: Add ¼ cup dried mushrooms (page 252), 1 cup chopped stewed tomatoes, and dried hot peppers (page 174) to taste at the start of step 4.

Slow-Cooked Bolognaise

SERVINGS: 6

EFFORT: 30 MINUTES

ELAPSED: 8–12 HOURS

FOR THE SAUCE:

4 cups beef stock

2 quart jars tomato sauce (page 332)

2–3 air-dried hot peppers (page 174)

3 bay leaves

½ tsp dried oregano

Lard or vegetable oil for cooking

2 lb coarsely ground meat (I use a
  combination of beef and pork or
  beef and game)

Salt

Black pepper

Ground cumin

3 cloves garlic, minced

1 cup onions, diced small
  then measured

½ cup carrots, diced small
  then measured

½ cup celery, diced small
  then measured

TO SERVE:

1½–2 lb fresh pasta

Finely grated hard cheese such
  as Parmigiano-Reggiano or
  cloth-aged cheddar

Hot sauce (page 176)

Fresh basil, to garnish

YOU WILL NEED

Slow cooker

If I could live on pasta dishes alone, I would. I've developed a love for slow-cooking tomato sauce, which I learned from cooking our vats of sauce. If you cook tomato sauce long and slowly, it develops a texture so thick that you can actually stack it well above the rim of a spoon.

1   Pour the stock into a pot, bring it to a boil, then turn down to a simmer, uncovered, to reduce to 1 cup or less, about 10–15 minutes.

2   While the stock simmers, prepare the sauce. Place the tomato sauce, hot peppers, bay leaves, and oregano in your slow cooker set on high heat.

3   Heat a heavy-bottomed pot on medium-high. Add the lard and heat until it just begins to smoke. Scatter ½ lb of the ground meat across the pan. Season liberally with salt, pepper, and ½ tsp of cumin. Allow the meat to sit, undisturbed, until it releases itself from the pan, about 2–4 minutes, then stir and brown it on all sides. Remove the meat with a slotted spoon and transfer it to the slow cooker. Repeat, adding fat if needed, until all the meat is browned.

4   Toss the garlic, onion, carrot, and celery into the pan you used to cook the meat (no need to clean it out). Cook until the onion is slightly translucent, 4–5 minutes. Transfer to the slow cooker using a slotted spoon, along with the reduced beef stock.

5   Place the lid on the slow cooker. Once it starts to simmer, lower the heat and simmer for 8–10 hours, with the lid on, stirring occasionally.

6   When the sauce is almost ready, cook the pasta until al dente. To keep the sauce from running, preheat your serving plate by running it under hot water for a few minutes and drying it before plating. Serve the pasta with the sauce and top with cheese, hot sauce, and basil to taste.

PANTRY RAID: Add chili oil to taste (page 174), 1 Tbsp tomato powder (page 332) when adding the sauce, or 1 pint pressure canned mushrooms (page 250) before serving.

Acknowledgments

By the time you hold *Batch* it will have been three years in the making. It has been the toughest, most personal project that either of us has ever worked on, and it would not be possible without the support of so many people for whom words will fall short to thank properly—but we will try.

Thanks to you for picking up this book and to all of you who have read the blog, commented, shared, or attended one of our Home Ec events (and to The Avro, Handlebar, HiLo and The Cannonball for hosting). Thank you for encouraging us, and sharing your feedback and passion for preserving. We are especially grateful to all those from around the world who volunteered as recipe testers, and provided feedback that made this book immeasurably better.

We owe a debt of gratitude to friends and family. When we chose this project, we knew it came with sacrifices that would impact them as well. Their support has been humbling. A special thanks to our parents, Ruth, Paul, Joyce, and Ken. To Kevin, Chris, Zoya, Susan, Patrick, and Jessie for helping with our backyard shoot—and a giant thank you to Aaron and Kelly, who always went above and beyond (including preserving samples into the wee hours with us). Thank you to Shawn, Val, Nat, Jen, Paul, and Paul for keeping us sane and getting us out during this process.

Sean Timberlake, of Punk Domestics, and Alison Fryer, of the dearly missed Cookbook Store, planted the seeds that made this book possible. This book wouldn't exist without them. Judy Linden and the Stonesong team fertilized those seeds so we had something worthy of sharing with the Random House team. Thank you, of course, to Robert McCullough, our publisher at Appetite by Random House, for championing us and seeing that we had something great we wanted to share with the world. Our amazing editor, and now friend, Zoe Maslow, has worked so hard alongside us the entire time (and has been adept at managing all the Joelisms and Danaisms with such patience). To the design and production departments, and especially our designer Kelly Hill, thank you for making it look even better than we could have hoped and for being great at working with a perfectionist designer (Dana) on her "baby."

Our core visual team was a dream team. To our food photographer, Reena Newman, whom Dana has dreamt of doing a cookbook with since we met—we did a cookbook! Margaret Mulligan did all the location and portraits, and constantly went above and beyond what we asked of her. Thanks to Claire Stubbs (food stylist) and Laura Branson (Still Life Props) for your amazing creativity, and to Brandon and Gus for all your help on the shoots. It was above all FUN to work with friends, and we made something beautiful we are so proud of.

Thank you to the many farmers, chefs, and small businesses who supported and/or inspired us through this process. Special mention must be made to Rob Poizner (The Cannonball), Andrew Poulsen (Bespoke Butchers), Dan and Kristin Donovan (Hooked), Jessie Sosnicki (Sosnicki Organics), Morgan Yew (Jam Factory), Laura Watt (Cubits Organics), Norm Hardie (Norman Hardie Winery and Vineyard) and the entire Merchants of Green crew. Matt Dean Pettit, Joshna Maharaj, Mark Cutrara, Matty Matheson, Arlene Stein, Matt DeMille, Scott Vivian, Dave Mottershall and Zane Caplansky have been more inspiring than they know.

Another thanks to the welcoming community of bloggers, writers, and editors who have helped us along the way. Cathy Barrow, Jennifer Bain, Sarah Hood, David Ort, Joel Solish, Ashley English, Ayngelina Brogan, Marisa McClellan, Tigress and all the Kidz, Gail Gordon Oliver, and countless others.

And thanks to our recipe testers, who made this book better with their feedback and support.

Finally, thank you to Shaeffer, our dog. He stayed relentlessly positive through this entire process, reminded us that it is important to play even when you think you can't, and that a cookie will help you conquer most goals.

Index

Note: Page ranges in **boldface** indicate the main preserving recipe sections for these ingredients. Recipes that appear within these sections are not individually listed as subentries.